FORGOTTEN FOOTPRINTS

UNTOLD STORIES OF HUMANITY'S PAST

Prateek Dasgupta completed his Master's in Materials Science from Pennsylvania State University, where he combined his interest in natural history with his fascination for metals to study iron-nickel meteorites. After a career in manufacturing, he is pursuing his lifelong passion for writing with an unmatched penchant for uncovering the stories from history that are often omitted from popular texts. He is curious about the lesser-known chapters of humanity's past, and through his writing, he is bringing us closer to the world of those who were overlooked in historical records. Prateek's primary interest lies in learning about societies from the Ice Age till the fall of the Mongol Empire in the "Old World," and before the arrival of Columbus in the "New World." He runs a newsletter called *Forgotten Footprints* on Substack (https://prateekdg.substack.com/) and is the editor of *Teatime History*, a publication on Medium. He has also written scripts for popular YouTube historical shows.

Praise for the book

"With so much written about ancient cultures, ruins and artifacts, it's no easy job to write a book filled with interesting, new material. Yet this is what Prateek Dasgupta has done in this fascinating and engaging work. As a historian of antiquity myself, I learned many things I hadn't known before, and Dasgupta has adeptly brought it to life. I highly recommend picking up a copy at your earliest opportunity. It's a great piece of writing to have on your bedside table."

— **Dr. David Miano**, Historian of the Ancient World, Host of the *World of Antiquity* Channel (YouTube), and Author

"A fascinating read. Prateek Dasgupta takes us on an exhilarating journey through history's greatest forgotten chapters, from the ruins of Göbekli Tepe to the rise of the Kushans. In vivid detail and brilliant prose, he breathes life into lost worlds of the steppe and reclaims the overlooked moments that shaped our past."

—**Sam Dalrymple**, Historian,
Author of *Shattered Lands*

"*Forgotten Footprints* takes us to some of our earliest civilizations and celebrates their rich lives and sometimes surprising customs."

—**Dr. Jon Hunner**, Emeritus Professor of History at
New Mexico State University,
Former Director of New Mexico History Museum

PRATEEK DASGUPTA

FORGOTTEN FOOTPRINTS

UNTOLD STORIES OF HUMANITY'S PAST

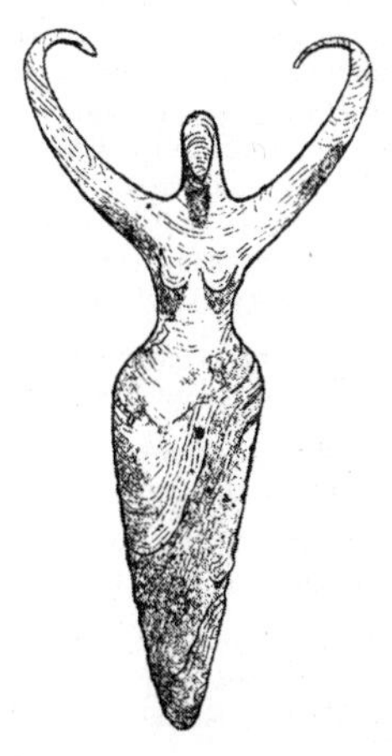

First published in 2025 by Hachette India
(Registered name: Hachette Book Publishing India Pvt. Ltd)
An Hachette UK company
www.hachetteindia.com

1

Print ISBN 978-93-5731-319-3
ebook ISBN 978-93-5731-502-9

Hachette Book Publishing India Pvt. Ltd
4th & 5th Floors, Corporate Centre
Plot No. 94, Sector 44, Gurugram – 122003, India

Typeset by Mukul Chand, Delhi

Printed and bound in India
by Thomson Press India Ltd.

To Ira

Contents

Section 3
Lost Cities

Section 4
Forgotten Empires

FOREWORD

PRATEEK DASGUPTA'S *Forgotten Footprints: Untold Stories of Humanity's Past* accomplishes several ambitious goals—he has discovered and brought to life stories about our distant past from around the globe. He has reconstructed these histories despite a lack of written texts. And he has convincingly challenged many myths about the distant past, especially that our ancestors lived complex lives. Dasgupta argues that they did not just survive, but they thrived.

Forgotten Footprints begins in what is now the Czech Republic. There, humans lived in permanent settlements, hunted mammoths and other big game, chipped stone tools, wove textiles and baskets, and carved figurines. They lived there 28,000 years ago, in the midst of the last Ice Age. From his extensive research, Dasgupta animates other Neolithic and Bronze Age societies in Europe, Africa, Asia, and the Americas. He has discovered the places where many human firsts occurred—the first cities, the first written language, the earliest pyramids, where hunter-gatherers became sedentary farmers, where early dentists and surgeons operated on patients thousands of years ago, the networks of trade routes, and even the invention of spoke-wheeled chariots. Dasgupta surprises us with these innovative civilizations where ancient humans invented vibrant societies of early agronomists, traders, religious leaders, city builders, architects, engineers, and astronomers. He takes us on a path to strange and foreign peoples and times.

Finding evidence to recreate these civilizations is not easy. Some of these societies lacked a written language, or if they did have written texts, they are now indecipherable. Some societies wrote on papyrus or other materials that disintegrated a long time ago. So, how did *Forgotten Footprints* recreate such detailed histories of the distant past? Prateek scoured through an impressive range of disciplines to gather the necessary information. He combed through reports from archaeological excavations, dove into findings from ground penetrating radars, and studied aerial photographs of ancient sites. He read recent research that used DNA evidence on the ancient bones, teeth, and residue left on cooking pots found during these digs to find out about diets. Other recent technologies, like an electron microscope scanning preserved cotton fibers, revealed that humans farmed it 7,500 years ago. Dasgupta also turned to geological history to look at how volcanic eruptions and sea level changes impacted these old civilizations. By using such multifaceted research across many disciplines, *Forgotten Footprints* presents a lively account of how humans lived in the distant past.

Of course, the primary treasure trove that reveals how humans lived in the past comes to light through archaeological excavations. Dasgupta researched a variety of these archaeological digs from around the globe, including many conducted in the last twenty years, to weave his fascinating accounts of our lost pasts. The excavations uncover the tools, jewelry, human and animal remains, and expose the cultural practices like burial traditions and living arrangements. Many of these archaeological finds and sites are illustrated in *Forgotten Footprints* with photographs and detailed maps. The use of all of these sources gave Dasgupta a deep understanding of how people lived thousands of years ago.

The civilizations uncovered in this book give us new insights into humanity's past. Studying times thousands of years old presents challenges since experts can disagree and offer conflicting theories about what happened and what it means. Even for historians using recent written records, it can be hard to predict the past. Thankfully, Dasgupta embraces this uncertainty by presenting competing theories and hotly debated interpretations about these societies and peoples. As Dasgupta states: "While studying a civilization, it is essential to keep an open mind and accept that new discoveries will challenge existing beliefs." *Forgotten Footprints* follows wherever the footprints lead, with all the unique detours and varieties of human experiences.

Forgotten Footprints is divided into four sections. In "Section One: Dawn of Civilization," we follow the footsteps of hunters living in towns almost 30,000 years before the present; of cotton farmers who practiced dentistry at least 7,000 years ago; and of burial practices from 9,000 years ago. "Section Two: Rise of Civilizations" explores some of the world's first metallurgists who smelted copper 7,000 years ago; the creation of the spoked wheel for chariots 4,000 years ago; and the world's first pyramids—not in Egypt but in Peru—5,000 years ago. In "Section Three: Lost Cities," we visit a 7,000-year-old city in Mesopotamia; another city 6,000 years old which tells us the story of the Egyptian Civilization's origins; a recently discovered urban area 2,500 years old in the Amazon; cities along the Silk Road; and even a Mound-builder metropolis in the United States some 1,000 years before now. In "Section Four: Forgotten Empires," we return to the Middle East to explore the location of the Hanging Gardens of Babylon; go to the earliest Steppe Empires; and examine the classical Greek influence on Buddhist art. In all of these sections and chapters, *Forgotten Footprints* walks along ancient pathways to help explain how early civilizations developed and have influenced who we are today.

Dasgupta has breathed new life into these ancient histories, confirmed as well as debunked some of the myths and common beliefs about early humans. Writing in a conversational tone, he has incorporated recent discoveries and advances in research technology, which animates these lost peoples. Finally, in his place-based histories, he has also shown how important the environment is in human development and how it impacts civilizations.

As *Forgotten Footprints* states, "The journey to civilization involves starts and stops." Dasgupta has created an entertaining and well-researched account of these past and often forgotten societies.

Dr. Jon Hunner,
Emeritus Professor of History,
New Mexico State University,
Author, *Inventing Los Alamos* and
J. Robert Oppenheimer,
the Cold War and the Atomic West

PREFACE

I WAS MESMERIZED BY THE HEADLESS SCULPTURE OF THE MAN. It was made of sandstone and stood about 185 cm tall. His kaftan robe nearly reached his ankles, and he wore well-defined cushioned boots. His right hand rested on a massive mace with finely crafted bands running from his waist to the floor. The club's end features a *makara,* a legendary sea creature from Hindu mythology that frequently appears in Hindu and Buddhist art. He had a hilted sword at his waist, on which his left hand rested. Near the end of the man's tunic, an inscription in Kharoshti reads "the great king, the king of kings, the son of God, Kanishka."

I was ten when I saw the headless statue of King Kanishka. He belonged to the Kushan dynasty, which ruled much of Central Asia and Northern India from the first century BCE to the third century CE.

The statue piqued my interest in learning more about the lives of people from the past for whom we have scant records. Although Kanishka is a popular male name in India, little was known about this mysterious ruler until the Rabatak Inscription was discovered in 1993, two years before I first saw the statue.

I have been captivated by history since I was a child. But as I read books, I couldn't help but question how much of our past is missing. How did the people who didn't make it to the records live? They could be kings like Kanishka or ordinary folk. Widespread adoption of writing is a relatively recent development. Hence, we still don't know most of our history. Historians have found it convenient to focus their research on civilizations that had extensive recordkeeping. But they are the tip of an iceberg, and not the complete picture of our past.

In this book, I aim to investigate some of history's lesser-known chapters through essays from the Upper Paleolithic period (roughly 50,000 to 12,000 years ago) to the twelfth century CE. *Forgotten Footprints* is not a traditional history book. It looks beyond themes, regions, and periods and focuses on the overlooked corners of humanity's past.

I have organized the book into four sections. We begin with the "Dawn of Civilization," in which we explore various milestones in the journey to the foundations of civilization. We'll encounter remarkable mammoth hunters who crafted fine ceramics and built permanent settlements during the Ice Age, several thousand years before the rise of agriculture. The section examines how ancient communities managed megalithic constructions before the rise of urban centers and practiced dentistry during the Stone Age.

The book's second section deals with the "Rise of Civilizations," where we will challenge some common perceptions about civilizations. Are there pyramids in the Americas that are older than those in Egypt? Did the Balkans have a script predating Mesopotamia? Could an obscure settlement at the foothills of the Ural Mountains transform human mobility for centuries? Was there a fifth river valley civilization in the "Old World" besides Mesopotamia, Egypt, China, and the Indus Valley? The third section, "Lost Cities," aims to unearth cities that were once magnificent metropolises but have since disappeared. No, we will not discuss the rise and fall of Rome, Athens, Harappa, or Persepolis. Instead, we will defy conventional wisdom by exploring the stories of cities that once dominated the expansive grasslands of the Eurasian

Steppes and the thick Amazonian jungles. We will visit a magnificent metropolis on the banks of the Mississippi that flourished long before European arrival and had a population comparable to that of London and Paris in its heyday.

In the book's final section, "Forgotten Empires," I pay tribute to long-lost empires that once controlled vast swathes of land but are often overlooked. Alexander the Great's exploits are well known, but did you know that long before Chinggis Khan, another ruler unified the warring Steppe tribes in the third century BCE and built an empire twice the size of Alexander's? Kanishka is well known, but where did his ancestors come from? These are some questions we shall address in the empires section.

Forgotten Footprints takes a multi-disciplinary approach to make cutting-edge academic research accessible for a wide readership. I do not claim to be an expert in any of the topics covered in the book. I have built upon the work of those who have dedicated their lives to studying each civilization or culture that has impacted the world we live in today. My expertise lies in stitching together stories from across the globe and different eras to present a narrative that is guaranteed to spark your curiosity about the past. Popular TV shows and documentaries often draw simplistic conclusions about historical events and archaeological findings. Their narratives lack nuance and depth. Without getting entangled in the details of academia, we can appreciate that events that occurred before us leave us with many questions. Yet, we also have many answers that can give us an idea about the lives of our distant ancestors. The civilizations I have studied remind me that greatness is fleeting and memory is a deliberate choice. Written history often ignores many voices from the past, but that can always change. The world before us was similar to ours, yet vastly different. Their rise and fall remind us of the fragility of our modern society, and many of the problems that affect us today have also plagued people in the past.

When I began writing this book, I aimed to cover as many ancient cultures as possible. However, I realized it is better to focus on a few areas so that I can do greater justice to them. You will find at least one civilization, culture, city, or empire from most corners of the globe. Owing to page limitations, I regretfully have not been able to include the amazing cultures of Mesoamerica and Oceania. I hope to cover them in the future.

Forgotten Footprints challenges many traditional narratives using an evidence-based approach. My hope with this book is to encourage you to learn more about at least one civilization, city, or empire that caught your attention, and educate at least one person you know, so that overlooked peoples of the past become a part of popular discussions.

Section 1

Dawn of Civilization

1

Gravettians: Mammoth Hunters Who Built the First Permanent Settlements

SOME 28,000 YEARS AGO, A LITTLE GIRL AND HER FAMILY SAT around a fire by a stream in Moravia, Czechia, as the winds howled. Gathered around the warmth, they braved icy temperatures to make clay figurines of the creatures they encountered. The sculptures were mostly of megafauna, including woolly rhinoceroses, cave lions, bears, and mammoths. They also featured foxes, owls, and horses.

One figurine stood out.

It was a tiny, featureless female figure with enormous breasts, hips, and a round tummy. The child gazed at it in amazement before her parents hurriedly took it away and threw it into the fire. It was one of several human and animal figurines that these mysterious people had crafted that night.

On July 13, 1925, archaeologists led by Karel Absolon excavated the Dolní Věstonice[1] site, in Moravia. Next to lumps of

1 Dolní Věstonice is pronounced as "Doll-nee" "vye-staw-nyee-tse."

clay by a fireplace, they found animal figurines and a shattered, curvaceous statuette covered in ash.

The faceless figurine's bulging breasts, wide hips, and distorted arms and legs left the excavators scratching their heads. What was the meaning of this object with odd proportions?

Or did people look like that back then?

Absolon and his colleagues discovered the world's earliest known ceramics and unearthed the first permanent human settlement, Dolní Věstonice, dating back approximately 27,000 years ago. People here didn't just survive the bitter cold of the Ice Age; they thrived.

The discovery leaves us with even more questions than answers.

How did humans struggling for survival during the Ice Age produce ceramics long before inventing pottery? Was there a specific class of people committed to creating such excellent art? Where did they get the food security to do so?

Our understanding of human history is often linear. We envision ancient humans as hunter-gatherers who began farming and building cities after the last Ice Age ended approximately 12,000 years ago. These urban landscapes grew into civilizations, nations, and eventually empires.

But the reality is much more complex.

The journey to civilization involved several starts and stops. Settled life began even before the discovery of farming. In some regions, such as the Americas, animal domestication predated agriculture, while in others, like Japan, pottery was invented before humans started cultivating crops.

Our path to evolution and modern life resembles multiple branches of a tree connected by a stem and roots. One such branch was in the Moravian basin, where hunter-gatherers during the Ice Age formed a settled community long before farmers from Anatolia introduced agriculture to the region.

These innovative early humans, who made exquisite ceramics, were the Gravettians. They were descendants of the first humans to colonize Europe and laid the groundwork for the rise of civilizations that blossomed thousands of years later.

We find glimpses of human progress in this forgotten period of our history. These enigmatic lords of the mammoth steppe braved frigid conditions to build permanent settlements, bake the earliest known ceramics, craft exquisite jewelry, depict their world through paintings, and perform elaborate burials, which would become hallmarks of human advancement millennia later. Let's explore the origins of these Ice Age mammoth hunters who provided us with humanity's first trailer of civilization.

ORIGINS OF THE GRAVETTIANS

The Gravettians were hunter-gatherers who lived in Europe and Russia between 33,000 and 21,000 years ago. This period is called the Upper Paleolithic or Old Stone Age.

The earliest known human settlers arrived in Europe about 57,000 years ago. They interacted and interbred with Neanderthals. Scientists refer to these individuals as Early European Modern Humans, commonly known as Cro-Magnons. The name originates from the Cro-Magnon Cave in France, where their remains were first discovered.

The descendants of the Cro-Magnons established the Aurignacian culture, the earliest widespread archaeological technocomplex.[2] Although no two cultural sites were identical, we observe a typical pattern during the Aurignacian period,

2 In archaeology of the Stone Age, a technocomplex or industry is defined by the type of tools produced. The tools such as hand axes, cleavers, and spears are identified by the way the rock is cut and finished.

which lasted from approximately 43,000 years ago to 28,000 years ago. The culture derives its name from the Cave of Aurignac, located in Haute-Garonne, France. The Aurignacians produced some of the world's oldest expressions of figurative art and Venus figurines. There was a slight overlap between the Aurignacian and Gravettian epochs.

Horse figurine from the Vogelherd Cave, Germany, dating to the Aurignacian period, approximately 35,000 years ago.

The Gravettians trace their ancestry back to the Aurignacians. A 2023 study that analyzed 356 hunter-gatherer genomes from 116 ancient skeletons across 14 countries in Central and Western Eurasia found a connection between the Gravettians and the earlier Aurignacian populations. Additionally, the researchers discovered that the Gravettians in Western Europe were genetically distinct from those in Central and Southern Europe.

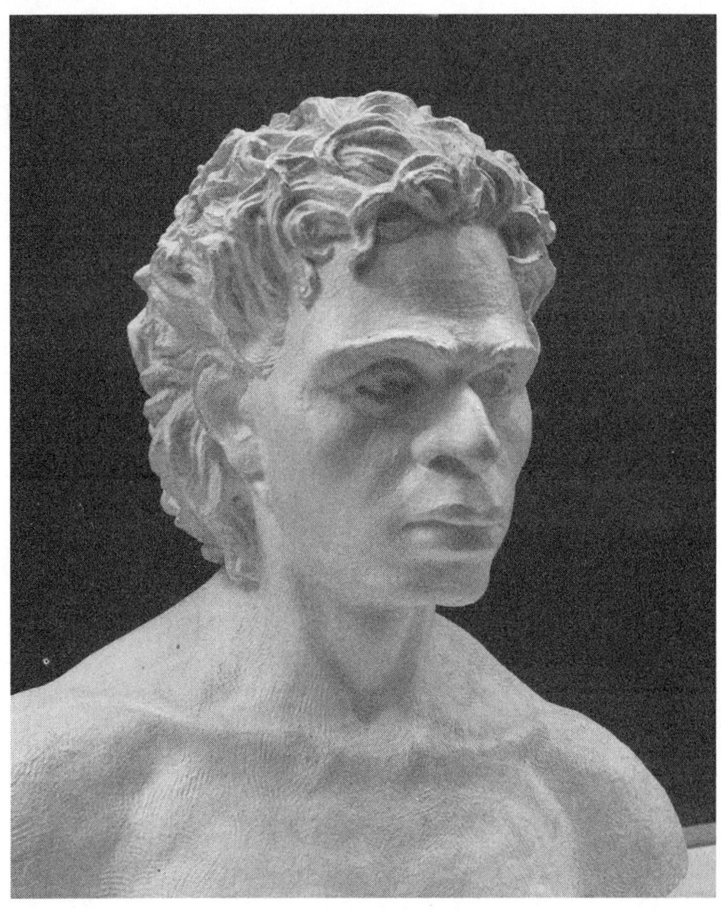

Reconstruction of an Aurignacian man from Kostenki-14.

The figure on page 8 shows that those who lived at Dolní Věstonice were a mixture of Eastern (Kostenki, Russia) and Western (Goyet, Belgium) Aurignacian groups. However, the DNA revealed that the Věstonice people were more closely related to the Eastern Aurignacian group than to the Western one.

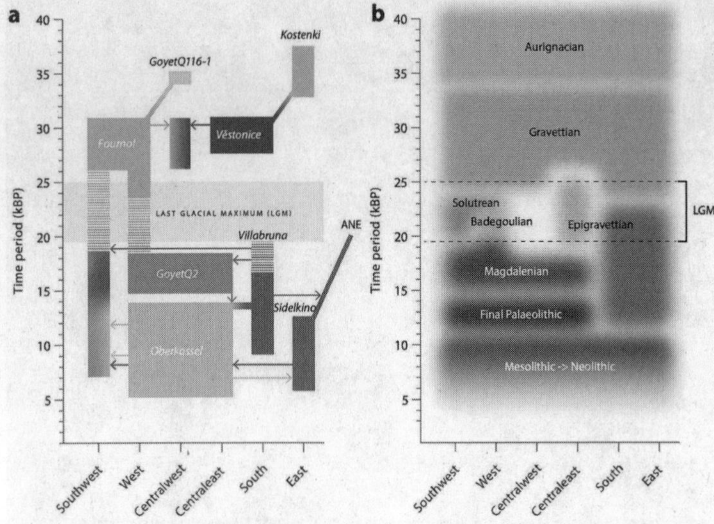

Interaction between different hunter-gatherer groups in Europe during the Upper Paleolithic period.
Credits: Posth et al. (2023).

In 2024, researchers from the University of Bordeaux, France, conducted another study and found that nine separate cultures existed across Eurasia during the Gravettian period. Although we consider the Gravettians a single group, their cultural traditions were diverse. So, why are they called "Gravettians"? What did they have in common?

The term "Gravettian" comes from the La Gravette archaeological site, where tools typical of this culture were first identified in 1880. According to archaeologist Natasha Reynolds from the University of Bordeaux, "Gravettian" defines the systematic production of backed lithic artifacts, including Gravette points, microgravettes, and shouldered points.

Stone tools found at Dolní Věstonice and Pavlov, dating to the Gravettian period.

What do we mean by "backed lithic artifacts," typical of the Gravettian culture? It is a technical term for stone blades with blunted edges that were sharp before. Usually, a stone blade has two sharp edges. Backing or blunting causes one edge to become blunt enough to fit into a tool, allowing the user to apply greater force on the sharper edge. The Gravettians always backed a previously sharpened edge of the flint. Among the backed blades, the period's most well-known tool is a small, pointed, slightly curved blade with a blunt back, known as the Gravette point. This remarkable invention helped the Gravettians hunt megafauna, a game changer in human evolution.

A Gravette point.

WHAT DID THE GRAVETTIANS EAT?

An illustrative representation of a mammoth hunt.

When we think of the Ice Age, images of hunters attacking giant beasts such as mammoths, bisons, and woolly rhinos come to mind. Pop culture has portrayed prehistoric humans as exclusive big-game hunters. In contrast, academics have been more skeptical. A documentary titled *Gravettian–The Birth of First Civilization (Moravia, Europe)* showed three starving humans walking past a mammoth despite having spears.

The depiction is unrealistic. During the Gravettian era, people ate a variety of animals, including both carnivores and herbivores. Megafauna, such as bisons, mammoths, woolly rhinos, bears, and cave lions, were hunted due to their immense calorific value.

A 2024 study suggests that hunting may have contributed to the eventual extinction of megafauna. So why were academics skeptical in the past?

Bones of reindeer, hyenas, wolves, foxes, and red deer, which were widely consumed, constituted the majority of the animal remains discovered in most Gravettian sites. In coastal areas, people ate shellfish, fish, and sea lions. About 20–30 percent of all food consumed in Italy and Wales was sea creatures.

However, the number of remains of a particular animal isn't always a fair reflection of people's regular diet. For example, one woolly mammoth provides as many as 3.6 million calories. Humans could have consumed mammoths much longer without having to hunt daily. Cold weather conditions meant meat preservation wasn't an issue.

A study analyzing the nitrogen content in bone collagen of human remains at the Buran Kaya archaeological site in Crimea found mammoth meat was the single most significant contributor of protein.

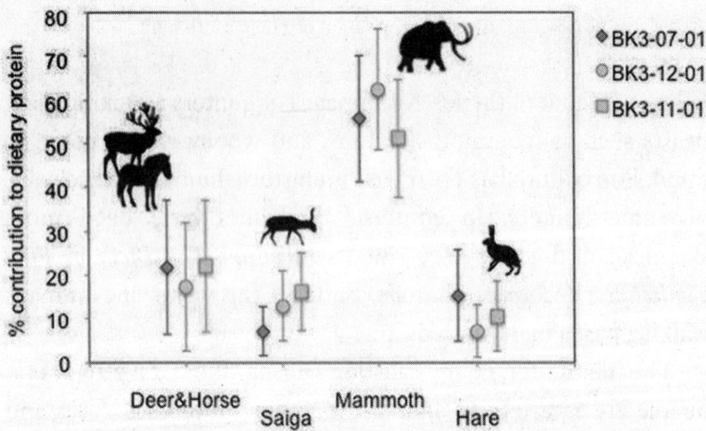

Analyses of bone collagen revealed the various animals consumed at Buran Kaya. Mammoths were the primary source of protein.

Credits: Drucker et al.(2017).

Hunting was not the sole means of subsistence. Excavations at Dolní Věstonice and Pavlov, another archaeological site in Moravia, revealed grinding tools, hinting that the Gravettians may have processed plant-based foods.

Archaeologists studied dental calculus from human remains at the sites and discovered that the Gravettian people ate starch, fiber, and plants. Could the eating habits of these mysterious Ice Age humans have contributed to their physical appearance?

The Gravettian men are among the tallest in history. The average height for males was between 179 cm and 188 cm (5'10" to 6'2"). They were muscular and slender, weighing around 67 to 73 kg. Females were much shorter, averaging around 158 cm (5'2") and weighing around 54 kg. Why was there such a significant variation between men and women?

Scientists continue to debate the reasons behind sexual dimorphism among the Gravettians, and no clear answers have emerged. Our samples may be biased since archaeologists have found only a few Gravettian burials, and these remains may represent the social elite of the time.

One explanation suggests that men primarily participated in hunting, which gave them access to more calorie-rich meats. At the same time, women relied on gathering and often settled for a less nutritious diet. However, such theories are far from conclusive in explaining the differences in stature between Gravettian men and women.

You may wonder why we need to learn about the diets of the Gravettians. Despite the harsh conditions of the Ice Age, hunting megafauna, in particular, provided a reliable source of food security. It also allowed people to build permanent settlements, focus on art, engage in long-distance trade, and organize elaborate burials.

To understand the lifestyle of the Gravettians, let us examine one of the most well-studied sites: Dolní Věstonice. It is worth noting that such open-air settlements were characteristic of Central and Eastern Europe. In contrast, Gravettians in Western Europe preferred to live in caves.

DOLNÍ VĚSTONICE: THE WORLD'S FIRST PERMANENT SETTLEMENT

Illustration of a day in at Dolní Věstonice based on "Life at Dolní Věstonice by Giovanni Caselli."

Social hierarchies, permanent housing, arts and crafts, and a division of labor are all characteristics of a settled society. In the twentieth century, archaeologists believed these changes only emerged after the First Agricultural Revolution, also known as the Neolithic Revolution.

While farming represented a significant advancement in human evolution, many aspects of settled life can be traced back to the Gravettian period, particularly to the site of Dolní Věstonice.

Dolní Věstonice, situated in the heart of Central Europe, provides an extraordinary glimpse into life 27,000 years ago. After its discovery, archaeologist Bohuslav Klíma led further excavations, revealing a treasure trove of art and human innovations. The village consisted of five huts constructed from mammoth bones, surrounded by a fence made from tusks, earth, and timber, with animal skins likely used for the roofs.

Life revolved around a central bonfire that likely burned day and night, keeping predators at bay. Inside the largest hut, families gathered around five hearths, one of which was cleverly rigged with mammoth bones to hold a spit for roasting meat. It's easy to imagine the hum of activity, the rhythmic tapping of tools, and the occasional burst of laughter.

At the top of the hill stood a smaller hut. Inside was a marvel of human ingenuity: one of the world's first kilns. The Gravettians mixed clay with powdered bone, shaped and threw the lumps in this dome-shaped oven, transforming them into durable ceramics.

Scattered across the floor were fragments of animal figurines—bears, foxes, and lions—and striking female figures, such as the Venus of Dolní Věstonice, with exaggerated curves that may have symbolized fertility or protection.

Excavations at Dolní Věstonice revealed the world's first woven textiles. Ninety particles of clay bore impressions of braided threads. Archaeologists also found evidence of basket weaving and net making at Pavlov.

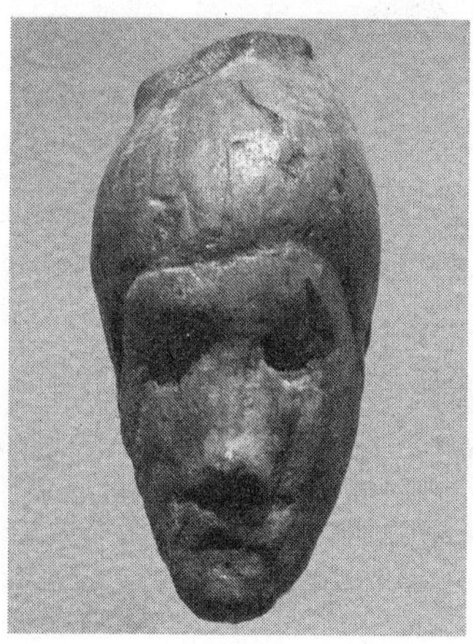

Ivory carved figurine of a woman, possibly a shaman, found at Dolní Věstonice.

One of the artifacts recovered at Dolní Věstonice was an ivory figurine of a woman with a scar on the left side of her face, possibly caused by a deformity. Her face was sagging to one side.

Who was she?

In 1949, archaeologists discovered a spectacular burial at Dolní Věstonice. Under the floor of a big hut, they found a shallow, dish-shaped pit containing the remains of a woman.

Her body was short and slender, about 160 cm (4'10"), and she rested on her right, her knees drawn to her chest. Before burying her, the community sprinkled her with red ochre, a pigment commonly used in prehistoric rituals. Two mammoth shoulder bones, one carved on the underside, covered the burial. Beside her left hand rested the bones of an Arctic fox, while her right hand clutched ten fox canines.[3] Next to her skull was a flint spearhead, probably placed as a mark of respect. The arrangement of the body with the grave goods hints that she was a shaman or a figure of spiritual influence in her community.

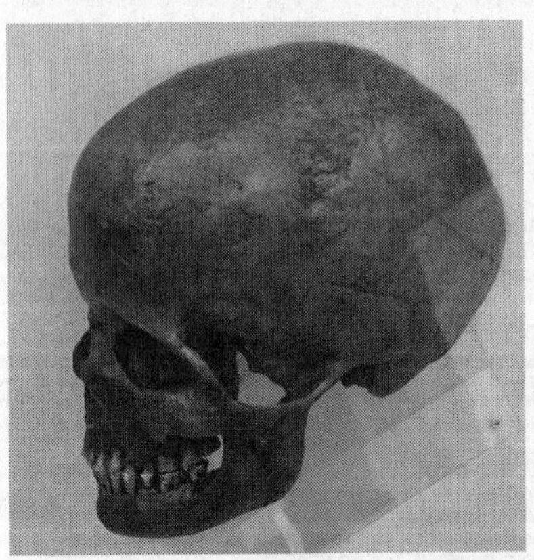

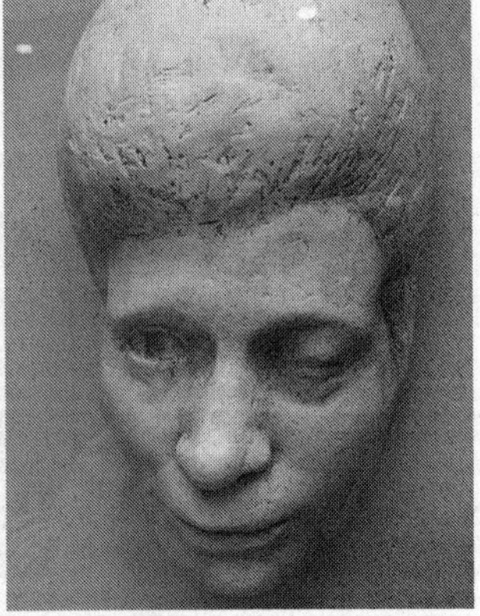

Reconstruction of the woman with the scar from Dolní Věstonice, from her cranium.

3 In many cultures foxes are vital for shamans as spiritual messengers, while fox furs are used by shamans as robes and for healing.

But the most interesting part about her was that the left side of her skull was disfigured, just like the ivory statuette. A coincidence? Maybe not. The carved ivory figurine was possibly the first known sculpture of a specific person, the shaman of Dolní Věstonice.

The shaman statuette with the scar is overshadowed by the more renowned Venus of Dolní Věstonice, one of the numerous Venus figurines discovered during the Gravettian era. These tiny idols give us a glimpse into the artistic expressions of people during the Ice Age. However, for a long time, there has been considerable controversy in interpreting these images, with attitudes towards them varying significantly between the archaeologists who first discovered them in the nineteenth century and the present day.

THE VENUS FIGURINES

Paul Hurault found the first Ice Age female figurine in Laugerie-Basse, France, in 1864. The figurine, approximately 8 cm in height, belongs to the Magdalenian culture and was made between 17,000 and 14,000 years ago. Hurault named it the *Venus Impudique*, which means the "immodest Venus" and refers to the Roman goddess of fertility. The term "Venus" stuck, and researchers continue to refer to these Ice Age artifacts as "Venus figurines."

Archaeologists have uncovered approximately 200 Venus figurines across Eurasia, dating from around 40,000 years ago to 10,000 years ago. Although the Gravettians weren't the first, or the last, to make them, most of the figurines discovered belong to the Gravettian era.

Most Gravettian artisans crafted Venus figurines from mammoth tusk ivory, while others used ceramics and various stones as materials. The stauettes exaggerate the female body, depicting huge breasts, thighs, hips, belly, genitals, and buttocks. Although the exact purpose of the Venus figurines is unknown, researchers have suggested several theories. Archaeologists in the

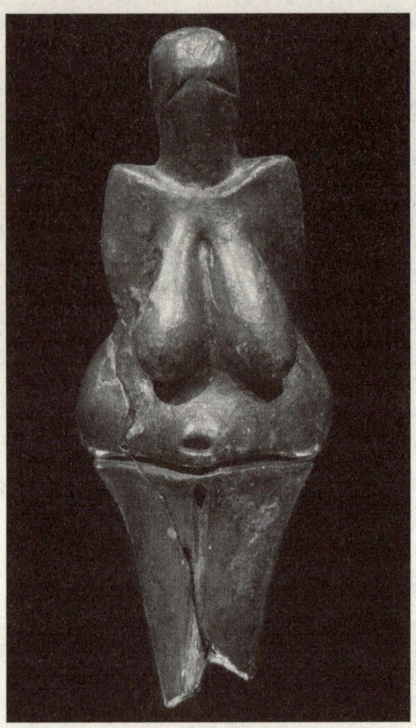

The Venus of Dolní Věstonice, dated 29,000 BP (before present) to 25,000 BP.

nineteenth century proposed that figurines were risqué Paleolithic art. However, in the twentieth century, such explanations were deemed male-centric, and several other hypotheses emerged.

According to a popular theory, these statues depict an earth mother goddess brimming with fertility. The fundamental flaw with this idea is that we don't know the religious practices of the time, and representations of the female body could have been stylistic rather than representing a pregnant woman. The discovery of multiple slim figurines raises the possibility that the Gravettians also depicted girls not yet of childbearing age, or women who weren't pregnant. The Venus Impudique is slender and graceful, offering a different perspective on these Ice Age figurines. Hence, the association of Venus figurines with fertility is far from certain.

Venus Impudique, the first discovered Venus figurine.

Another hypothesis suggests that the Venus figurines represented the beauty standards of the era. Did the Gravettians find a specific body type more attractive than others? Why so?

During the Ice Age, the danger of starvation was real. Hence, it is unlikely that all women could have possibly looked like the depictions on most Venus figurines. Yet, people also had access to millions of calories, such as when a mammoth was hunted. An ideal beauty standard may have emerged where greater fat distribution was associated with childbearing, which people may have found attractive.

Art historian LeRoy McDermott hypothesized that pregnant women looking down from their bodies crafted these figurines, which explains why they lack a face and feet. Mirrors were not available; therefore, the figurines served as a substitute for self-reflection. Many have questioned McDermott's idea because women could have readily looked at their reflection in bodies of water as a substitute for mirrors.

At the beginning of this chapter, I shared a story of a child holding the Venus of Dolní Věstonice. A 2004 tomography scan revealed the fingerprint of a child between seven and fifteen who had handled the figurine before dropping it in the kiln.

Could these figurines be amulets, children's toys, or good luck symbols?

The source material for the most well-known Venus figurine, the Venus of Willendorf, found in Willendorf, Austria, provides a clue supporting this theory.

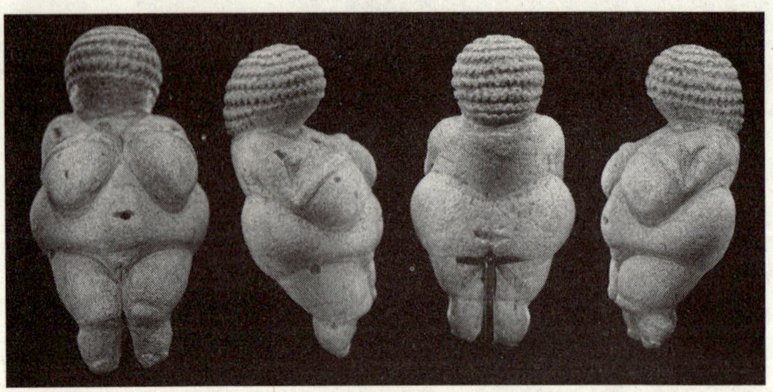

The Venus of Willendorf was made of limestone from Italy or Ukraine.

A 2022 study revealed that the Venus of Willendorf was made of limestone sourced from either Lake Garda in Italy or eastern Ukraine. The likelihood of the material originating in Italy is greater due to its proximity to Austria. Regardless of where the limestone originated, the figurine was likely a product of long-distance trade.

Could the item have been produced in Italy and transported across the Alps to Austria? We can't rule out the possibility, which would lend credence to the theory that Venus figurines may have served as good luck charms or children's toys.

Venus figurines were not the only art from the Gravettian period.

The earliest examples of sculptures from the Aurignacian era include the Vogelherd Horse and the Löwenmensch (lion-man) figurine, both made from mammoth ivory and discovered in Germany. The Aurignacians also left behind numerous cave paintings, such as those found in Chauvet, France; Coliboaia, Romania; and El Castillo, Spain.

Gravettian era art depicting horses, from the Cosquer Cave, France.

The Gravettians expanded on the artistic traditions of their ancestors, carving animal and human objects from ivory, ceramics, and stone. A prominent example of cave paintings from this era is found in Cosquer Cave in France, featuring hand stencils that date back 27,000 years ago and vibrant animal depictions from approximately 19,000 years ago. These illustrations showcase bisons, ibexes, horses, seals, and what could be auks and jellyfish, creating a stunning gallery.

Gravettians used the canines of animals such as Arctic foxes, shells, and beads to carve intricate jewelry. Archaeologists have discovered these decorative items in Gravettian graves, which suggests they could've belonged to the elite.

A Gravettian necklace from Brillenhöhle Cave, Germany.
Thilo Parg/Wikimedia Commons; License: CC BY-SA 3.0

The Gravettian period marked a significant transition in human evolution. Though we have earlier evidence of Homo sapiens and Neanderthals burying their dead, during the Upper Paleolithic we see elaborate burials.

The Aurignacians buried their loved ones, but the evidence of a widespread practice is limited. The Gravettians displayed a profound connection with the deceased. Archaeologists have found around 50 burials from this period across Eurasia. The burial practices indicate that the Gravettians had a social

The Löwenmensch sculpture, dated 35,000 BP–41,000 BP, found at Hohlenstein-Stadel, Germany.

hierarchy and exhibited care for the dead in ways that would not become common until approximately 12,000 years ago, after the end of the Ice Age.

RITUAL BURIALS OF THE GRAVETTIANS

The triple burial at Dolní Věstonice

On August 13, 1986, archaeologists made an incredible discovery at Dolní Věstonice: a triple burial dating back around 28,000 years ago. The grave held the remains of three young men between sixteen and twenty-five. For a long time, people thought the central figure was female, but DNA testing later revealed it was male.

The burial was anything but ordinary. The bodies were laid in a line, carefully covered with charred spruce logs and branches. Perhaps the grave was set on fire, resulting in the burning of the wood.

The central figure was placed first, with the other two positioned on top of or alongside him. One lay face down, and

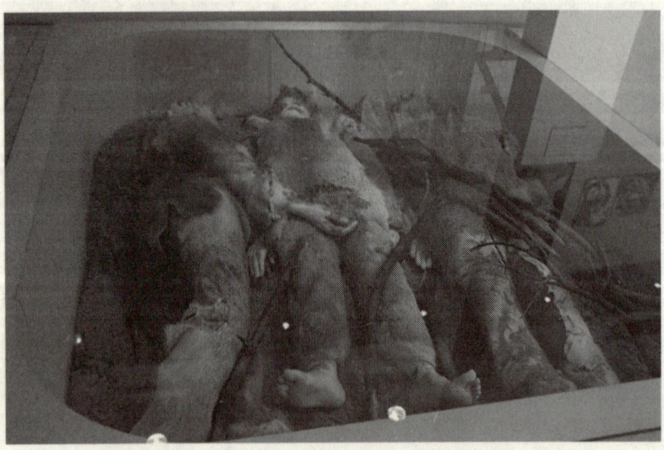

Reconstruction of the Triple burial at Dolní Věstonice.

the other was on his side, his hands resting near the middle individual's pelvis.

Red ochre added a splash of color to the scene. All three buried individuals had ochre on their heads, and the central figure also had the pigment sprinkled around his pelvis. The young man in the middle stood out in another way: his legs were curved because of a genetic condition.

Were these individuals related?

All three were missing the frontal sinus, had benign tumors in their ears, and a distinct positioning of their wisdom teeth has led to theories that they were relatives.

Is it possible that they died together?

A hypothesis suggests that one of them died, possibly the person with the deformed legs, and the other two joined him in a ritual sacrifice, either voluntarily or forced.

The triple burial has puzzled experts. The cause of death for the three individuals remains undetermined. Nevertheless, this unique grave illustrates the social complexities of the period.

Il Giovane Principe

Let us visit Arene Candide (Cavern of the White Sands) in Liguria, Italy, for our next burial. Excavations revealed 19 burial pits, dated to the Paleolithic period. One of them stands out, the *Il Giovane Principe*, meaning the "young prince."

Il Giovane Principe is a remarkable burial of a 15-year-old boy, dating back 23,500 years ago. He was buried with care, and his people made extensive arrangements for his journey to the afterlife. The young prince's grave was deep in the ground, 6.7 meters (22 feet) below the surface, and was filled with a layer of red ochre before laying him to rest. His body faced south, and he was surrounded by an astonishing array of grave goods, which included a cap made of deer canine and shells adorning

The Young Prince, a Paleolithic burial from Italy.

his head. Before burying him, his people covered him in shellfish and mammoth ivory jewelry. Four beautifully crafted deer antler batons were found nearby, with a 23-cm (9.1-in.) flint blade in his right hand. The flint was sourced from southeastern France, hinting at long-distance trade.

Before the final burial, the grave was sprinkled with yellow ochre, adding another layer of ritual significance.

Because of the wealth of grave goods, archaeologists have speculated that he may have been a young leader or the son of an influential shaman. The story of the young prince's death is a sad one. He suffered serious injuries to his jaw and shoulder, possibly from an encounter with a bear or a cave lion. Isotope analysis of his teeth revealed that approximately a quarter of his diet consisted of marine protein.

The fascinating burial of the young prince reveals the special treatment of the deceased elite. Funerary rituals were elaborate, and the Gravettians settled in the region took extra care to ensure the young man's journey to the afterlife was smooth.

Extensive grave goods weren't limited to the young prince. Intricate jewelry found at the Sunghir archaeological site,

200 km east of Moscow, gives us further information about the burial practices of the Gravettians.

The Sunghir burials

The Sunghir site, discovered in 1955 while digging clay pits, provides a fascinating insight into the lives of Gravettian communities located east of Moravia. It reveals a story of cultural and genetic continuity. After 16 field seasons, from 1957 to 1977, archaeologists uncovered evidence of human habitation at Sunghir that dates back between 32,000 and 24,000 years ago.

The presence of surface dwellings suggests that the site was used seasonally, possibly as a gathering place at certain times of the year. Unlike Dolní Věstonice and Pavlov, it was not a permanently occupied site.

Two burials at Sunghir—Graves 1 and 2—are among Europe's most exciting Gravettian discoveries. Grave 1 held an adult male adorned with ivory-beaded clothing, jewelry, and spears. Grave 2 contained two adolescents buried head-to-head with an adult femur filled with red ochre.

The adolescents were long thought to be twins. However, later genetic analysis revealed that they shared a maternal

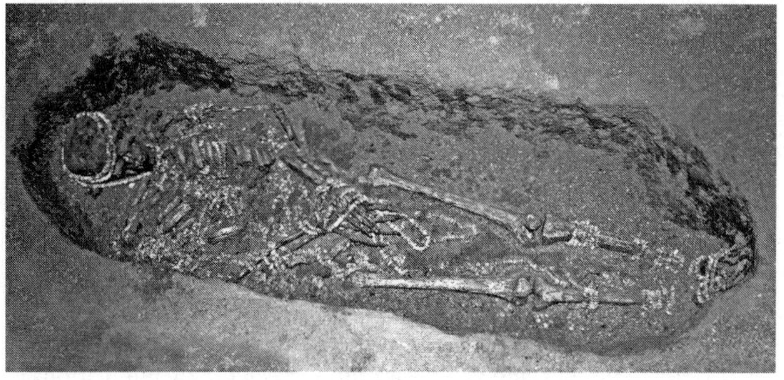

Burial of an adult male at Sunghir.

lineage but were not siblings. They may have been victims of ritual sacrifice.

Archaeologists found over 13,000 tiny ivory beads in these graves, an extraordinary number that would have required 10,000 hours to create. The remarkable skill and labor involved demonstrate the significant investment people had in these burials.

Earlier, we discussed two distinct origins of the Gravettians, one from the East, in Russia, and another from Belgium. Genetic studies revealed that the Sunghir individuals shared a close affinity with the people at Dolní Věstonice. They contain the haplogroup C1,[4] common among ancient West Eurasians but rare in modern Europeans.

The genetic variation tells us how people migrated from West Eurasia to the heart of Europe during the Ice Age, only for the lineage to die out eventually.

END OF THE GRAVETTIANS

Most elements of the Gravettian culture disappeared 22,000 years ago, though some persisted till 17,000 years ago, closer to the Last Glacial Maximum. The Solutrean culture in France and Iberia, and the Epigravettian culture in Italy, the Balkans, and Eastern Europe succeeded the Gravettians.

Genetic studies show that Epigravettians were distinct from Gravettians. However, the Solutrean culture continued

---

4 Y-chromosome, or male, haplogroup C1 is one of the two primary branches of the haplogroup C, which is found in the indigenous ancient populations of Siberia, East Asia, Central Asia, North America, Australia as well as some populations of Japan and the Levant. The subclade C1a2 was found in Paleolithic populations of Czech Republic, Belgium, and Sunghir.

the Gravettian traditions, incorporating more advanced tool-making techniques.

The Gravettian era was humanity's earliest hints towards civilization. In the frigid conditions of the Ice Age, these incredible people imagined settling down, building permanent houses to keep themselves warm, and making ceramics and art. They also manufactured clothes, baskets, nets, and jewelry, and had elaborate burial practices.

Their attempts towards a settled life were imprinted in human memory as hunter-gatherers of future generations began cracking the code of civilization. One such group of hunter-gatherers started settling in the Near East, pioneering the development of farming and urbanization.

2

The Mysterious Builders of Göbekli Tepe

Göbekli Tepe, in Türkiye's Şanliurfa Province, is one of the most widely discussed archaeological discoveries of the twenty-first century. Yet, much controversy surrounds the identity of the builders of the mysterious megaliths at the site. These structures have become the subject of a heated discussion regarding the origins of organized religion and farming. The megaliths erected between 9600 BCE and 8200 BCE have also piqued the interest of alternative historians who postulate that survivors of a lost Ice Age civilization built the monuments. Others have proposed that Göbekli Tepe was the Garden of Eden, while some believe that Sumerian mythical beings, the Anunnaki, built it. However, evidence doesn't support such theories.

Göbekli Tepe, meaning "pot-bellied hill" in Turkish, was discovered during an archaeological survey conducted by the University of Chicago, in 1963. Unfortunately, the site didn't receive much attention, and it wasn't until 1995 that archaeologist Klaus Schmidt "re-discovered" Göbekli Tepe and began excavation. Schmidt's initial assumption was that hunter-gatherers built the remarkable megaliths. He also suggested the site was the world's first temple.

He passed away in 2014, and since then, significant developments have taken place, challenging our initial understanding of Göbekli Tepe. Some ideas, such as whether it was a temple as first proposed, are now less definite. Given that only a tiny section of the site has been excavated, much of the present information could be outdated in five years, which is the beauty of archaeology.

The megaliths at Göbekli Tepe.

After our journey to the first permanent human settlement at Dolní Věstonice, we will learn about the enigmatic people who built Göbekli Tepe. The megaliths are one of the earliest examples of monumental architecture in history and have challenged traditional assumptions about human evolution. We have little information about who built these magnificent structures, but with the help of recent archaeological finds, we might be a step closer to understanding what society was like and how they completed such a massive project without the help of an organized state.

GÖBEKLI TEPE: AN OVERVIEW

Göbekli Tepe is in Taş Tepeler (Stone Hills), at the foothills of the Taurus Mountains, overlooking the Harran Plain. Taş Tepeler has several archaeological sites, including Göbekli Tepe, Nevalı Çori,[1] Karahan Tepe, Hamzan Tepe, Sefer Tepe, Kurt Tepe, Harbetsuvan Tepe, Sayburç, and Ayanlar Höyük – all from the Pre-Pottery Neolithic (PPN) period.

As the name implies, PPN refers to a period in the Neolithic era[2] before the discovery of pottery. Crop and animal domestication were in their early stages of development.

We can classify PPN into two periods: PPNA and PPNB.

PPNA corresponds to the early part of the era, roughly 10,000 BCE to 8700 BCE, whereas PPNB lasted between 8800 BCE and 6500 BCE.

Göbekli Tepe dates back to the PPNA era, when a hybrid lifestyle with elements of sedentism, and hunting and gathering began taking shape.

The aerial view of Göbekli Tepe shows four circular complexes, Enclosures A, B, C, and D, with diameters varying from 10 to 30 m. Geophysical surveys found 16 more similar enclosures. We can also notice some smaller rectangular compounds.

Each circular enclosure has two giant T-shaped pillars (5.5 m tall) in the center, flanked by multiple smaller T-pillars. Surveys show that there may be around 200 similar pillars at the site. The larger pillars weigh an average of 8–10 tons.

How did people carry such massive structures?

Göbekli Tepe sits on a limestone Plateau, where workers quarried stones for its massive pillars. The location was suitable

---

1 Ç in Turkish is pronounced as "ch," as in church. Hence, Nevalı Çori = Nevali + Chori, and Sayburç = say + burch.

2 The Neolithic or the New Stone Age in the Near East lasted from 10,000 BCE to 5500 BCE, and in some places like southern Levant upto 4500 BCE.

Aerial view of the site showing circular enclosures A, B, C, and D. The rectangular structures could have domestic purposes.

for quarrying because the limestone layers were naturally separated by fault lines, making it easy to chisel pieces without digging beneath them. The limestone was hard and crystalline, ideal for sculpting with basic tools such as flint and wood.

Workers utilized these tools to carve channels in the limestone that matched the dimensions of the finished object. Wooden beams and wedges were most likely employed to hoist the finished pieces. However, not all attempts were successful as workers abandoned several nearly completed pillars and blocks because of faults or fissures. The rejected pieces enable archaeologists to investigate quarrying operations firsthand. The largest unfinished pillar discovered is 7 m long and 1.5 m thick, likely abandoned because of a fissure or its sheer size.

Archaeologists studied the ethnographic records from Nias, Indonesia, to understand how the builders transported these massive pillars. In the early twentieth century, 525 men hurled a megalith over 3 km using wooden sleds. Though the giant structure in Indonesia was considerably smaller, scholars believe hundreds of laborers transported the pillars at Göbekli Tepe using comparable techniques.

Reconstruction of the central pillars from enclosure D. Arms are visible on the main shaft.

Göbekli Tepe's T-shaped pillars aren't unique, as other PPNA sites in the region, such as Nevalı Çori, contain similar structures. However, the distinctive feature of the pillars at Göbekli Tepe is their rich detail, containing depictions of animal figurines, including foxes, ducks, vultures, serpents, scorpions, cranes, and lizards. The majority of the animals carved on the pillars were predators. The prominent depiction of beasts of prey on the pillars led Schmidt and archaeologist Joris Peters to hypothesize that the predators may have been made to ward off evil and functioned as totems.

Looking at the pillars, we can see different parts of the human body carved onto them, such as the elbows, shoulders, and fingers. Each pillar has a draped loincloth around it. In Enclosure D, pillar 43, we see a decapitated man with an erect phallus. What could these abstract human-like depictions represent? Though we may never know the exact answer, an earlier structure provides hints.

The Urfa Man is the earliest known life-sized statue depicting a human. Standing over 6 feet tall and carved from limestone, it dates back to 9000 BCE. Found near Göbekli Tepe at the Urfa Yeni-Yol archaeological site, it has a quiet presence—hands folded, obsidian eyes gazing into eternity. Was it a deity, an ancestor, a shaman, or a high-ranking member of society venerated later in the T-pillars at Göbekli Tepe? Did the vague human depictions in the megaliths honor the Urfa Man?

Current research is focused on interpreting the imagery and symbolism of the pillars. As we will see later, they could represent stories and creation myths important to the people who gathered at the site.

Göbekli Tepe's early phase (c. 9500 BCE) included enclosures A, B, C, and D, featuring T-pillars. The people most likely used the areas for community or ceremonial functions. They lacked

The Urfa Man, the world's first human sculpture.

fireplaces and other indicators of everyday life, implying that they served as gathering spaces for special occasions. The building of additional walls within the circular enclosures resulted in a reduction of their area over time.

Later, smaller rectangular structures became increasingly common. These had lime-plastered floors and strong walls, and were constructed in clusters, frequently sharing walls with adjoining structures. Archaeologists suggest these structures were contemporaneous; most date to around the same period, built approximately at the beginning of the ninth millennium BCE.

Unlike the earlier spherical enclosures, these rectangular ones served a practical purpose for daily activities. People used them to grind grains and prepare meals, and the flat roofs most likely acted as workstations. How did people enter the houses? Chances are the entrances were on the roofs, a feature

Enclosure C at Göbekli Tepe.

we'll encounter and discuss in greater detail in Chapter 3 on Çatalhöyük.

There was a time when both rectangular and circular styles of buildings coexisted. Some ancient circular buildings were still operating, but newer rectangular structures came up nearby. When the builders abandoned earlier constructions, they meticulously filed them with tools and carvings, maybe as ritual closure.

Schmidt first thought Göbekli Tepe was a temple where hunter-gatherers came together for rituals. He concluded that the architects of Göbekli Tepe could not have lived sedentary lives because of the lack of water sources and minimal evidence of homes. The absence of domesticated animal bones and the presence of a significant amount of wild grains further support his arguments. Hence, Schmidt hypothesized that the people who used the site gathered for religious activities and feasting.

But how valid is this assumption?

DID PEOPLE LIVE AT GÖBEKLI TEPE?

According to popular belief, people first lived in nomadic hunter-gatherer societies before settling down and cultivating land some 11,000 years ago, when global temperatures rose and the climate was ideal for farming.

But this narrative isn't backed by archaeological evidence.

In the previous chapter, we discussed the world's first permanent human settlements at Dolní Věstonice, 26,000 BP (before present), during the pinnacle of the Ice Age. Our transition to sedentism was a long, drawn-out process with many starts and stops.

Before farming began, humans cultivated and processed wild grains for thousands of years. Cereal processing in the

Near East dates back to 23,000 BP, and the Paleolithic Ohalo II[3] archaeological site in northern Israel has one of the earliest

Sickles and tools for harvesting wild grains found at Ohalo II, 23,000 BP.

3 Ohalo II was in a transition stage between the Upper Paleolithic and Epipaleolithic periods and is attributed to both eras. Epipaleolithic in the Near East is defined as the period between Upper Paleolithic to the Neolithic approximately 20,000 to 10,000 BP.

examples. Located near the southwest shore of the Sea of Galilee, we have evidence of some of the first brushwood dwellings and cultivation of wild plants. Humans experimented with agriculture long before the so-called "agricultural revolution." Archaeologists found five glossed flint sickle blades and knives used during harvesting and discovered grinding tools for processing nearly ripe or semi-ripe grains.

After Ohalo II, the first clear evidence of sedentism was seen a few millennia before the PPNA period in the Natufian culture (15,000 BP to 11,500 BP) in modern-day Israel, which was semi-sedentary. Its inhabitants lived in settled communities, processed wild grain, hunted animals, and brewed beer. Despite living in settled communities, the Natufians depended on hunted animals, wild plants, and grains for subsistence.

At the Tell Abu Hureyra site, in Syria, we see the dawn of agriculture during the PPNA period. The Natufians inhabited Abu Hureyra 14,000 years ago and sowed the seeds of agriculture by exploiting wild cereals. The innovative Natufians were also among the earliest brewers in history. Evidence of the world's first beermaking process was discovered at Raqefet Cave in Mount Carmel, Israel. They were sophisticated and displayed several aspects of settled life that would become commonplace thousands of years later.

The achievements of the Natufians led archaeologists to question whether agriculture was necessary for humans to settle down, as there are several contradictory examples that we'll encounter throughout this book.

Around the end of the Natufian culture, the world experienced the Younger Dryas, a geological episode of severe cooling that occurred between 12,900 and 11,700 years ago. Some experts believe the Younger Dryas's near-glacial conditions significantly impacted megafauna, leading to the late Pleistocene extinctions. Others argue that megafaunal extinctions began much before this time. In the Near East, the Younger Dryas may have prompted the last Natufians to adopt a more mobile lifestyle, as their access to game and wild cereals decreased due to increased aridity. However, by the beginning of the PPNA period, the number of small wild game had exceeded that of the early Natufian period, and small cultivated lands supporting dense populations began to emerge.

Though it is tempting to connect the end of the Younger Dryas to the birth of agriculture in the Near East, there isn't a strong correlation between the two events. Why would humans start farming when wild game numbers exceeded those of the early Natufian era? Hence, the period immediately preceding the rise of Göbekli Tepe witnessed the emergence of a hybrid lifestyle, where people hunted and cultivated wild crops. As the lines between nomadism and sedentism were blurry, Schmidt initially theorized that hunter-gatherers must have assembled at the site as part of a religious ritual and built the T-pillars. He based this hypothesis on the lack of water sources, but more recent findings paint a different picture.

During the initial excavations, Schmidt and his team found no natural water sources near the site. The nearest water source, in the village of Edene Köyü, is about 5 km northeast of Şanlıurfa. Acquiring a consistent water supply across this distance would have been impossible for those living at Göbekli Tepe, assuming they lived there.

At Göbekli Tepe, Schmidt discovered a 6-m-deep funnel-shaped cistern with a large storage volume of 60 cubic meters, which is still in use. However, he deemed it unsuitable for a year-round water supply, as the quantity needed by the dwellers would be greater.

A recent geophysical survey indicates that the water table was higher during the PPNA period and may have contributed to the nearby springs, which are now inactive. The primary cistern for collecting rainwater was linked to multiple cisterns beneath the site's bedrock, and the potential for water storage would have been substantially greater.

In 2007 and 2009, field investigations revealed 61 rock-cut cisterns at the site. There was a doubt as to whether the residents of Göbekli Tepe built these structures or whether they were natural limestone deposits. The researchers used dynamic probing, a test used to determine depths. They found the pits were 2 to 5 meters deep, strategically placed beneath the primary water catchment. The arrangement allowed water collected in one pit to overflow into another interconnected cistern. Furthermore, channels were carved into the bedrock to connect the cisterns, similar to modern drains, indicating that the design wasn't accidental but a visionary water collection system.

The researchers concluded that the rock pits were indeed cisterns that stored water using an ancient rainwater harvesting technique.

The cistern network suggests a well-planned approach to permanent settlement at the site, rather than relying on accidental limestone deposits. The residents could have stored water for an extended period of habitation, anticipating the shortage during the drier months. The rainwater storage system at Göbekli Tepe may be the world's oldest surviving drinking water storage facility. Why would hunter-gatherers take so much trouble to harvest and store rainwater when they could've moved to the nearest spring?

At Göbekli Tepe, we see a hybrid semi-sedentary culture. In addition to cisterns, the presence of detailed stone masonry, workbenches, hearths, grinding stones for plant processing, and limestone vessels for food storage suggests that people may have occupied the site for a significant part of the year. The inhabitants were going through a transitional period. They were finally settling down, but hunting was crucial to their diet.

In midsummer, as part of what archaeologist Oliver Dietrich terms "work feasts," the numerous individuals who built the megaliths would gather to hunt and prepare meals. As Schmidt hypothesized, the site held religious significance, but it is also possible that people lived in the area where they prayed. We should remember that the idea of a place of worship separate from one's home is a modern, secular concept. People living in Göbekli Tepe 10,000 years ago may not have made such a distinction. This blurring of boundaries between domestic and religious functions becomes even more pronounced in the PPNB period, as we will explore in the next chapter.

We can imagine people living in Göbekli Tepe, at least for most of the year. The rectangular compounds near the circular enclosures were household structures, further hinting at a semi-sedentary lifestyle.

Although we have moved on from Schmidt's "hunter-gatherer" theory, it is undeniable that Göbekli Tepe predates the rise of full-fledged agriculture and animal domestication. People may have figured out how to cultivate wild grains and herd wild animals, but they still needed leaders to coordinate the construction of the megaliths. Which brings us to our next question: Did the people of Göbekli Tepe have an elite class that directed the mega projects?

Who were they?

THE INSPIRED INDIVIDUALS OF GÖBEKLI TEPE

There was no pharaoh or priest-king to direct megaprojects during the PPNA era. We are looking at cultures before state formation. In the absence of a figure of authority, what drives people to complete challenging tasks?

Lee Clare, one of the site's lead archaeologists, argues that charisma played a significant role in encouraging prehistoric societies to undertake such monumental projects.

Citing Jacques Cauvin, an influential French archaeologist renowned for his monumental research on the prehistory of the

The totem pole at Göbekli Tepe is proof of shamanic influence.

Near East, Clare notes that in prehistoric communities, specific "inspired individuals" possessed a natural superiority that enabled them to exert power during certain phases. For example, several Paleo-Indian tribes had war leaders only when the conflict was ongoing. Once the conflict was over and peace prevailed, the tribe disbanded the "war chief" position. At Göbekli Tepe, some people may have led others during construction and ritual feasts, thus forming the society's elite.

Clare divides these "inspired individuals" into three groups: the ritually adept, the storyteller, and the hunter. However, some people may have belonged to more than one category.

Archaeologists have theorized that shamans, or, as Clare terms them, "the ritually adept," were influential at Göbekli Tepe. Shamans played a vital role during the Paleolithic era, and as humans settled, they transitioned from animistic shamans to full-fledged priests. A new world order was emerging, characterized by an established priestly class, organized religion, and a distinct social hierarchy. The shamans may have assumed the leadership of the world in transition.

What proof do we have of the power of shamans at Göbekli Tepe?

One argument in favor of the increasing influence of the shamans is the widespread representation of death at the site. They played a vital role in interpreting death and the afterlife in prehistoric societies. We have evidence of a death cult, that is, a funerary cult focused on the veneration of ancestors, at Göbekli Tepe and the surrounding PPNA sites.

You will notice visible ribs on some animal and human figurines found at Göbekli Tepe and neighboring sites. Scholars say this represents the removal of an individual's flesh before interment. This method is known as excarnation, and some communities, such as the Tibetans, still practice it during sky burials.[4] A panel depicting vultures with a headless human body could further solidify the argument in favor of excarnation.

---

4 Sky burials are a Tibetan Buddhist burial practice where the corpse is de-fleshed and placed on a mountaintop for consumption by birds of prey, primarily vultures.

A predator (possibly a leopard) hunting a boar. Notice the visible ribs of the predator.

Though we can't conclude with certainty if the bare ribs represent excarnation, the depictions associated with death are hardly questionable.

We see evidence of human skull worship and the early stages of a skull cult at Göbekli Tepe, which expanded throughout the Fertile Crescent during the PPNB period, as we shall see in Chapter 3. In cultures where shamans hold significant power, skulls are revered and preserved. The skulls symbolize courage, and their worship is associated with respect for the deceased and their venerated status in society.

Besides the shamans, storytellers had a vital role at Göbekli Tepe. Clare claims that the depictions on the T-pillars were part of oral traditions passed down through generations. The

The vulture stone relief possibly depicts a Neolithic myth.

representations were crucial in passing on knowledge of the past and preserving cultural traditions.

Clare further proposes that the narratives discovered in each pillar were unique and belonged to a particular clan in the community. Each narrative was independent and unrelated to the stories seen on other pillars.

If this is a valid hypothesis, what kind of stories did the people of Göbekli Tepe leave behind for future generations on the megaliths?

Archaeologists believe that significant portrayals of death represent legends of the death cult passed down across generations. In particular, the image of a vulture carrying a round object, with a headless man next to it, could be a Neolithic myth associated with death.

Traditional storytellers may have risen to higher social ranks by utilizing their inherited wisdom and narrative mastery to

Animal head found at Göbekli Tepe.

influence listeners and win people over. They garnered respect and were the favored choice of social partners. Clare suggests that prestige and power may have propelled the storytellers to elite rank, but we don't have archaeological evidence to support this theory. Though the proof for a distinct class of storytellers is lacking, it is not unimaginable that people would be influenced by the power of narrative, as even in the modern world, compelling narrators can be the difference between the success and failure of a brand's campaign or political messaging.

The animal figures at Göbekli Tepe are primarily predators or hostile species, including foxes, wild boars, scorpions, leopards, and aurochs.[5] We see them in frightening stances, preparing to attack. There are non-threatening creatures, such as cranes and ducks, but they do not make up most of the images.

The emphasis on powerful predator imagery brings us to the next elite class: hunters.

The Sayburç relief.

Could the depictions of ferocious beasts show that hunting was considered respectable and that the society revered outstanding hunters?

A relief discovered at the Sayburç archaeological site, near Göbekli Tepe, in 2021, depicts a human with an aurochs. In the second half of the panel, we see the same individual holding his phallus and flanked by two leopards.

5 Aurochs is an extinct bovine species which was the wild ancestor of modern domestic cows.

In the first scene, the man seems to tease the aurochs. He is holding a snake-like object that archaeologists initially assumed was a rattlesnake or another animal's tail. However, Clare proposes that the thing is a severed penis and testicles of an aurochs. He concluded this by comparing the object in the man's hands with the genitalia of bulls. Other archaeologists disagree with the interpretation and suggest the snake-like item is a slingshot used to hunt the aurochs.

The depiction at Sayburç could be a "coming of age" event or an initiation rite in which hunting dangerous creatures was valued in society, reflecting the hunter's elite status. Depictions of kings and prominent aristocrats hunting wild animals are a consistent historical theme; hence, it is imaginable that hunters held a significant influence in the society at Göbekli Tepe.

Our knowledge of Göbekli Tepe has grown considerably in recent years. We have a better understanding of who erected these stunning megaliths. They were shifting from a hunter-gatherer lifestyle to a settled life and were on the edge of domesticating plants and animals.

Archaeologists believe that shamans, storytellers, and hunters, who were all charismatic members of the community, formed the social elite and managed the project during this pre-state era.

We have learnt a great deal about this mysterious site, but there is still much more to discover. Archaeologists have excavated only a fraction of the site, and further digs may completely alter our understanding of the mysterious megaliths and their builders.

Many interpretations of the stories are subjective. As Oliver Dietrich has aptly summed up in a social media post, if we were to examine the painting of the *Last Supper* without knowing its context, we would see a group of people eating and could add any interpretation to it. That's what is currently happening at Göbekli Tepe.

3

The Cult of the Dead at Çatalhöyük

On a chilly November afternoon in 1958, British archaeologist James Mellaart spotted a mound 450 m long, covering 32 acres, on the Anatolian Plateau near the city of Konya, in Türkiye.

Between 1961 and 1966, Mellaart excavated the mound, revealing an incredible human settlement. Rectangular, mud-brick houses arranged in a geometric pattern gave the impression that they were the ruins of an ancient metropolis. The earliest digs revealed rectangular mud-brick houses with painted walls, sculpted bullheads, burials beneath homes, and female figurines. Other artifacts included obsidian mirrors and daggers with elegant bone handles.

Did Mellaart discover a long-lost civilization?

Mellaart identified the site as a Neolithic commune. However, its size led many to question whether Stone Age people could have built such a complex settlement that almost resembled an urban center. Further excavations confirmed that the site did indeed date back to the Neolithic period, dispelling any doubts.

The mound that Mellaart found was called Çatalhöyük.[1] It was humanity's first venture into urban life, with the settlement at its peak, housing up to 8,000 people. Excavations at Çatalhöyük reveal 18 layers of continuous habitation from 7400 BCE to 5200 BCE. Unlike Göbekli Tepe, where massive megaliths and pictograms caught our attention, Çatalhöyük is all about the people.

ÇATALHÖYÜK: A BIRD'S EYE VIEW

The Çatalhöyük archaeological site.

After 1966, no further excavations took place at Çatalhöyük. Mellaart was involved in a scandal of alleged smuggling of antiquities, known as the Dorak Affair. Mellaart claimed to have encountered ancient relics, which he termed the "Dorak Treasure," after seeing a young girl wearing a unique armband. He published photos of the treasure, but when Turkish authorities investigated the case, they found that the address of the young girl where Mellaart claimed he saw the treasure was a commercial building, leading the press to accuse him of smuggling the antiquities. The Dorak Affair prompted the Turkish government to prohibit Mellaart from excavating sites

1 Çatalhöyük is pronounced as "Chatal + Hoyuk," "ch" as in "church."

in Türkiye in 1964. But the authorities later overturned the ban, allowing him to excavate only at Çatalhöyük with a local government-approved assistant.

Fortunately, Ian Hodder, one of Mellaart's students at the University of Cambridge, was inspired by his lectures about Çatalhöyük and obtained permission to begin digging the site in 1993. Hodder, who led the Çatalhöyük Research Project until 2018, made significant contributions to our understanding of this Neolithic settlement.

At Çatalhöyük, the houses were crammed together in a labyrinth because no streets connected them. One had to use the roof and a ladder to enter and exit a dwelling. Each house was occupied for 80 years, after which the residents deliberately razed it and built a new home over the demolished structure.

The dwellings were similar in design, each house having two rooms. The kitchen, situated near the entrance, featured a hearth and an oven. It was part of the main room and included a raised platform for domestic tasks. Beneath this platform were the burial chambers. A small storage space beside the main room housed grains and animal hides.

The walls of the central area feature enormous sculpted bullheads with horns pointing at the viewer. The walls are plastered and depict scenes of hunting stags, aurochs, and wild boars. They also have murals featuring giant vultures flying over headless humans, a theme we encounter in Göbekli Tepe.

Despite the abundance of hunting depictions in the dwellings, the inhabitants primarily relied on sheep and goats for meat. The residents of Çatalhöyük were early farmers who had just started domesticating plants and animals. However, recent studies suggest that they depended on wild grains, plants, legumes, and game meat, such as deer, to supplement their diet.

A recent discovery provides further insight into the diets of the people at Çatalhöyük. In March 2024, archaeologists discovered

Reconstruction of a mural depicting the hunting of an aurochs.

an 8,600-year-old bread at the site. The uncooked bread was inside an oven-like structure, along with wheat, barley, and pea seeds. Analysis of the bread at Necmettin Erbakan University dated it to 6600 BCE, making it the oldest known evidence of a whole loaf.[2] There was a finger impression in the center of the bread, indicating that the preparation techniques were similar to those used today. Scanning Electron Microscope images revealed air spaces in the dough. Surprisingly, though the baker had fermented the bread and it was ready, it remained unbaked. Maybe it was an oversight, thanks to which we have definite proof of an essential staple of Çatalhöyük's people.

The discovery of bread helps us appreciate how the transition from a hunter-gatherer stage to farming was gradual. At Göbekli Tepe, we encountered semi-sedentary individuals. By the PPNB period, they had settled and begun to farm, though they still

2 Evidence of breadcrumbs were found in Naturfian sites and were dated 14,000 years ago but unlike the find at Çatalhöyük a complete bread loaf or dough wasn't discovered.

valued hunting and considered collecting wild grains an essential part of their lives. An analysis of eight seed samples found at the site confirms that the exploitation of wild grains was as vital to the residents of Çatalhöyük as farming.

One of the primary features of Çatalhöyük is the abundance of remarkable female figurines, which Mellaart and the initial excavators imagined to be part of a fertility cult. The most famous among them is the clay figurine of the Seated Woman of Çatalhöyük.

A FERTILITY CULT?

The Seated Woman of Çatalhöyük depicts a nude, corpulent female seated on two feline armrests, likely representing either leopards or lionesses. Due to the posture of a prominent figure atop a throne, Mellaart interpreted it as a "mother goddess" and proposed that the society at Çatalhöyük was matriarchal.

More recent research, however, has cast doubt on this theory. Mellaart claimed that he found the "goddess" in what he called a "shrine." Later excavations revealed that most of the animal and human clay figurines were in trash heaps, along with plant and animal remains. The discovery raises the question of whether they were indeed significant from a religious perspective. The area of the houses with plastered walls and sculptured bullheads can be assumed to be of spiritual importance, or a "shrine," as Mellaart would call it. However, further digs near the so-called shrines didn't reveal any clay figurines.

Why would people throw holy idols in the garbage?

Hodder's research moves away from binary interpretations of patriarchy or matriarchy at Çatalhöyük, focusing instead on the evidence discovered. Less than 5 percent of over 2,000 figurines found at the site are female. The vast majority of them are male. There are ample depictions of men with erect genitalia, which

The Seated Woman of Çatalhöyük, with two felines, possibly leopards or lionesses.

could indicate this was a period in history where human self-expression was evident. Erect phalluses and buxom females may also be associated with fertility.

Further analysis of the diets and customs related to death reveals that men and women shared an equal social status. Naturally, the high-status individuals had access to better food and the choicest meats. People venerated the elite after their death. Based on the treatment of the influential individuals following their demise, Hodder theorizes that the Seated Woman of Çatalhöyük was just as likely to be associated with death as she is with life.

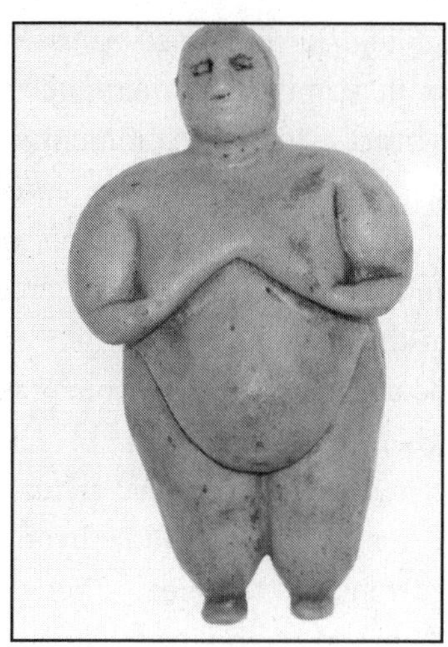

Reconstruction of a limestone figurine of an overweight woman found at Çatalhöyük.

In 2016, Hodder's team found a statuette of a voluptuous woman in Çatalhöyük. The well-preserved limestone figurine dates between 6300 BCE and 6000 BCE. The find is rare since most figurines from the site are made of clay and have deteriorated over time. The stauette, approximately 17 cm long and weighing 1 kg, is remarkably detailed, featuring characteristics such as fat rolls, distinct limbs, and an undercut belly. It showcases the skill of a veteran artisan, utilizing fine tools such as flint or obsidian. The archaeologists found the figurine in a large house, placed on a platform alongside an obsidian blade, a second, less refined figurine made of yellow limestone, and a piece of galena.

Interpretations of ancient artifacts always depend on the archaeologist and their worldview. Hodder prefers not to associate these figurines with divinity. Hence, the theory that this represents a "goddess" is debatable. Instead, Hodder believes the image could be of an older woman who was a part of the social elite. In this context, his team interprets the high body fat as a symbol of her superior social standing. She likely performed little to no manual labor associated with farming, hunting, and construction, and may have directed rituals within the community.

Further, Hodder believes the figurine represented a societal shift as Çatalhöyük was moving away from an egalitarian society. Houses became more independent, and increased agricultural output resulted in the concentration of power in the hands of a few. The figurine of the voluptuous woman was discovered in the later layers, when the proto-city had reached its peak, and fatness was associated with high social status. During this era, burial beneath the homes ceased. Hodder hypothesizes that such figurines may have replaced the idea of burial beneath homes, and that placing them was symbolic of their ancestral traditions.

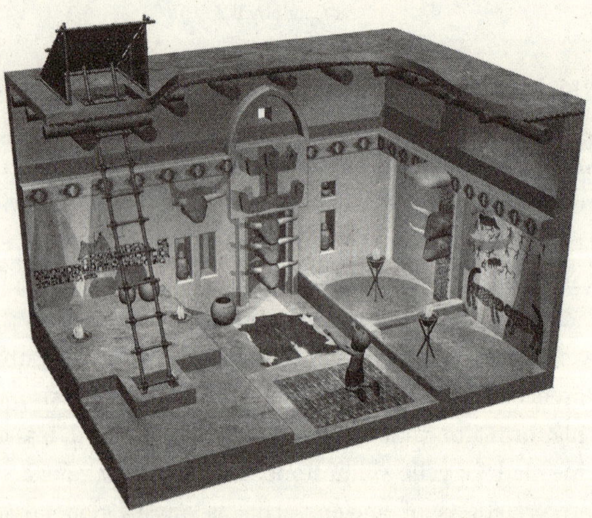

A 3-D reconstruction of a Çatalhöyük house showing a resident involved in ritual prayers.

At Çatalhöyük, archaeologists haven't found evidence of public buildings or a priestly class. Hodder hypothesizes that people linked sacred rituals to domestic activities and did not distinguish between a religious setting and their homes. As discussed in the previous chapter, the boundaries between living spaces and places of worship are a modern concept. Rituals dictated people's lives. Some of these customs influenced their attitudes towards death.

Although Çatalhöyük lacked a distinct social hierarchy, burials indicate specific individuals received preferential treatment. Let's learn more about the different types of burials and the potential social stratification that may have existed.

BURIALS AT ÇATALHÖYÜK

Reconstruction of a typical house at Çatalhöyük. The entrance and exit were through the roof, accessible only with a ladder.

If you've lost a loved one, you probably have a photo of them somewhere in your home. Many also carry the deceased's cremated remains in an urn. Pictures and urns evoke memories of those who have passed away.

Although we enjoy remembering special moments with those who are no longer with us, we prefer they rest far away from our living spaces. The dead are laid to rest in cemeteries or cremated. Around 9,000 years ago, the residents of Çatalhöyük buried the dead beneath their houses. The deceased were family to them, and the modern boundaries separating the dead and the living didn't exist.

During the Neolithic era, burying people beneath houses in the Near East was a common practice. We encounter intramural burials[3] at other Neolithic sites such as Nevalı Çori, Aşıklı Höyük, and Jericho.

However, the scale of burials seen at Çatalhöyük is unparalleled, with some houses containing as many as 60 graves. We can envision it as a prehistoric town on top of a cemetery.

Since 1995, archaeologists have unearthed more than 800 skeletons at Çatalhöyük. The excavations revealed that some members of the society buried their dead in specific areas of the house. The home's north was for adult male and female interments. The people of Çatalhöyük rarely buried adolescents, infants, and newborns in the north. Most of the sub-adult burials occurred in the storage room, though one can find their graves scattered throughout the house. Some, both adults and children, were buried outside the dwellings. I am sure you're wondering why they didn't bury the children in the north and why they opted to bury some people outside their homes. I will explain it later.

Sub-adult burials comprise 57 percent of the total, with adult burials accounting for 43 percent. There is one exception to burying adults in the northern part of a home. Genetic research shows visitors from nearby settlements who died at Çatalhöyük didn't have the privilege of a burial in the house's north portion. Regardless of age, people buried them in the storage rooms.

---

3 Intramural burials are interments beneath the dwellings like we encounter at Çatalhöyük and were also seen at other sites in the Near East during the PPNB.

Perhaps there was an early concept of "citizenship," with burial privileges in the north reserved only for adults born in Çatalhöyük.

Some burials contained complete skeletons, and others had disturbed remains. To get a clear picture of the depositions,[4] archaeologist Peter Andrews classified the human remains into three categories.

The first category includes primary burials, articulated skeletons[5] found in their original place of interment. The next category comprises secondary burials, which involve the relocation of articulated or partial skeletons from their original burial sites and redeposition in a different location.

The final group consists of primary disturbed burials. These are articulated skeletons that have been disturbed by the residents. For example, a skeleton is sometimes lifted and reburied to make room for other bodies in its original burial place.

Primary disturbed skeletons accounted for 52 percent of the bodies analyzed, while primary skeletons comprised 42 percent, and secondary skeletons made up 6 percent. It appears that most funerals involved moving and reburying the bodies, suggesting several burials occurred in the same place.

I am sure you're wondering how humans lived among the dead. Didn't the smell annoy them?

Before burying a person, the people at Çatalhöyük conducted several rituals. Most skeletons were discovered in a crouching or fetal position, showing that the interment occurred after the first 24 hours of death. After death, a human's muscles become stiff, a phenomenon known as rigor mortis, lasting for one to two days.

---

4 In the context of burials, depositions refer to how the body is placed after death.

5 An articulated skeleton is a complete skeleton where the bones are connected at the natural joints the way it is in a living human.

Thus, one had to wait between 24 hours and a few days after death to make the body flexible enough to be folded.

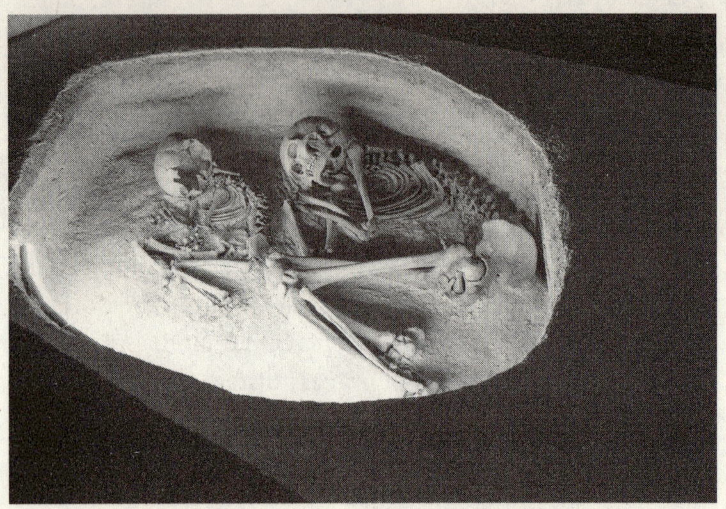

Reconstruction of a typical burial position at Çatalhöyük.

So, the next obvious question is: What happened between death and interment? Archaeological evidence suggests that everyone received some form of treatment during this period.

Phytoliths found on the adult remains indicate that people bound them in plant fibers before burial. Phytoliths are hard, tiny silica formations found in plant tissues and were deposited at the point of contact between the plant fiber and the dead body. In contrast, infants were frequently wrapped and placed in baskets. These funerary baskets also contain grave goods, including necklaces, anklets, beads, and textiles.

Pigments such as red and yellow ochre, as well as cinnabar, were used to treat dead bodies and decorate burial chambers. We see more color used in children's funerals than in those of adults.

However, the use of pigments was a standard practice for all age groups. We do not know the significance of the dyes.

Researchers believe red ochre and cinnabar, two of the most commonly used pigments, may have represented blood and life.

Evidence of feasting in Çatalhöyük suggests that the community may have organized funerary feasts to honor the deceased. It's unclear whether the feasts were directly linked to death or a house's life cycle, as demolition and the building of a new home could've sparked celebrations. Given the importance of death in the settlement, archaeologists believe feasts to honor the departed were common.

One fascinating fact about the skeletons in Çatalhöyük is that many lacked skulls. Headless remains are common in single

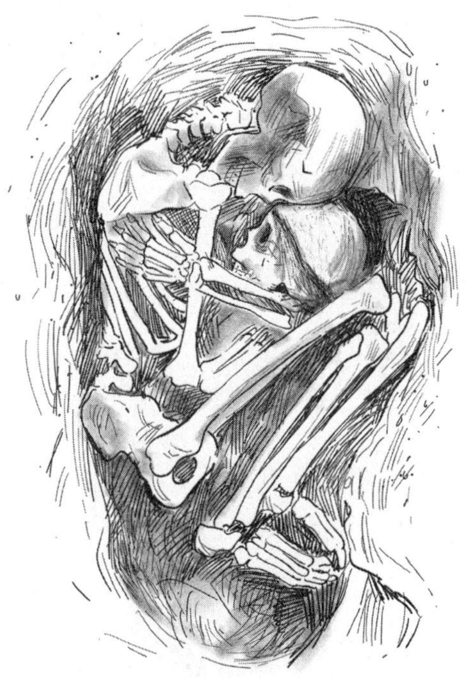

Illustration of an adult female holding a plastered skull painted with red ochre inspired by the reconstruction of the burial in Boz and Hager (2013).

interments, and though we find such bodies in all age groups, they are more common in adults.

In one burial, a woman was found tightly clutching a skull. It could've belonged to someone close to her. The skull was plastered and painted four times to regenerate the deceased's facial features.

The removal and plastering of skulls were prevalent in the pre-pottery Neolithic sites of the Near East, most famously seen in Jericho and Ain Ghazal in the Levant. The practice of preserving skulls can help us understand the relationship Çatalhöyük's residents had with death.

RELATIONSHIP WITH DEATH AND THE CULT OF THE DEAD

Head of a 9,000-year-old ancestor statue found at Jericho. Ancestor veneration was common during the PPNB period.

Ancestor veneration is the most popular explanation for removing heads from the body. However, other archaeologists have challenged this notion, citing the evidence that people also removed infant skulls. Hodder proposes a more straightforward yet logical theory, according to which the skulls serve the same purpose as pictures today: to create a link between the living and the memories of the deceased.

Some archaeologists have suggested that skull preservation may have been an act of trophy hunting. However, this theory is implausible as there is no evidence of violence in Çatalhöyük.

Hodder suggests that skulls are removed only in the context of specific funerary practices. We also observe additional body parts, such as limbs, taken from the deceased. Hence, we may need to go beyond skulls to grasp the rituals related to death. Further research is required to understand why Çatalhöyük's residents removed body parts.

In December 2023, archaeologists from Anadolu University discovered a unique skull of an 18- to 19-year-old male. There was a 2.5 cm hole in his skull made either after he died or when he was about to die. The hole was on the side of the skull and may have been for therapeutic purposes. This practice of drilling a small hole and removing a portion of the skull is known as trepanation, and was common in the ancient world. People believed that trepanation cured headaches, hemorrhages, and mental disorders, and the young man's skull was the earliest evidence of the practice in Anatolia. Archaeologists believe that people at Çatalhöyük drilled the skull of the ailing teenager because they thought it would alleviate his pain. However, there is no clear evidence that he was alive during the procedure, raising the question of whether the skull drilling may have had a ritual context connected with death.

The various traditions we have encountered at Çatalhöyük provide insight into the society and how rituals influenced their daily lives. We have learnt how the residents of Çatalhöyük wanted to memorialize the dead. But it is equally possible that they tried to overcome the pain of losing a loved one by forgetting their death. Maybe after the interment occurred, they didn't want to think about the deceased, especially in the case of infant deaths.

The death of children is heartbreaking, and one way to cope with the grief is to bury them away from the main room. An alternate interpretation is that they did not want their departed kids disturbed by placing them beneath the main room, where everyone could come and go. Hence, people preferred the quieter storage areas.

According to archaeologists Basak Boz and Lori Hager, burying children beneath the storage rooms was a symbolic link between a new life originating from the womb and food as a source of sustenance. They also theorize that the storage rooms may have been simply convenient for burying newborns, which explains why a large number of them were found in the side room.

Outdoors had multiple burials of both adults and children. These graves may have been a way for the society to show disregard for their deaths, or perhaps the individuals died from an incurable disease, and the people wanted to prevent its spread.

We learnt about burial practices and customs at Çatalhöyük to gain insights into the society's perspective on death. However, there is one hypothesis that could help us piece together the puzzle and understand the relationship between the living and the dead.

Some houses had as many as 60 skeletons, whereas the others had none. Why was the burial distribution so uneven? Was it related to status? Did more funerals per dwelling indicate a higher social standing?

One theory suggests that graves in certain homes were associated with relatives or clans. The hypothesis sounds reasonable, as we can imagine members of a clan gathering in an influential person's home to bury their dead. In 2011, anthropologists Marin Pilloud and Clark Spencer Larsen examined the teeth of individuals buried in various houses. They found that bodies buried in specific homes didn't always share kinship, challenging previous assumptions.

You may wonder why anyone would bury their loved ones in someone else's home. Çayönü, a Neolithic site in southern Türkiye, also shows uneven burial patterns. Researchers searched for clues in communities with similar funerary traditions to Çatalhöyük.

In Göbekli Tepe, we encounter depictions of decapitated bodies and skulls painted in red ochre. Skull plastering, as previously mentioned, was popular in Ain Ghazal and Jericho. A clear pattern emerges, where societies revered death, known as the cult of the dead.

Depiction of headless humans attacked by vultures next to an intramural burial at Çatalhöyük.

The death cult appeared in the early PPNA and spread throughout the Near East during the PPNB. People in PPNB sites, like Çatalhöyük, were bound by a cult of the dead and rituals associated with death. As evidenced by the number of burials, particular residences held greater significance in relation to death. People may have chosen to bury the dead in such homes; hence, we don't always see a shared kinship among the skeletons recovered from a house.

Wolfgang Palaver, a professor specializing in violence and religion in ancient societies, suggests the death cult was a unifying factor at Çatalhöyük. This shared bond of being united together by the cult of the dead kept the fear of death away.

According to Palaver:

> "The people at Çatalhöyük were most likely united not by fighting outside enemies or scapegoating outsiders among them, but by their hunting rituals and by a cult of the dead that immersed each individual in a hero-system that connected them via their house with the ancestors and kept death fear at bay."

END OF AN ERA

We live in a world with clear distinctions between the living and the dead. At Çatalhöyük, 9,000 years ago, there were no such boundaries; people's homes served as both places of worship and burial sites. Adults were buried in the house's northern part, whereas beneath the storage room were the children's burials.

Before burying the dead, elaborate rituals were performed, including binding and treating the body with paints like red ochre and cinnabar. Skulls were often removed from the skeletons and plastered, suggesting veneration of ancestors.

The cult of the dead unified the inhabitants of Çatalhöyük, helping them overcome the fear of death and welcoming the deceased as family members.

Around 5200 BCE, people living in Çatalhöyük abandoned their settlement. The causes of this remarkable Neolithic settlement's collapse are poorly understood. Hodder believes that with the increasing influence of agriculture, communities may have thrived independently and didn't need to depend on Çatalhöyük. One study suggests that climate change may have been a crucial factor in the settlement's collapse, although further studies are required to establish this theory.

The extraordinary rise of Çatalhöyük served as a model for future cities in the Fertile Crescent, where humans would start their next journey and build sprawling urban centers that would last for thousands of years. In the book's third section, we'll move on to cities and look at some of the early urban centers and towns that were once glorious but vanished without a trace.

4

The Cotton Farmers Who Practiced Dentistry: Mehrgarh and the Dawn of Civilization in the Indian Subcontinent

Around 5500 BCE, locals buried two individuals in the Kachi Plain in the Balochistan province of present-day Pakistan. One was an adult male lying on his side with his legs flexed backward. At his feet was a child, one or two years old. A low mud-brick wall enclosed their burial chamber.

Thousands of years later, in the 1990s, archaeologists from the French Archaeological Mission in Pakistan uncovered this grave. Located adjacent to the adult's left wrist was an unusual artifact. Eight copper beads, formerly part of a bracelet, lay alongside his hand. The burial was one of only two in the region to contain a copper relic.

A team from the Center de Recherche et de Restauration des Musées de France (C2RMF), led by anthropologist Christophe Moulherat, who specializes in the study of ancient textiles, examined the beads in greater detail. When they split one of the beads, they were surprised to find vegetable fibers within it.

Further research confirmed that the fibers were cotton.

The copper beads examined by Moulherat were proof of the world's earliest known use of cotton. The remarkable people who made the copper bracelet belonged to the settlement of Mehrgarh, where farming originated in the Indian subcontinent.

Mehrgarh's people established a vibrant culture that laid the groundwork for the Indus Valley Civilization, one of the most important Bronze Age civilizations in history.

Who were these enigmatic farmers of Mehrgarh, and where did they come from? How did they start cultivating cotton? Let us turn the clock back to 7000 BCE and find out.

THE FIRST FARMERS OF THE INDIAN SUBCONTINENT

The ruins of Mehrgarh.

Bolan Pass, situated south of the Hindu Kush Mountains, marks the boundary between the Indian tectonic plate and the Iranian

Plateau. Nestled at the foothills of the Bolan Pass, in the northern part of the Kachi Plain, is Mehrgarh.

Strategically situated between the fertile Indus Basin to the east and the hilly Iranian Plateau to the west, the Kachi Plain serves as a transition zone. The dry area experiences intense summers, often recording the highest temperatures in the Indian subcontinent. But there is a lifeline.

The Bolan River runs through this arid land, making its banks ideal for farming. Around 7000 BCE, Mehrgarh emerged on the riverside as a small farming community of over a hundred inhabitants. The archaeological site of Mehrgarh consists of several settlements along the Bolan River. The river changed its course over time, leading to the construction of new dwellings and the abandonment of older ones. The deserted homes were buried under the river's sediments and exposed again when its course changed. One such shift in Bolan's course led to the discovery of the Mehrgarh archaeological site in the 1970s.

Two theories exist about the origins of Mehrgarh's farmers.

According to the first hypothesis, Anatolian farmers introduced agriculture in the Indian subcontinent. Before Mehrgarh, there was no indication that the region's people were cultivating wild plants or herding wild animals. The Indian subcontinent's indigenous hunter-gatherers lived on the Kachi Plain. We know this from the relics of microliths (tiny stone tools, usually made of flint, about 1 cm long and used as projectile points such as arrowheads and spearpoints) dating back to before 7000 BCE.

The transition to agriculture at Mehrgarh is in stark contrast to human evolution in the Near East, where people gradually shifted from hunting and gathering to a semi-sedentary lifestyle before fully settling down. The change at Mehrgarh from a nomadic to a settled way of life seems abrupt, suggesting that migrant farmers from the Near East may have introduced agriculture to the Indian subcontinent. Several pieces of evidence support this perspective. For instance, the wheat varieties found at the site originated in the Near East, where wild wheat was native. Mehrgarh's circular fire pits were filled with pebbles similar to Neolithic settlements in the Near East, and its granaries mirror their Mesopotamian counterparts. Moreover, even the burial practices exhibit parallels. The positions of skeletal remains in Mehrgarh are identical to those at the Ali Kosh archaeological site in the Zagros Mountains, in southwest Iran.

Based on these arguments, can we conclude that the early farmers in Mehrgarh must have been migrants from the Near East, just as Anatolian farmers introduced agriculture to Europe?

Not quite.

Some archaeologists argue that human migrations from the Near East to South Asia are difficult to explain since they require crossing the vast Iranian Plateau before reaching the Bolan Pass's foothills. The journey to Europe was shorter and less challenging. But if humans can go to Australia, the Arctic, and the Americas, why can't they reach the Indian subcontinent?

The Anatolian origins of Mehrgarh's farmers appear plausible, but genetic studies and archaeological finds have cast doubt on this.

Mehrgarh's agriculture and animal domestication have indigenous origins. Jean-François Jarrige, the archaeologist who discovered the site in 1974, analyzed the animal bones unearthed there. He determined that the skeletal bones of cattle and sheep grew smaller over time, indicating a local domestication process. Had Anatolian farmers brought livestock, their bone sizes would have remained unchanged.

A dental analysis of Mehrgarh's people revealed their teeth were identical to those of South Asia's indigenous hunter-gatherers. Neolithic farmers in the Near East developed tooth cavities due to a diet of coarsely ground cereals rich in carbohydrates.

Surprisingly, cavities were absent among the farmers of Mehrgarh. Their teeth were bigger and healthier than those of their Near Eastern counterparts. The dental structures revealed a continuity in the transition from a hunter-gatherer to a settled farming lifestyle. However, the natural fluoride in the Bolan River could also explain the robust dental health. We'll see later in this chapter that Mehrgarh's residents were particular about tooth care.

Recent genetic studies examined the DNA of Neolithic (7200 BCE to 2500 BCE) and Chalcolithic[1] (4500 BCE to 1000 BCE) populations in Iran and South Asia. The researchers discovered that while Neolithic Iranian farmers shared DNA with Anatolian farmers, South Asian farmers lacked this component. After 6000 BCE, there was very little gene flow from the Iranian Plateau into the Indian subcontinent. The lack of migrations from the west suggests that farming was a local development in the Indian subcontinent.

So, which theory about the origins of Mehrgarh's farmers is correct?

Although a few people may have come from the Iranian Plateau, the lack of DNA from Anatolia suggests there were no mass migrations from the Near East. The domestication of cattle and crops occurred locally. Cotton was one of the crops cultivated by Mehrgarh's people. But before we discuss the cotton found at the site, let's learn about the lives of its inhabitants.

LIFE AT MEHRGARH

The exact date of the original settlement is unknown, but by 7000 BCE, several multi-roomed rectangular mud-brick homes had cropped up along the riverbank.

---

1 Chalcolithic or Eneolithic period, also known as the Copper Age, saw a transition to using both stone- and copper-based tools, setting the stage for the gradual transition to the Bronze Age.

There were four different room plans: two-room, four-room, six-room, and ten-room buildings. The four-roomed houses were the most common in the early days of the settlement. The walls of the houses were plastered inside and out with a 2-cm-thick clay mortar. There is evidence that the residents may have colored the walls with red ochre. Some of the houses had fragments of collapsed roofs. Each home had a square storage room.

Warm hearths once blazed in these rooms. Residents built fireplaces within their homes, using them for heat and cooking, as evidenced by traces of fire use, such as soot-stained walls. The open spaces between the houses also featured fire pits with diameters ranging from 40 to 60 cm and a depth of 35 cm. Mehrgarh's residents filled the firepits with pebbles, and Jarrige suggests that their purpose must have been to bake bread, as using stones for breadmaking is still prevalent in Balochistan.

Courtyards, where residents did household chores, separated the dwellings. The symmetrically designed houses with open spaces separating them were a marked contrast to the closely packed Neolithic settlements of the Near East, as we saw in Chapter 3.

The courtyards also served as burial sites. While the idea of living with the dead is unthinkable today, humans in Europe, the Near East, and South Asia buried their dead beneath their houses or in courtyards during the Neolithic period.

Arrow points, stone knives, scraping tools, wooden bowls, and sacrificed animals are among the items in Mehrgarh's graves. Archaeologists also found seashells, lapis lazuli, limestone, sandstone, and turquoise, and several bead-making workshops containing ornaments made of these materials.

The discovery of lapis lazuli, mined at Badakhshan, Afghanistan, and seashells from the shores of the Arabian Sea suggests that Mehrgarh's residents were active in long-distance trading. These trade networks would be crucial later for the rise and prosperity of the Indus Valley Civilization.

The burial rituals at this Neolithic site depict a culture that cherished its deceased, similar to what we witnessed at Çatalhöyük, displaying a unique blend of tradition, artistry, and compassion. Archaeologists discovered 318 tombs spread across 9 archaeological layers, 179 of which had grave items.

Initial burials in Mehrgarh took place in the courtyard, but as the town expanded, the residents constructed a formal cemetery which housed 150 graves.

Crystals of lazurite, the main mineral in lapis lazuli, from the Sar-i Sang mining district of Afghanistan.

Interments were constructed underground, with bodies in distinct chambers separated by mud-brick walls. To place a new corpse inside a chamber, one had to break down the walls, causing existing skeletons to shift. After placing a fresh body, people rebuilt the wall and shut the tomb. Scholars believe such burial rituals represent the value of family bonds, as each family wanted to bury its deceased members together. Bodies were buried in a curled, flexed position, and more than three-quarters of the graves were oriented east-west, though we also come across other directional alignments.

In the earlier levels, simpler graves often contained red ochre on the chamber floor, possibly symbolizing life or rebirth. The burial of a young woman revealed she had a necklace of seashells,

Painted pottery found at Mehrgarh with distinct animal and plant motifs (3000 BCE–2500 BCE).

and next to her lay vertebrae from a bovine tail, perhaps once used as a flyswatter.

In another grave, there were four baby goats alongside the deceased. As time passed, the burials became increasingly elaborate. Graves from the middle levels included ornaments made from lapis lazuli, turquoise, and seashells. One headband was intricately woven from tiny dentalium shells, while a belt-like ornament included polished beads and pendants.

Remember the funerary chamber of the adult male and child we talked about at the beginning of the chapter? As we'll see later, the bracelet found in their burial had the earliest evidence of a cotton thread.

We see evidence of pottery at Mehrgarh from 5500 BCE onwards. Around 4000 BCE, with the introduction of the potter's wheel, pots began replacing stone vessels. The ceramic designs became more sophisticated around 3500 BCE, with prominent animal and plant motifs. Over the years, Mehrgarh's pottery underwent several changes. Copper and bronze vessels started to replace traditional clay pottery around 2500 BCE.[2]

The developments in new pottery technologies suggest people were gaining scientific knowledge and unlocking new achievements.

The people of Mehrgarh made human figurines using terracotta. The sculptures from 4000 BCE show an obvious development of the feminine form: breasts are more visible, and braided hairstyles become popular.

Scholars debate the meaning of these figurines. Like most Neolithic farming societies worldwide, Mehrgarh may have been the site of a fertility cult. Experts have linked the female figurines to a "fertility goddess" or a "mother goddess." Some scholars

---

2 The later stages of Mehrgarh overlap with the rise of the Indus Valley Civilization.

Female figurine of cultic importance from Mehrgarh around 3000 BCE.

have interpreted them as representations of women holding babies, thereby connecting them with motherhood.

Another school of thought holds that they may have been toys or representations of everyday women. Yet another possibility is that, though people worshipped them, they were unrelated to fertility. For example, some figurines may have been lucky charms. They may have had some sort of religious significance, but the evidence isn't conclusive. Excavations revealed one clay figurine in the grave of a female, who was holding onto it. Could this be evidence in favor of the "lucky charm" theory? While we won't know for sure, burying the woman with the figurine suggests that such objects were significant enough to be associated with death.

Most of the initial figurines were female. Male figurines appeared only around 3000 BCE, and their numbers increased in later years.

Figurines, long-distance trade, and pottery were standard in the Neolithic cultures of the Near East, Central Asia, and Europe. What made Mehrgarh special?

DENTISTRY AND SCIENTIFIC BREAKTHROUGHS AT MEHRGARH

Over the years, analysis of the skeletal remains at Mehrgarh has revealed that the people of this farming community were quite innovative. When scientists analyzed the bodies of nine people from a grave in Mehrgarh, they found eleven drilled molar crowns. The farmers of Mehrgarh performed dental work using flint tools.

The molar crowns of Mehrgarh are the earliest known examples of dentistry in history. The people practiced a form of proto-dentistry, possibly using a type of filing. As the filing didn't survive, it is challenging for us to guess the material used.

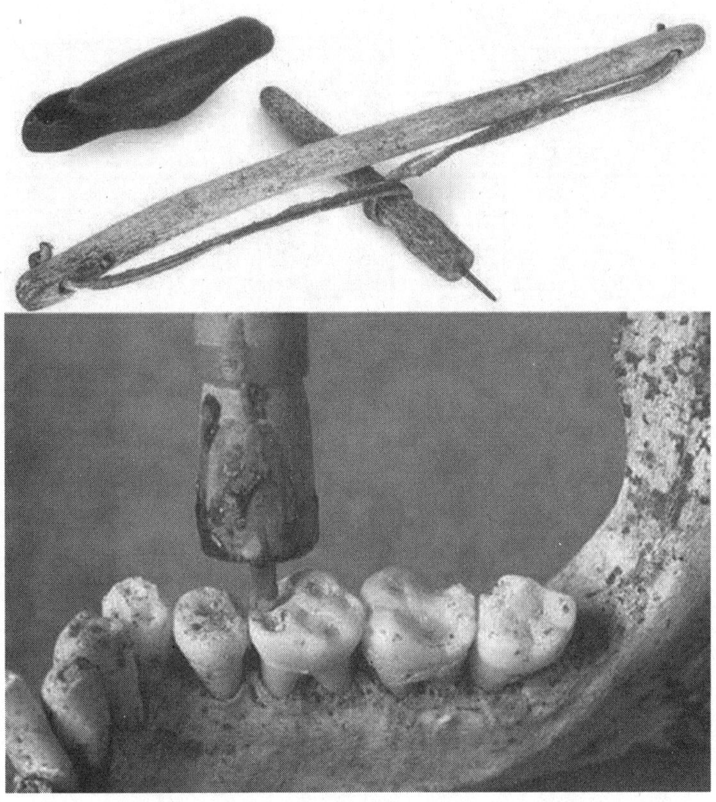

Reconstruction of dental drilling equipment at Mehrgarh

The next significant achievement of this remarkable farming settlement was the discovery of the lost-wax casting process.

Mehrgarh is home to the earliest known example of lost-wax casting, dating between 4500 BCE and 3600 BCE, as evidenced by a wheel-shaped copper amulet unearthed on the site. In the lost-wax technique, artisans of Mehrgarh made a model of the object with wax, encased it in clay, heated the mold to drain the wax, and then poured molten copper to create the final artifact. Later, the

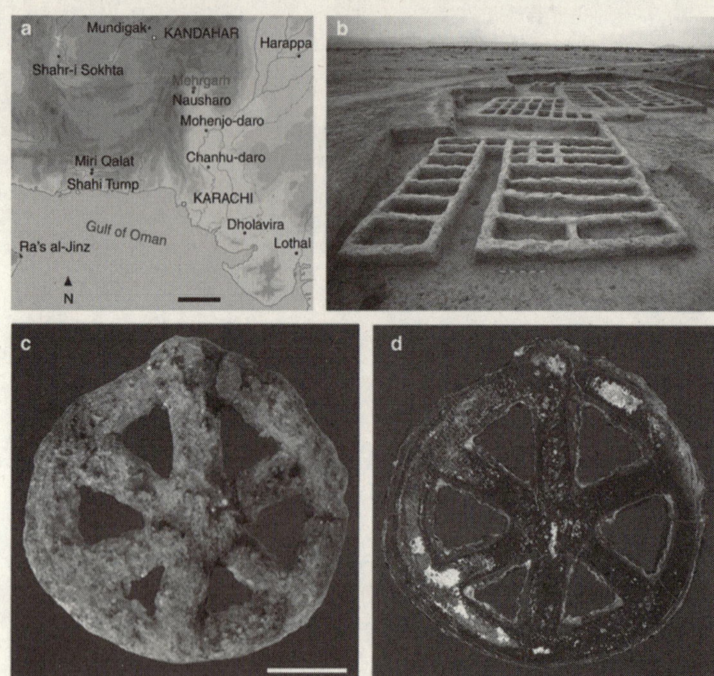

Amulet made using the lost wax process found at Mehrgarh.

people of the Indus Valley adopted the method (probably from the people of Mehrgarh) to make the dancing girl of Mohenjo-daro, one of the unique figurines of the civilization.

As we discussed in Chapter 1, food security plays a key role in the development of technology and the arts. The earliest archaeological layers at Mehrgarh reveal bones of 12 wild species, including wild asses, boars, wild goats and sheep, gazelles, elephants, and wild buffaloes. Wild animals became scarce over time, and we see more remains of domesticated animals.

There is evidence that the people of Mehrgarh domesticated the humped zebu cattle, a native of the Indian subcontinent. Cattle were the dominant livestock by the sixth millennium BCE and people used them for plowing, transportation, milk, and meat. Abundant sheep and goat bones suggest herders raised them to supplement cattle. In the burial of a young woman, there were bones of five kid goats sacrificed and placed around her legs, which could indicate some sort of ritual associated with the beginnings of pastoralism. Mehrgarh initially relied on wild game, but later transitioned to livestock, and ceremonies associated with this new lifestyle may have developed.

The dancing girl of Mohenjo-daro, an example of a figure made using lost wax-casting.

A seal from the Indus Valley Civilization showing a zebu bull.

The decline in the reliance on hunting is evident in the gradual decrease in the use of microliths over time. Hunting tools are less common in the later archaeological layers. Additionally, a nutritious diet and a low-stress environment positively impacted the health of the residents. Males averaged 170 cm in height, and females 160 cm, with some women reaching an impressive 175 cm.

At Mehrgarh, barley was the main harvest, followed by wheat. Archaeologists discovered cotton seeds inside the cereal storage facilities and found dates and jujube seeds elsewhere at the site. The people of Mehrgarh were the world's first cotton farmers, and they valued the oil-rich seeds of this crop. Cotton was crucial in the region's economic transformation, and today it is the world's most extensively manufactured textile material.

THE FIRST COTTON THREAD

Moulherat's discovery of cotton threads in a copper bracelet at Mehrgarh was a unique find. It pushed back the date of cotton

G. arboreum, or tree cotton, is the most common cotton species in the Indian subcontinent.

domestication by several thousand years. Earlier scholars believed the Indus Valley Civilization was the first to make cotton products.

Because cotton fibers do not last long, it's hard to say precisely when cotton farming began at Mehrgarh. The copper bracelet discovered in a burial from 5500 BCE is the earliest evidence of cotton use, but residents likely cultivated and utilized it long before this date. The artifact was unusual because the copper had corroded, releasing metallic salts that replaced the organic compounds in the cotton. Consequently, the thread got encased in the bead, which preserved it.

How did Moulherat know it was cotton?

His team removed a 5 sq. mm section of the bead and coated it with gold, allowing them to examine the substance under a Scanning Electron Microscope (SEM). SEM analysis reveals the sample's composition.

Moulherat's team set the sample in resin and polished it with a diamond paste. They cut sections from the sample and examined the fibers under a microscope.

By measuring the thickness of the fibers' cell walls, the scientists concluded that the thread had both ripe and unripe cotton. They had identified the world's earliest known cotton thread, though they couldn't tell if the cotton had been domesticated or wild.

So, is the term "cotton farmers" appropriate?

Did the Mehrgarh inhabitants cultivate cotton or gather it from wild plants?

Fifty species of cotton are recognized, classified under the genus *Gossypium.* However, only four cotton species are cultivated, each evolving independently in different parts of the world. Among these four species, we are interested in *G. arboreum,* also known as tree cotton, which most likely originated somewhere between East Africa and the Indian subcontinent.

As there are no known wild varieties of *G. arboreum,* Moulherat concludes that the inhabitants of Mehrgarh were either familiar with domestic cotton or may have domesticated it themselves. This is evident from their skill in making threads.

Archaeologist Steven Mithen believes cotton production at Mehrgarh is unsurprising because Neolithic farmers in the Jordan Valley, who had economies and technology similar to those of their South Asian counterparts, produced fabrics as early as 8000 BCE.

Another indicator of cotton farming was the storing of cotton seeds. Large-scale cotton cultivation resulted in a surplus of seeds that the farmers stored for later use in designated cereal storage areas. The seeds were probably processed into oil or fed to cattle.

MEHRGARH DECLINES, AND A NEW CIVILIZATION RISES

Mehrgarh was innovative for its time, as nothing like it had been seen in the Indian subcontinent before. The people made significant breakthroughs in science, commerce, religion, and art. Though they lacked a distinct social hierarchy and a government, the residents of Mehrgarh had sown the seeds for a sophisticated civilization.

Over the next 4,000 years, the Bolan River changed course, prompting new settlements to spring up along its banks while inhabitants abandoned others. Mehrgarh continued to expand, shifting its position on the Kachi Plain. Cotton, advanced pottery, and long-distance trade facilitated economic growth, laying the foundation for the Indus Valley Civilization.

Around 2600 BCE, the people of Mehrgarh abandoned their community and relocated to Nausharo, about 8 km away, as the Indus Valley Civilization began to expand into the region.

Section 2

Rise of Civilizations

5

Vinča Culture: The Stone Age Metallurgists

IN 2004, LEADING LINGUISTS, HISTORIANS, AND archaeologists convened in Novi Sad, Serbia, for an international conference. One prominent speaker was Shan M.M. Winn, a former professor of anthropology at the University of Southern Mississippi. In 1981, he published a landmark study, *Pre-Writing in Southeastern Europe: The Sign System of the Vinča Culture*, which brought him recognition among scholars.

Winn surprised his audience with a bold claim.

He argued that a script existed in Europe two thousand years before writing appeared in Egypt and Mesopotamia. However, in the 1970s, most scholars rejected any challenge to the widespread belief that Mesopotamia was the cradle of civilization. Winn carefully worded his thesis to describe the script as "pre-writing," knowing that if he called it a script, his peers would not take him seriously.

Fortunately, researchers no longer have to walk on eggshells. Most historians and archaeologists now believe that civilizations developed independently around the world. However, a European civilization thousands of years before the Minoans,[1]

1 A Bronze Age civilization based in Crete which thrived between 3100 BCE to 1100 BCE.

with a written script and advanced metallurgy, remains a subject of controversy.

To this day, academics studying ancient Mesopotamia do not accept the idea that a society existed that knew how to write before the Sumerians or Egyptians.

Winn focused his research on a civilization called the Vinča culture,[2] a society that flourished in the Balkans between 5400 BCE and 4500 BCE. These remarkable people smelted copper during the Neolithic era, making them one of the world's earliest metallurgists.

However, their most controversial legacy is inventing a writing system that continues to divide experts. While some believe it is a script, others refuse to accept the argument, terming the Vinča symbols as "proto-writing" or "pre-writing."

Vinča isn't a new civilization. Archaeologists have excavated its sites since the late nineteenth and early twentieth centuries. Yet, discussions of the culture outside the academic circles of the Balkan nations are limited. Despite this wealth of evidence and research, why is the Vinča script so divisive, and the civilization seldom discussed beyond academia?

Let us explore how the Vinča people changed the course of early human history. Before examining the Vinča culture's writing system, it's essential to understand who they were and their social organization.

THE ORIGINS OF THE VINČA CULTURE

In the book's previous section, we witnessed the rise of agriculture in Anatolia and saw the earliest farming settlements

---

2 Vinča culture is pronounced as Vin+cuh. It is also known as the Turdaș culture, or Vinča-Turdaș culture, after the Turdaș archaeological site in Romania.

that flourished in the Near East. Around 7000 BCE, a group of these Neolithic Anatolian farmers crossed over to Greece and into the Balkans, introducing agriculture to Europe.

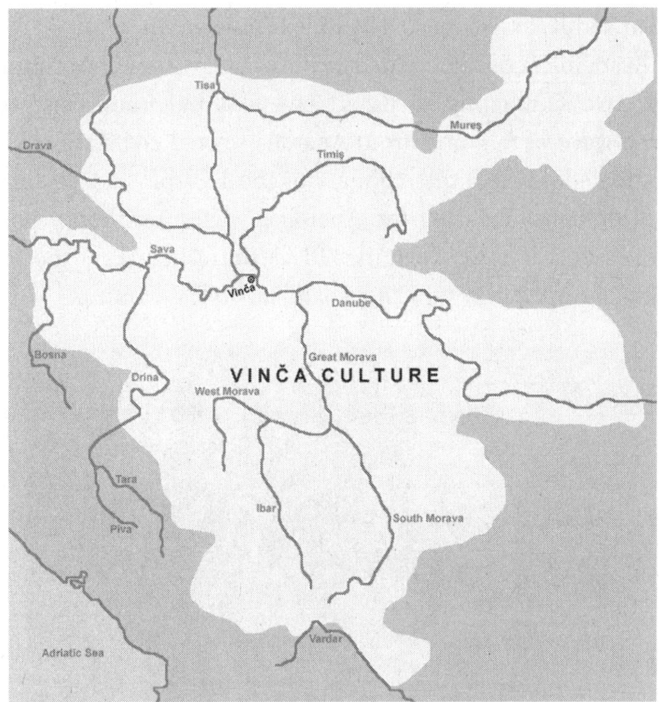

A map showing the extent of the Vinča culture.

They migrated north and northwest, entering North Africa through the Iberian Peninsula. We refer to this group as the Early European Farmers (EEF). They mixed with the European Hunter-Gatherers, also known as Western Hunter-Gatherers (WHG), and over the next few millennia, transformed Europe into an agriculture-driven economy, with several farming communities emerging across the continent. One such group formed by the descendants of EEF was the Vinča culture.

The Vinča culture thrived in the Balkans, encompassing present-day Serbia and Kosovo, as well as parts of Romania, western Bulgaria, eastern Macedonia, and southern Hungary. The civilization takes its name from the Vinča-Belo Brdo archaeological site in Serbia, first excavated by Miloje Vasić in 1908.

Academics continue to debate the origins of the Vinča culture, with two competing theories. The first hypothesis suggests that a wave of migrants from Anatolia started civilization after the preceding Neolithic cultures of the Balkans had declined. Archaeologists favoring the Anatolian migration theory point to the similarities between the "Black Burnished Ware" pottery found in early Vinča sites and Anatolian-style ceramics.

Reconstruction of Vinča pottery with lid.

Other scholars favor a local origin, suggesting that Vinča emerged from the Neolithic Starčevo culture,[3] which lasted from approximately 6200 BCE to 4500 BCE.

The Starčevo culture originated in present-day Serbia, on the banks of the Danube, as a result of migrating Anatolian farmers who first settled in Greece and then moved north into the Balkan heartland. One of the more striking discoveries at the Starčevo archaeological site is a "red-haired goddess" figurine with large buttocks and small breasts, possibly a continuation of Neolithic statuettes found in Anatolia.

Red-haired goddess figurine, Starčevo.

3 Starčevo is pronounced as Star + Chevo.

The Starčevo pottery was primarily coarse, featuring globular-shaped vessels that occasionally bore rustic, ornamented designs. Bone spatulas were discovered at the site, hinting at the widespread use of flour. Vinča exhibits pottery styles similar to those of the preceding Starčevo culture, suggesting continuity. Further, early Vinča residents built their homes on top of Starčevo settlements.

Recent studies suggest that both theories regarding the origins of the Vinča culture may be valid. The Vinča Civilization incorporated characteristics of both migratory and indigenous people, and the academic debate has evolved beyond the competing binary ideas.

Regardless of which hypothesis you believe about its origins, the Vinča culture pioneered several innovations previously unheard of in Europe. Let us review the social structure that allowed them to do so.

THE PEOPLE AND THE SOCIETY

Vinča-Belo Brdo site, the most well-known settlement of the Vinča culture.

The people of the Vinča culture were European Neolithic farmers. DNA tests revealed they were an admixture of primarily Anatolian farmers and a small genetic component of European Hunter-Gatherers.

Farming and animal husbandry were the primary sources of sustenance for the Vinča Civilization, with hunting and fishing supplementing the diet. The residents cultivated oats, wheat, and barley more intensively than their predecessors in Neolithic cultures.

Based on indirect evidence, archaeologists infer that the Vinča farmers were skilled in using the plow. The largest settlements are found in regions with heavy soils that require plowing, suggesting that mastery of this technique enabled farmers to support large, populous communities.

Adopting the plow and increasing agricultural output freed people to pursue a variety of professions. The increased crop yields also enabled residents to invest significant time in producing textiles from plant products and utilizing animal hides for clothing.

Animal figurines found at several locations suggest cattle were more important to the Vinča people than sheep, goats, and pigs. At the Vinča site, several houses featured painted cattle skulls fixed to the walls, a practice also observed at Çatalhöyük. The reverence for cattle may also indicate that ox-driven plowing techniques helped residents achieve high agricultural yields.

Vinča houses were rectangular, with mud-plastered walls and wooden flooring. They usually had an oven in the home, but some had a fireplace outside. A few houses had an upper floor.

Vinča was the largest site in the civilization. Situated on the banks of the Danube, it covered 29 hectares and, at its peak, housed 2,500 people.

In the later phases, Vinča had large buildings (40 x 60 m^2) with distinct rooms featuring fixed furniture, including benches, waterwheels, and tables. The settlement was likely a ceremonial

Reconstruction of the Stubline settlement of the Vinča culture.
Credits: Miloš Spasić/Belgrade City Museum.

center for the entire region, as evidenced by the abundance of ritual objects and anthropomorphic figurines found at the site. Other cult objects, such as a "mushroom amulet" and animal head jewelry, originated at Vinča and then spread to other settlements in this civilization.

Vinča was a walled community with houses organized in straight streets. The Stubline archaeological complex, established around 4700 BCE, features approximately 200 homes arranged in rows and connected linearly, similar to those found at Vinča. Plenty of open spaces and circular ditches surround Stubline.

The homes had clear groupings. Archaeologists believe that each dwelling cluster belonged to a particular clan. Stubline's walls feature bucranium (cattle skull) decorations, similar to those found in Vinča.

Archaeologists have discovered several Vinča culture sites across the Balkans. The largest settlements had between 300 and 650 houses. The Divostin archaeological site in Serbia has 1,028 homes.

Some of the settlements of the Vinča culture were fortified with ditches and palisades. Could the defense systems indicate that the residents feared invaders attacking their grain and livestock? Earlier, most archaeologists believed the Vinča Civilization, like other Neolithic cultures of Europe, was an egalitarian society free from warfare. However, recent discoveries have challenged this view.

Neolithic figurines discovered at Stubline, Serbia.

Credits: Miloš Spasić/Belgrade City Museum.

A 2011 study led by Adam Crnobrnja of the Belgrade City Museum analyzed the location and position of several figurines discovered at the Stubline archaeological site. The statuettes depicted individuals holding maces, hammer axes, and other tools that may have been used in a conflict. The researchers concluded the figurines represented a hierarchical society in Vinča culture, with individuals having assigned roles.

There is no consensus on interpreting these figurines. A 2014 study by Miloš Spasić suggested they could represent invading warriors. He argues that figurines depicting people of the Vinča culture show detailed clothing, jewelry, and hairstyles. But the set of figurines holding clubs, hammers, and maces is abstract. The representation is deliberate and serves as a way for the people of this early Balkan civilization to indicate that these were foreigners they were unfamiliar with; hence, their depiction is ambiguous.

Although we can not conclude whether there were possible conflicts at Vinča, another activity of the residents could provide a clue.

The people of the Vinča culture burned their houses, a practice common in Neolithic Europe that archaeologists refer to as the "Burned House Horizon." The reasons behind setting their residences ablaze are debatable. Some scholars suggest it was a premeditated ritual. Other academics argue that raids by rival tribes could have caused the destruction of the houses, and the burning may not have been a pre-planned activity.

The argument for social hierarchy is persuasive. The focus on metallurgy and crafts at Vinča was driven by the community's food security, as evidenced by the numerous artifacts discovered. Specialization in professions likely led to the emergence of social classes.

COPPER SMELTING AND UNIQUE CRAFTS

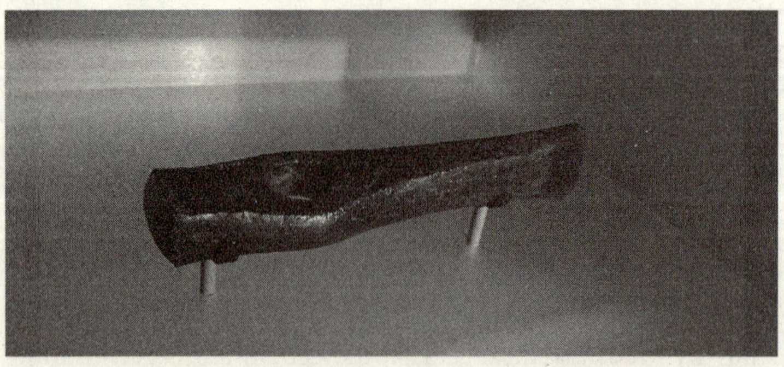

Copper axe from Pločnik, around 5000 BCE.

Vinča was a Neolithic civilization. Yet, we witness a remarkable growth in metalworking during this period in the Balkans. Initially, the Vinča culture used copper as a valuable commodity for trade. Later, they hammered copper ores into metal items and jewelry. They eventually figured out how to process and extract copper from ore and cast it into objects.

The earliest evidence of copper smelting in history was discovered at the Pločnik and Belovode archaeological sites, in Serbia, dating back to approximately 5500 BCE to 5000 BCE.

Malachite (green) and azurite (blue) copper ores were abundant at both sites. Malachite beads and pendants are the most common discoveries at Belovode. They were also found in mixtures with ash and charcoal, on home floors, storage jars, and porcelain shards.

At Rudna Glava, in Serbia, miners bored shafts into the hills and then added scaffolds to access the copper ore veins.

You must be wondering how the ancient people mined ores from the rocks. Their method was pretty straightforward. They set fire to the ore-rich stones, a technique known as firesetting, and then poured cold water. The rapid temperature difference caused the rocks to crack, exposing the metal ore. There is clear evidence of copper smelting at Belovode. Several ceramic "chimneys" were discovered at Belovode, used for melting the ore and separating the slag from the metal.

The archaeological site of Pločnik has some of the world's earliest known copper tools. Although copper smelting had begun, its use was not widespread, and people preferred to make their tools from chipped stones, bones, and antlers.

The Vinča culture is known for its distinctive anthropomorphic figurines. Unlike previous Neolithic art, these sculptures were found in significantly greater quantities and are more detailed in their design. Earlier Neolithic figurines were mostly plain. However, the Vinča style featured realistic

An anthropomorphic figurine from the Vinča culture, dated between 4500 BCE and 4000 BCE.

Two-headed anthropomorphic statue found at Gomolava archaeological site (c. 4000 BCE–3800 BCE), Serbia.

depictions of jewelry, clothing, and faces. Some statuettes have unusual appearances, such as human bodies with animal-like heads. Many have a distinctive red paint, typical of the Vinča culture.

The exact meaning of these figurines is subject to debate. Most were discovered in people's homes and may have had spiritual and ritual significance.

One interpretation of the statuettes' peculiar facial features is that they were masks worn by shamans who played a crucial role in Vinča society. Ritual masks are still used in many cultures

The Vidovdanka anthromorphic figurine, c. 5100 BCE.

and are often associated with funerary customs. Shamans of the Vinča culture were influential religious figures and may have been among the civilization's elite.

Among the most noteworthy discoveries is Vidovdanka, an anthropomorphic figurine found at Vinča. The artifact, about 30.6 cm tall, is made of terracotta. The figure is a female, yet her face is not human.

Vidovdanka's face has been interpreted as a mask used for ceremonial purposes. The lack of discernible distinction between the face and the mask raises concerns about whether masks were used during religious rites. However, at the Liubcova site, a clay figurine was discovered holding what appears to be a mask. Masks were commonly worn in contemporary Neolithic communities, which adds to the argument. The fragmented remains of a mask were found at the Romanian archaeological site of Uivar, where the Tiszapolgár culture thrived (4500 BCE to 4000 BCE). We can think of the human-like figures as representations of the high-status people in society, such as shamans or perhaps the emerging class of metallurgists. They may have worn masks on special occasions as a distinct marker of their social standing.

"Goddess on the Throne," an anthropomorphic figurine discovered in Pristina, Kosovo.

In 1956, excavations at the Tjerrtorja spinning mill in Pristina, the capital of present-day Kosovo, revealed a unique anthropomorphic figurine. Dated between 5700 BCE and 4500 BCE, this 18.5 cm statuette depicts a female seated on a stool. Archaeologists dubbed the artifact "Goddess on the Throne" and interpreted the find as representative of a female deity common among Neolithic farming societies in Europe. She could represent an Earth mother goddess, which we encountered in the previous section of the book. It is an important cultural symbol in Kosovo. Since 2002, the deity has been on display at the Kosovo Museum in Pristina. You'll also find the figurine on Pristina's flag.

We don't know the exact religious beliefs of the people of the Vinča culture. However, religion played a significant role in Neolithic Europe and could have sparked another vital discovery: writing.

VINČA SYMBOLS: SCRIPT OR PICTOGRAPHS?

One of the Tărtăria tablets.

In 1961, an archaeological team led by Nicolae Vlassa of the National Museum of Transylvanian History unearthed three tablets and a burned pit of bones at the Neolithic site of Tărtăria in Romania. The discovery divided the archaeological community.

The clay tablets contained the Vinča symbols, also known as the Danube script. They were dated between 5370 BCE and 5140 BCE, over two thousand years older than the earliest evidence of writing in Mesopotamia and Egypt. Some scholars believe the Tărtăria tablets are the world's first known proof of writing.

Vinča symbols were first discovered in 1875 by Baroness Zsófia Torma, a self-educated archaeologist and paleontologist from the Austro-Hungarian Empire, at Turdaş, present-day Romania. She found fragments of pottery with unknown symbols inscribed on them. In 1908, Miloje Vasić unearthed artifacts with similar symbols at Vinča. These discoveries, along

One of the Gradeshnitsa tablets.

with other findings from the region, led V. Gordon Childe to propose that there was a "Danubian" Civilization in Europe before the migration of Indo-Europeans. Several linguists and archaeologists support this theory. Excavations at Gradeshnitsa in Bulgaria also revealed clay artifacts with incised marks.

Was writing widespread in the Balkans? Linguists and archaeologists who argue in favor of an early writing system in Europe term the Vinča symbols as the Danube script. According to linguist Harald Haarmann, the Danube script is one of the earliest independent writing systems, originating without influence from previous scripts. He states that, based on current evidence, no other form of writing existed in Southeast Europe prior to its emergence, nor was it introduced to the region from external sources. He also notes that by the late sixth millennium BCE, the Danube script represents the only known experiment with writing in the Old World. It was, he says, another 2,000 years before writing first appeared in ancient Egypt and Mesopotamia.

How does the Danube script compare with the rest of the ancient world's writing systems? The Indus script contained 400 characters, the Sumerian script had 770, the Egyptian script had about 700, and the Danube script had 720.

Most of the inscriptions in the Danube script were brief and contained only a few symbols. There are larger sequences of 10 to 20 symbols, although uncommon.

So, why is this script so controversial?

Not all archaeologists, especially those researching Near Eastern civilizations, agree that the Vinča symbols can be called a script. They claim the symbols are pictographs and do not represent a developed communication language. Others share a less definitive position, arguing that the Danube script may have been a form of proto-writing. Another controversy that plagues the debate on the origins of writing in the Balkans is that most Vinča symbols were found to be dated between 4500 BCE and

4000 BCE, after the decline of the Vinča culture. The Tărtăria tablets push the date back to the Vinča period, but some scholars have questioned the accuracy of its dating.

Yet another theory suggests that the symbols may share a tenuous link with early Sumerian city-states, which are largely credited with inventing writing. Archaeologist Colin Renfrew, who specialized in the prehistory of languages, argued that the comparisons between the symbols on the Tărtăria tablets and those of proto-literate Sumeria hold little substance. He points out that such symbols are simple pictographs, and a depiction of a goat in one culture will naturally resemble a similar depiction in another. To label these Balkan symbols as "writing," he suggests, would imply they carried an independent meaning capable of being understood without verbal context—a notion that Renfrew found doubtful.

Many academics, including Haarmann, have raised objections to Renfrew's claim. They propose that the Vinča script was developed for religious purposes by shamans who held significant power in the ancient Neolithic societies of Europe. To support his argument, Haarmann points to the medium used for writing. He states that the Vinča script is commonly found on sacred pottery, miniature altars, clay figurines, and stone artifacts, including loom weights and spindle whorls.

Archaeologists found the Tărtăria tablets in the grave of a female shaman, which further supports Haarmann's theory.

The Vinča script differs from ancient Mesopotamia, where the primary purpose of writing was for temple inventory and administrative purposes.

Unfortunately, scholars have yet to decipher the Vinča symbols. Many ancient scripts, such as Minoan Linear A and the Indus Valley writing system, remain undeciphered. But we don't doubt that these are scripts.

There is no academic consensus on whether Vinča symbols constitute a script, but many linguists, archaeologists, and historians believe they do. According to Shan Winn, some academics are still unwilling to acknowledge the possibility that Europe may have developed a writing system about 2,000 years before Mesopotamia.

Winn's arguments are plausible. Accepting Vinča symbols as a script may challenge traditional ideas about the origins of civilizations. The purpose of this chapter is to challenge conventional views about the origins of civilization and propose that ideas may have developed independently across the world without much cultural contact. However, questioning the status quo and changing people's perceptions takes time.

END OF VINČA

The fall of the Vinča culture is as mysterious as its rise. Between 4600 BCE and 4500 BCE, the Vinča culture began to decline and eventually disappeared from the archaeological record. We see fewer figurines typical of the Vinča. One of the proposed theories behind its decline is that intensive farming reduced soil fertility, and the complex societies that depended on agriculture moved out, leading to a collapse in trade networks. Fire destroyed many of the Vinča sites. Warfare could have also caused the fires, but the evidence remains speculative.

The Vinča culture was undoubtedly Europe's first attempt at a full-fledged civilization. It boasted a well-defined social hierarchy, advanced agricultural practices, extensive long-distance trade networks, and pioneered the use of copper metallurgy. The residents may have independently invented writing. Yet, the civilization's achievements are seldom discussed in popular discourse. Hopefully, further research will help us settle the debate about the Vinča script.

While studying a civilization, it is essential to keep an open mind and accept that new discoveries will challenge existing beliefs.

6

The First Pyramid Builders of the New World

In 1994, archaeologist Ruth Shady Solis, of Peru's National University of San Marcos, was traveling north from Lima when she discovered a large mound. The region is an arid desert, located approximately 23 kilometers from the coast of Peru.

Shady realized she had made an important discovery. Unearthing it would be a challenge, especially with her limited excavation budget. She could not afford to pay her assistants and often worked alone in the empty valley. She occasionally slept in her car, a decision that posed significant risks. Once, she almost got robbed when assailants tried stealing her vehicle and shot her in the knee.

Yet, she did not give up.

Lacking official support, Shady rallied 25 Peruvian army personnel to assist in her digs. Her tenacity paid off when she discovered a stunning 5,000-year-old city containing arguably one of the world's earliest known pyramids.

Wait, did I say one of the world's first pyramids?

In Peru?

When we think of pyramids, we imagine the gigantic structures built by the ancient Egyptians. The "New World" is unlikely to cross your mind. Pyramids in the Americas? It must be the Chichén Itzá or the Pyramid of the Sun.[1] They are old, but not that old!

Shady's discovery shattered our long-held beliefs about the New World's monumental architecture and Peru as a cradle of civilization. She had discovered Caral, an ancient city that was part of the Norte Chico or Caral-Supe Civilization, one of the world's earliest independently developed civilizations, which was over 5,000 years old. Are you wondering why we have two names for the same civilization? In English scientific literature, researchers commonly refer to it as "Norte Chico," a name derived from the coastal region of north-central Peru, where it was first discovered. Spanish academics favor the term "Caral-Supe," named after Caral, in the Supe Valley, the most extensively studied city of the civilization. We do not know what the civilization's original inhabitants called themselves; these are modern archaeological terms.

I will use Caral-Supe in this chapter, following Peru's official and UNESCO's terminology. To date, archaeologists have unearthed approximately 30 sites belonging to the Caral-Supe Civilization.

Before we discuss the origins of civilization in Peru, there is an interesting observation about the region's geography. Most civilizations sprang up near a river during the Bronze Age, but Caral is an exception. The area has little vegetation, which makes us wonder: How did a sophisticated ancient culture thrive in one of the world's driest regions?

---

1 The Pyramid of the Sun, located in Teotihuacán is one of the largest buildings in Mesoamerica, constructed around 200 CE.

To find the answer, let us examine the geography of the Peruvian coast, which will help us understand what distinguished Caral-Supe from Egypt, India, China, and Mesopotamia.

GEOGRAPHY OF THE PERUVIAN COAST

Most of the Peruvian coast is arid and lacks vegetation.

Most of the Peruvian coast, situated between the Andes and the Pacific Ocean, is exceptionally arid and barren. It is the last place one would expect a flourishing ancient society.

The Peruvian Andes comprise two parallel mountain ranges: Cordillera Negra (the Black Range) and Cordillera Blanca (the White Range). The Santa Fe River separates the ranges. Moisture-laden winds from the Amazon rainforests in the east flow towards the Pacific, striking these mountains and leaving little room for rainfall in the coastal region.

Surprisingly, the Pacific winds don't help either. The warm winds from the west meet the chilly air from the Humboldt Current, which moves north along the South American coast, causing a temperature inversion. A temperature inversion prevents cold air from rising and warm air from falling, resulting in no moisture shedding. Despite their proximity to water, the Peruvian coast and the Atacama Desert in northern Chile are among the driest regions on Earth.

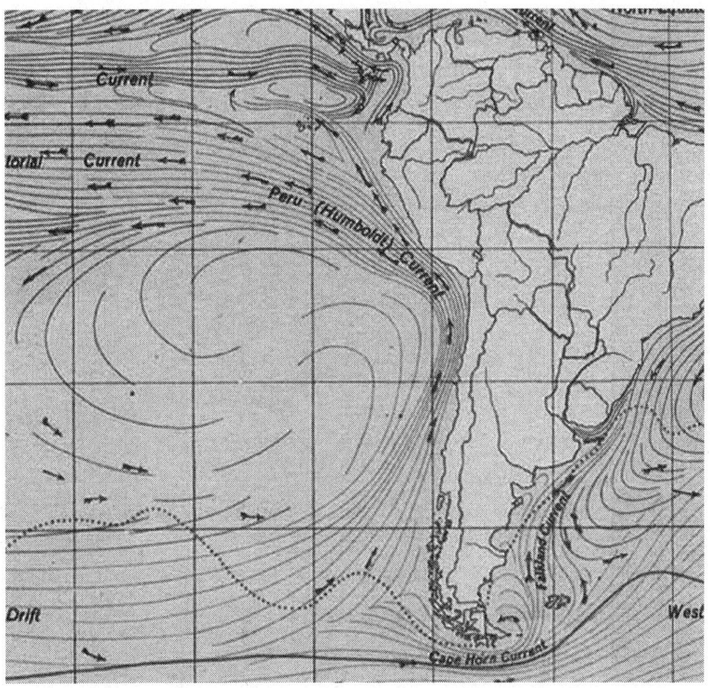

The Humboldt current is responsible for low rainfall along the Peruvian coast.

Learning about Peru's geography sparked my curiosity. How could a civilization emerge in this barren coastline? Despite being arid, the Peruvian coast is not an empty desert devoid of life.

A closer look reveals 50 rivers, fed by the melting ice from the Andes, which travel across the Peruvian coast and flow into the Pacific. Along the banks of these rivers are fertile lands ideal for irrigation and farming.

But as we will see, the conventional mode of agriculture did not develop along the Peruvian coast. Instead of grains, it was cotton and fish that fueled the rise of the Andean civilizations.[2]

ORIGINS OF CIVILIZATIONS IN PERU

The two main pyramids at Caral.

The earliest confirmed archaeological evidence of human habitation in Peru comes from the Guitarrero Cave in the Ancash region, dating from 10,500 BCE to 8000 BCE. However, there is evidence that people may have lived there even earlier, as a human mandible and teeth found in the cave were dated to 10,610 BCE. The cave is in a hilly area at an elevation of 2,580 meters above sea level. The first humans lived in the Andean foothills and migrated to the coast during the winter. At Quebrada Jaguay, on Peru's southern coast, these early inhabitants caught fish and clams, taking their catch to their base about 8 km inland from the coast.

2 A broad term for civilizations that flourished near the Andes such as Caral, Chavin, Nazca, Moche, Tiwanaku, Chachapoyas, Wari, and the Inca.

By 8000 BCE, Peru's hunter-gatherers settled in mountain caves, hunting Vicuña, a deer-sized camelid.[3] They caught fish from the mangrove swamps, and a small group moved to the coast and started living off the catch from the sea. We refer to this period of Peru's prehistory as the lithic stage.

Around 6000 BCE, small sedentary populations formed and began farming. During this era, three distinct groups emerged: hunter-gatherers in the high Andean regions, farmers in the inter-Andean valleys, and fishermen who lived along the coast. Subsequently, significant development occurred during the pre-ceramic period,[4] which began around 3500 BCE.

The Peruvian coast comprises four narrow river valleys: the Huaura, Supe, Pativilca, and Fortaleza. Something extraordinary happened in this region between 3500 BCE and 3200 BCE. Sophisticated cities with pyramids, temples, and residential complexes sprang up. Scholars consider the growth of civilization on the dry Peruvian coast an aberration.

According to archaeologists Winifred Creamer and Jonathan Haas, who have extensively researched the Caral-Supe Civilization in the Norte Chico region, it stands out as a unique epicenter of early Andean civilization due to its unparalleled concentration of ceremonial and residential sites.

While occasional, moderately sized communal architecture existed sporadically across the Andes during this period (3000 BCE–1800 BCE), the Supe Valley housed at least 25 large ceremonial centers, a density unmatched elsewhere in the region. Creamer and Haas compare the Andes to a landscape of scattered granules of sand, with occasional small anthills representing modest communal sites. Amidst this obscure landscape, the Caral-

3 Camelids include llama, alpaca, camels, guanacos, etc.

4 Some archaeologists suggest Andean pre-ceramic age started in Zaña Valley of northern Peru by 4700 BCE.

Supe Civilization rises dramatically like a volcano, dominating the archaeological landscape. What drove the birth of an isolated civilization in an arid region of South America?

The Peruvian coast is rich in seafood, while cotton was the primary agricultural product along the riverbanks. Cotton and seafood played a significant role in the rise of the Caral-Supe Civilization. Besides textiles, cotton was also an essential component of ancient Peruvian fishing nets.

In 1975, archaeologist Michael Moseley, studying the ancient coastal city of Aspero in Peru, suggested that the settlement was a fishing center and the birthplace of Andean civilizations. Aspero was built around 3000 BCE and was a couple of centuries older than Caral.

Moseley proposed that ancient Peruvians migrated from the shore to inland regions because they were predominantly fish-eaters who later discovered agriculture. Thus, the origins of all major Andean civilizations, before the Incas, were not found in the foothills of the Andes but rather in the coastal region of Peru, which was abundant with fish and seafood. This theory, known as the Maritime Foundation of Andean Civilization (MFAC), was a radical archaeological proposal. Aspero being older than Caral strengthens the MFAC theory, as one could argue that the residents of Aspero founded cities like Caral later.

Other archaeologists opposed the assumption that the sea was the principal source of nutrition. A lifestyle dependent entirely on seafood was deemed economically unviable for a large civilization. Yet, according to Moseley, sites like Aspero show very little evidence of consumption of anything besides fish and seafood. Shady noted that the animal remains at Caral exclusively consist of anchovies, clams, and sardines, adding further credence to MFAC.

But does a predominance of seafood in animal remains necessarily mean they were the prime source of subsistence?

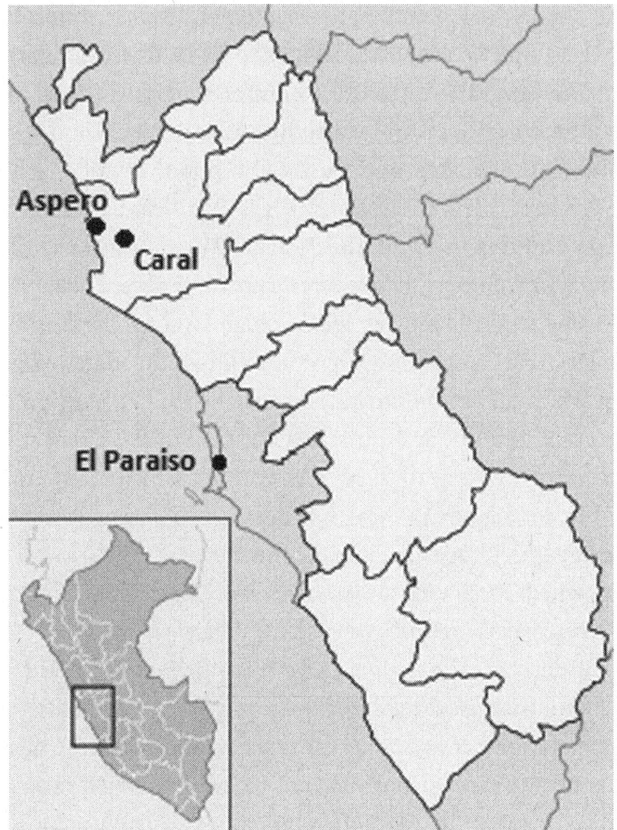

The locations of Caral, Aspero, and El Paraíso.

Shady, Haas, and Creamer proposed an alternative hypothesis: the inland sites developed concurrently with Aspero and were not dependent on the coastal city. They suggest that agriculture was the primary source of subsistence for the Caral-Supe people. The researchers believe that since Caral dominated the cotton trade, which was vital for the fishing industry, Aspero must have depended on Caral.

Shady, Haas, and Creamer discovered that the riverside settlements of Caral-Supe planted squash, beans, peppers, guavas, and sweet potatoes to supplement their seafood-based diet. Haas and Creamer cite evidence of seeds from fruits and vegetables found in Aspero to support their theory of the agricultural origins of Andean civilizations. In Caral and Aspero, we also find evidence of corn consumption. Initially, scholars hypothesized that maize played a less significant role in earlier Andean cultures, such as the Moche, Wari, and Inca, than it did in later cultures. However, in 2013, Haas, Creamer, and colleagues studied ancient fecal remains (coprolites), pollens, and stone tool residues. They combined the data with 126 radiocarbon dates and concluded that maize consumption was widespread in the Caral-Supe region. One of Peru's most well-known contributions to the world, without which many cuisines would be unimaginable—the humble potato—was missing from the list of agricultural products found at Caral.

So, which theory about the origins of Caral-Supe is correct?

To resolve the conflicting ideas, Moseley proposed that if over 50 percent of the diet came from fish and seafood, then MFAC holds. A 2022 study of the bones of 52 individuals from Aspero and Caral found that plant-based foods were the primary source of nutrition at both sites. In Caral, up to 70 percent of the diet in the early settlement phases consisted of produce, while in Aspero, the proportion varied between 55 percent and 68 percent. In the later stages of Caral, the dependence on seafood further decreased. These discoveries dealt a significant blow to the MFAC.

Further evidence supporting widespread crop growth was found in irrigation canals in the region. The Zaña Valley in northern Peru is home to the earliest known canals in the Americas, dating back to approximately 4700 BCE. We also have evidence of terrace farming on the hillsides, indicating that agricultural produce was vital, contrary to the MFAC's assumptions.

While archaeologists disagree on the importance of agriculture for supporting the population of Caral-Supe, two things are clear: seafood remained crucial to people's diet, and the fishing industry relied on inland sites, such as Caral, for cotton.

Aspero and Caral had an established trade in which the inland city exchanged cotton nets for fish and seafood. The commerce was mutually beneficial for both. Cotton and fish played a crucial role in fostering the growth of a complex culture that built the first pyramids in the New World and became the first civilization of the Americas. Caral's pyramids were contemporaries of the Egyptian pyramids, and some sites may have even older pyramids than Egypt's.

THE SEAT OF THE GODS: CARAL

"When I first arrived in the valley in 1994, I was overwhelmed. This place is somewhere between the seat of the gods and the home of man." —Ruth Shady

Ancient city of Caral.

Several sites in north-central Peru are part of this splendid civilization, but none is as well-researched as Caral.

Shady's excavations at Caral revealed a sprawling 150-acre area filled with monumental architecture. The city had six large pyramids. There were two circular plazas possibly used for religious activities, and the metropolis had large stone buildings with residential complexes of varying sizes.

The main pyramid temple complex, known as Templo Mayor, measures 150 m in length, 110 m in width, and 28 m in height. The earliest radiocarbon dates place the city's foundation at about 2800 BCE, with monuments constructed around 2600 BCE. This pyramid is located in the center of Caral, allowing society's elite to monitor the city's functioning.

The building had a sunken circular plaza and stepped platforms. The temple complex included a square altar with a fireplace and underground ventilation ducts.

Pyramids similar to Caral's were also found in Aspero, dated to around 3000 BCE. Thus, the pyramids of Aspero would be older than Egypt's first pyramid (dated 2670 BCE), while Caral's would be contemporary.

The construction of the Egyptian pyramids remains one of humanity's greatest mysteries. Scientists, engineers, and conspiracy theorists have proposed numerous explanations for how the Egyptians built them, but none have provided a satisfactory answer.

Fortunately, we have a better understanding of how the residents of Caral-Supe built their pyramids. Workers carried stones in reed bags called shicras, and they used these stones to build the pyramids' walls with mortar and plaster. By radiocarbon dating the shicras, archaeologists have been able to guess the age of the monuments.

Among the notable monuments at Caral is a large, walled amphitheater-temple complex. Like the Templo Mayor, it has

Shicra bags were used to carry stones for construction.

a circular plaza, the largest in the city. To the southeast of the amphitheater, there is a building within the outer wall, which was probably the residential quarters for the city's elite. A passage separates this house from the amphitheater, but a stairway north of the house connects to the temple.

The officials lived next to the public buildings, and their houses were attached to the larger structure, similar to the one we saw in the amphitheater temple complex. These houses were larger than other residential units and had spacious rooms with platforms, fireplaces, and intricately designed walls.

While the city's ruling class resided near the temples, the rest of the residents lived in housing units divided into subgroups. Shady classifies the residential complexes into four categories. The largest was the greater residential complex, located near the central temple and spanning an area of 20,236 sq. m. The lesser residential complex was the next in size, approximately 5,000 sq. m, and is located near the amphitheater. Two smaller residential subgroups were on the city's outskirts, and they most likely housed agricultural workers.

The people of Caral built a magnificent planned city, one of the earliest in the ancient world. What can we learn about Caral's society from these superb structures?

SOCIETY, RELIGION, AND GOVERNMENT

A panoramic view of Caral.

The monumental architecture and the differences in the sizes of residential quarters show that a social hierarchy existed at Caral. Objects belonging to the elite, such as textiles, sandals, quartz arrowheads, and axes, were found in their homes and tombs.

The elite must have been part of a government that commissioned the construction of the pyramids. In contrast to the Old World, the government in Peruvian cities did not originate from a need to protect people from common enemies. The towns of the Caral-Supe didn't have defenses or signs of warfare. In the absence of significant signs of violence, how did the elite encourage the people to participate in their grand projects?

Scholars link the ruling class's authority to religion and economics. It was a theocratic state whose officials promoted social cooperation and instituted a reward system for project completion.

Religion played an essential role in Caral-Supe. We can trace the roots of the Andean religion, as seen in later civilizations such as the Nazca, Moche, Wari, Tiwanaku, and the Incas, to the Caral-Supe.

Shady uncovered 32 stylized flutes made of pelican and condor bones depicting monkeys, snakes, and birds. These musical instruments may have been used during sacred ceremonies. In 2002, Haas and Creamer discovered a painted gourd in the Pativilca Valley that had a distinctive image. When they presented the object to their Peruvian colleagues, they were stunned. The image was a fanged, staff-wielding figure, likely an early portrayal of the Staff God, one of the most important deities in the Andean pantheon.[5]

Staff God at the Gate of Sun, Tiwanaku.

5 The earliest undisputed evidence of the Staff God comes from the Tiwanaku culture (peaked between 500 CE and 900 CE), centered in present-day Bolivia. The Tiwanaku Staff God was possibly the precursor to Viracocha, the creator and supreme deity in pre-Inca and Incan mythology.

The early depiction of the Staff God, who later became an important religious figure in Andean cultures, reveals a continuity in spiritual practices that dates back to the Caral-Supe Civilization. There is some controversy surrounding this figure. Some researchers suggest that, though the gourd is ancient, the drawing was carved onto it much later, between 900 CE and 1300 CE. Haas and Creamer disagree with this theory.

While the debate regarding the dating of the Staff God found at Pativilca remains, we observe similarities in religious structures, such as temples and pyramids, in later Andean civilizations. Hence, the hypothesis of religious continuity in Andean cultures, starting from Caral, is a plausible explanation.

We have evidence of human sacrifice in Caral and Aspero. Both adults and infants were sacrificed, and such rituals were a part of the religious ceremonies of the society. In Caral, the body of an adult male was discovered in a ceremonial room. Skulls were found in some buildings, and archaeologists suggest they were placed as offerings during construction activities.

At Caral-Supe, we find the burial of infants under the walls or floors of the houses of the elite and in specific areas of the Central Pyramid. There were elaborate offerings, including textiles and semi-precious stones. In Aspero, archaeologists discovered two burials: one of a newborn and another of an eight-year-old child. Both children were sacrificed and buried with grave goods that reflected their high status.

In Caral, archaeologists unearthed 26 vertebrae belonging to a blue whale and 3 vertebrae belonging to a fin whale. They were 23 cm high and 38 cm in diameter, polished and painted, and one had holes drilled in it. These vertebrae were found along with tree trunks of the pacay tree, which is native to the Andean Valley. The placement of the whale vertebrae with the tree trunks suggests they may have served a ceremonial purpose.

Vertebrae of blue whales were used in a ceremonial context at Caral.

Caral-Supe was the birthplace of several technological innovations that later appeared in other Andean civilizations, but it was unique in many respects. Let us examine some findings that laid the groundwork for succeeding civilizations.

THE UNIQUE TECHNOLOGIES OF CARAL-SUPE

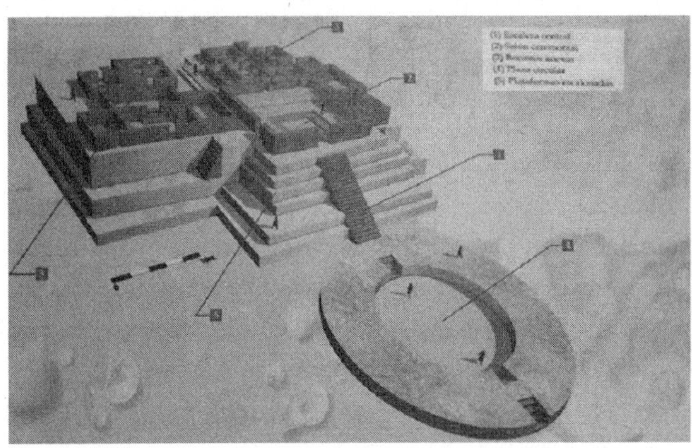

Reconstruction of a pyramid in Aspero.

Archaeologists discovered something unusual in the Caral-Supe cities: there was no pottery. The sites lacked pots, pans, storage containers, and cooking vessels. As there were no ceramics, we can assume the people roasted their food. Hence, this era in Peruvian history, spanning from 3500 BCE to 1600 BCE, is known as the pre-ceramic period.

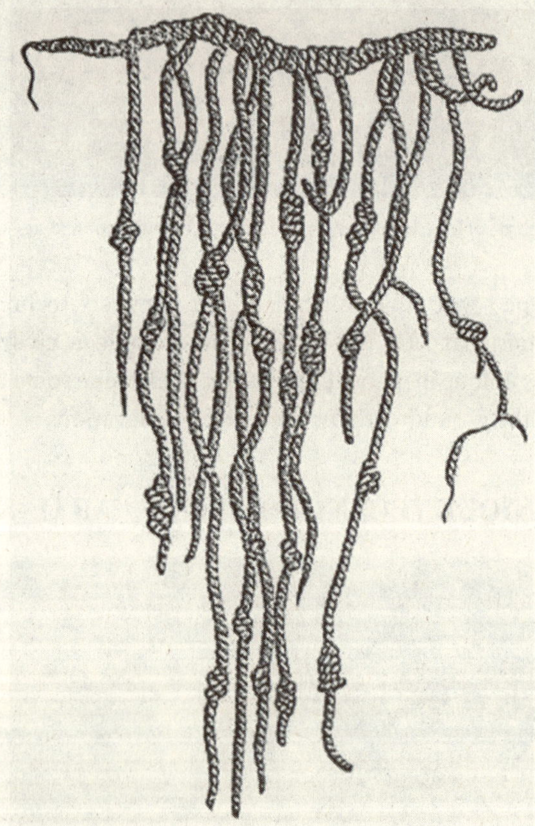

A *quipu* was discovered in Caral.

The residents of Caral lacked knowledge of pottery, but they had a comprehensive system for record-keeping. You may be familiar with the *quipu*, the Incan recording technique that employed knots in fiber strings to store information. The Incas used quipus to collect data and track their military, inventories, and census. The quipu is considered a form of writing or proto-writing.

Quipus were first used in Caral-Supe, and were made of cotton. A pallet containing offerings to the gods, including a quipu, was recovered in one of the Caral pyramid complexes. The discovery suggests that quipus were widespread, indicating that the residents had a well-established system for maintaining records.

Shady also suggests that the people of Caral-Supe studied astronomy and measured time. Astronomy helped them make annual and medium-term plans, and the festivities were centered around such calculations. They also applied their knowledge of astronomy to plan public buildings and determine the direction they should face.

La Huanca monolith in Caral.

A monolith in Caral, La Huanca, stands in a public square, surrounded by three pyramids and their adjacent residential units. The Huanca may have been used for astronomical studies. Shady suggests geoglyphs[6] found in the desert at strategic locations, along with underground structures that may have served as observatories, and monoliths planted above the ground at specific locations as evidence of the people of Caral-Supe practicing astronomy.

Altar of the holy fire on Templo Mayor.

Archaeologists discovered a packet of brown fiber in the shicra bags used for carrying stones to build pyramids. The fiber was from the Espostoa cactus plant, which grows in the higher reaches of the Andean Plateau (Altiplano).

6 Geoglyphs are large-scale ground markings, usually longer than 4 m. Nazca lines from the later Nazca Civilization are among Peru's most well-known geoglyphs.

Espostoa cactus was utilized to sustain fires for a longer duration. Its use, nearly 5,000 years ago, indicates that the people of Caral procured it through long-distance trade to fuel their altars.

Besides cactus, the innovative people of Caral came up with another ingenious idea to fan the flames of ritual fires. Five altars were discovered with underground ventilation ducts, which allowed the wind's draft to pass, keeping the fire alight.

END OF AN ERA

Pyramid at El Paraíso archaeological site.

Undoubtedly, Caral-Supe established a sound foundation for the succeeding Andean civilizations. Quipu, irrigation systems, and monumental architecture are just a few examples of technological breakthroughs that we can trace back to the Caral-Supe Civilization.

Caral-Supe's cities were abandoned between 1800 BCE and 1600 BCE. People painted their houses black and went inland.

The specific causes are unknown, but drought and famine are the best explanations.

Another theory is that as Peru entered the ceramic age, agriculture expanded, and dependency on marine resources for sustenance decreased. Cultivation moved closer to the Andes, providing people with greater food security. Recent evidence suggests that Caral-Supe had a robust agriculture, making it unlikely that a reduction in fish supplies contributed to its collapse.

I was astonished when I first learned about Caral. Incredibly, one of the driest places on earth supported such a sophisticated culture. Even more astounding was that they erected pyramids and preserved records before the discovery of pottery. The pyramids are among the world's oldest structures, raising serious concerns regarding whether the Americas should be called the "New World."

For the people of Caral, the concept of a government in which citizens give up some of their liberty for protection was foreign. Instead, they built a society centered on collaboration and rewards. Maybe we can learn something from their ruling class, which relied on social cooperation rather than a brute exercise of power.

We know very little about Peru's pre-ceramic past. El Paraíso (3500 BCE to 1800 BCE), located in the Chillón Valley in central Peru, has pyramids that may be older than those in Caral-Supe. Unfortunately, in 2013, property developers destroyed one of the pyramids. Police intervened to prevent the demolition of more pyramids, but the damage was permanent.

Ancient Peruvians likely erected pyramids older than the ones at Caral in other places, but we know little about them. Archaeological digs are underway throughout the Peruvian coast, which could reveal further information about the rise and fall of the Caral-Supe Civilization. As recently as July 2025, Shady and her team discovered the city of Peñico near Caral, which is dated to around 1800 BCE to 1500 BCE. The city's dating reveals that a significant urban center flourished after the collapse of Caral-Supe. Peñico was located at the center of a trade route connecting the Pacific coast with the Andes and the Amazon Basin. The discovery hints that Caral's legacy didn't disappear, but its successors continued the tradition of building sophisticated urban centers, laying the groundwork for future Andean civilizations.

7

Sintashta's Revolution on Wheels

THE EURASIAN STEPPES, 2100 BCE. AN ENTOURAGE OF warriors gathers outside a fortified settlement south of the Ural Mountains for their leader's funeral. He is about to be buried in a timber grave. The warlord is armed and prepared, poised for his journey to the afterlife. His burial contains copper and bronze axes, daggers, bronze socketed spearheads, flint arrowheads, javelins, and arrow tips. Ceramic containers and simple gold and silver ornaments are also placed beside him.

Despite his considerable wealth, weapons were his primary grave goods rather than gold and silver. People of his tribe sacrifice sheep and oxen to accompany him to the otherworld. After dying in combat as a hero, he will ride to the afterlife on his chariot. The tomb is sealed with a large *kurgan*,[1] or tumulus, measuring 85 m in diameter and 4.5 m in height.

These cemeteries dotted the Eurasian Steppes during the Bronze Age. However, this warlord's burial is unique because it contains evidence of the world's earliest spoked wheel chariot.

---

1 Kurgans are burial mounds constructed over a grave. They are typical of the Eurasian Steppes, and are associated with the burial traditions of the Indo-Europeans.

The horses buried with the warlord were the ancestors of the modern domestic horse.

Four thousand years ago, a little-known military-industrial center on the grasslands south of the Urals, near today's Russia-Kazakhstan border, sparked a revolution that shaped human mobility for millennia. This society, known as the Sintashta culture, invented the spoked wheel chariot and bred the ancestor of the modern horse. These innovations, born out of survival necessities, profoundly impacted both warriors and ordinary people for generations to come.

The Sintashta culture had around 20 settlements, which thrived between 2100 BCE and 1800 BCE. Soviet archaeologists discovered their remains in the 1970s. They termed the culture "Sintashta," after its type site by the same name in Chelyabinsk Oblast, Russia. It was a circular fortified town with a diameter of around 140 m.

The Sintashta people were more than just pioneers in mobility. Their descendants played a crucial role in disseminating Indo-Iranian languages across South and Central Asia. These languages include Bengali, Persian, Sanskrit, Hindi, Punjabi, Balochi, and many more. Today, over 1.5 billion people worldwide speak Indo-Iranian languages.

In our previous chapters, we saw how archaeological research has challenged conventional views about cities, writing, and pyramids. In this chapter, we will focus on another invention credited to the Near East that occurred thousands of kilometers away in the vast grasslands of the Eurasian Steppes: the chariot.

Unlike the debate surrounding writing and the emergence of the first cities, the archaeological consensus is that the world's earliest known chariots were invented in the Sintashta culture. Let us learn about these enigmatic warlords from the Eurasian Steppes and their historical impact. We will begin our journey by exploring their origins.

THE ORIGINS OF THE SINTASHTA CULTURE

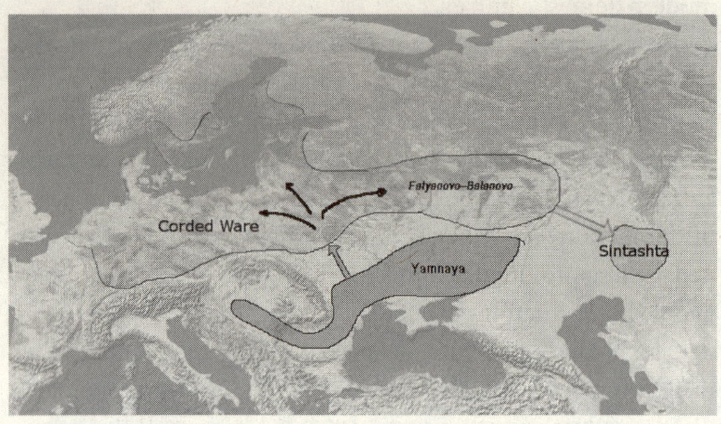

Migrants from the Corded Ware culture of Europe started the Sintashta culture.

The remains of *kurgans* in present-day Ukraine.

Archaeologists have offered various explanations regarding the origins of the Sintashta culture. To understand them, we must roll back the clock to 3000 BCE in the region between the Dnieper and Dniester Rivers, in present-day Ukraine, where

The Kernosivsky idol, a *kurgan* stele associated with the Yamnaya culture, mid-third millennium BCE.

extensive interactions occurred between the Corded Ware culture, Globular Amphora culture, and the Yamnaya culture.

Several cultures existed in the Eurasian Steppes during the Bronze Age, but we'll discuss the most relevant. A comprehensive discussion of Eurasian Bronze Age cultures is beyond the scope of this book; however, it is essential to be familiar with a few key cultures to understand the origins of Sintashta.

The Yamnaya culture (3400 BCE to 2600 BCE): Archaeologists identify the Yamnaya culture, based in the Pontic-Caspian region, by its kurgans. The population was an admixture of Eastern Hunter-Gatherer (EHG) from Eastern Europe and Caucasian hunter-gatherers (CHG) from the Caucasus or Iran. This new genetic population is known as the Western Steppe Herder (WSH). Recent research suggests that dairy consumption from sheep, cows, and horses fueled their migrations across Eurasia. The Yamnaya were among the earliest horse riders in history, a practice that the Sintashta people mastered.

Globular Amphora culture (3400 BCE TO 2800 BCE): Archaeological culture between the Elbe River (west) and the Vistula River (east). As the name suggests, their pottery is characterized by a globular shape and features two to four handles. They were an admixture of Early European Farmers (EEF), who originated from Anatolia, and Western Hunter-Gatherers (WHG), hunter-gatherers from Western and Central Europe. Globular Amphora had little genetic similarity with the Yamnaya.

Corded Ware culture (3000 BCE to 2300 BCE): A vast archaeological horizon stretching from present-day Belgium to Ukraine between the Rhine and the Volga Rivers. Cord-like impressions on pottery and crouched or fetal-position burials are typical identifiers of the Corded Ware culture. Recent genetic studies have revealed that the Corded Ware people were

Pottery typical of the Globular Amphora culture.

Corded Ware pottery, c. 2500 BCE.

a complex admixture of local hunter-gatherer populations and individuals from the Yamnaya and Globular Amphora cultures.

The intricate web of cultural interactions between the three distinct peoples gave birth to a fascinating array of regional cultures that stretched into the forest-steppe zone. Notably, the Middle-Dnieper (2800 BCE to 1800 BCE) and the Fatyanovo culture (2900 BCE to 2100 BCE) were the outcomes of this cultural exchange.

Fatyanovo emerged on the northeastern edge of the Middle-Dnieper culture. Its economy was based on cattle herding. Their pottery showed a mixture of Globular Amphora and Corded Ware cultures.

The Fatyanovo were mobile pastoralists, and some continued to migrate eastward down the Volga until they discovered copper ores at the foothills of the Ural Mountains, near the Kama River. They settled in this Volga-Kama region, converting it into a mining and metallurgical center, and the culture became known as the Balanovo culture.

Just south of the Fatyanovo-Balanovo horizon was the Abashevo culture in the forest-steppe zone,[2] which emerged around 2500 BCE. Their pottery bore a resemblance to the Corded Ware style, and their economy relied heavily on cattle breeding.

The Abashevo took advantage of the copper ores in the Ural Mountains and began large-scale metallurgy. Archaeologists discovered only two fortified Abashevo settlements among over 200 unearthed so far. Ultimately, the Abashevo people would move eastward and give rise to the Sintashta culture. Archaeologists have concluded this based on the continuation of Abashevo pottery styles in the Sintashta region. Further, a 2015 genetic study confirms

---

2 The forest-steppe zone in the Eurasian Steppes spans across Europe, from Ukraine through the Volga and the Urals in Central Russia to the eastern fringes of Siberia.

archaeologists' observations of this eastward migration pattern. The Sintashta people were genetically similar to the Corded Ware culture.

A common question that comes to our mind is, if the Abashevo people moved east, why not simply call it the Abashevo culture? Why Sintashta? Why do we need a unique name for the eastern migrants of the Abashevo?

The distinction between Abashevo and Sintashta lies in their large, fortified settlements. In contrast to Abashevo, all Sintashta settlements were surrounded by circular reinforced ramparts. Each residence had a metalworking furnace. Archaeologists have not discovered anything comparable to the Sintashta dwellings from the Bronze Age in the Eurasian Steppes. Each settlement had approximately 200 to 700 people, but some, such as Arkaim, had as many as 1,500 to 2,500 residents.

Contrary to the popular image of the Steppes as the domain of hardy horseback nomads, the Sintashta people led a sedentary lifestyle. They were not as mobile as their Corded Ware ancestors, but rather pastoralists living in settled communities. However, they didn't farm, and their subsistence depended entirely on livestock.

The lifestyle of the Sintashta people is crucial to understand why they invested heavily in building fortified settlements.

THE FORTIFIED TOWNS OF SINTASHTA

The climate in the Steppes became colder after 2500 BCE, and the grasslands became drier around 2000 BCE. Archaeologists determined the impact of this climate change on the ecological zone by studying ancient pollen grains. Forests retracted, grasslands expanded, and marshlands became more concentrated as their numbers reduced.

Marshy areas were a lifeline, providing crucial livestock feed during the unforgiving winter. This led to fierce competition among various tribes to establish control over these marshlands in the Steppes. The consequences of losing cattle were dire, which meant facing starvation during the winter. This desperation drove migrants to settle around these marshlands, ensuring the survival of their cattle. The situation was so desperate that they had to give up the nomadic lifestyle of their Corded Ware ancestors and adopt a more settled, permanent existence.

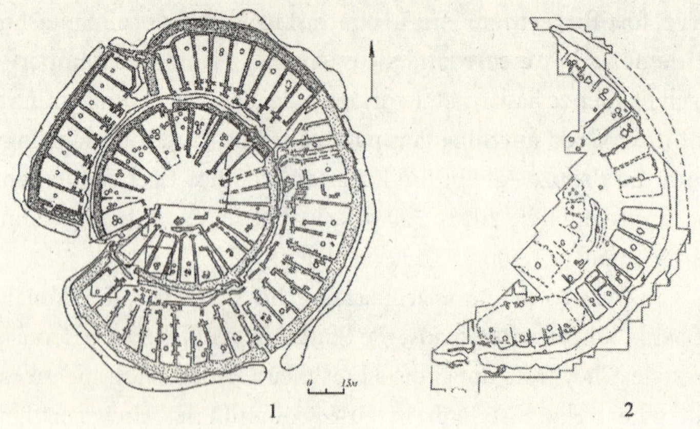

The ground plan of Arkaim (left) and Sintashta (right).

The competition for limited resources spurred the Sintashta people to adapt and build robust defenses along the marshes, a more challenging terrain than the defensible hills adjacent to the marshlands. Unlike prior cultures, which had constructed temporary defensive structures, the Sintashta people built massive, long-lasting fortifications.

Earthen walls reinforced with timber and V-shaped ditches protected the settlements. For added security, the residents topped off the walls with wooden palisades. Watchtowers, tall structures with a commanding view of the surrounding area, were erected strategically to detect potential threats.

Archaeologist David W. Anthony theorized that people built forts to protect their limited resources.

In 2021, archaeologist Igor Chechushkov proposed an alternative explanation for the fortifications, suggesting that they were warmer than the surrounding open plains and helped keep animals safe throughout the winter. You can imagine the Sintashta settlements as gigantic cattle pens.

Both views regarding the purpose of fortifications are sensible and not mutually exclusive. The well-being of the animals was as crucial as keeping intruders out. During 2100 BCE, violence was no longer limited to cattle raids. We see the rise of ritual warfare and the emergence of a warrior class dedicated to protecting the community and its resources.

Archaeological excavations of the burials at Sintashta reveal that among the 242 individuals found in 181 graves, 65 graves contained people buried with weapons.

Excavators identified a total of 79 graves as those of adults; among them, 43, or 54 percent, of the adults were interred with weapons rather than gold and silver, highlighting the value of arms at Sintashta.

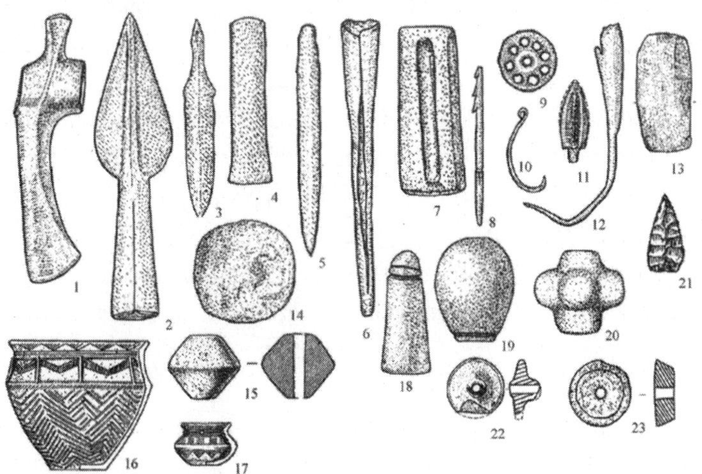

Weapons and artifacts from Sintashta graves.

As Anthony states in his book, *The Horse, the Wheel and Language,* "What was impressive in these graves was weaponry, vehicles, and animal sacrifices, not crowns or jewelry."

We can trace the origins of Sintashta's reverence for weapons to Abashevo. Excavations at Abashevo settlements yielded cast shaft-hole axes, knives, socketed spears, and socketed chisels. Burial with weaponry was not a new practice in the region. However, the sheer number of weapons found at Sintashta's graves surpasses those from Abashevo and Fatyanovo.

Many of the weapons found in Sintashta's graves, such as bronze or copper daggers, flat axes, shaft-hole axes, polished stone maceheads, and flint or bone projectile points, were a continuation of preceding cultures.

But we also see newer weaponry emerge.

Continuing the innovation in flint weapons, Sintashta's artisans significantly contributed to warfare technology by inventing a new type of point. This point, characterized by a contracting stem, defined shoulders, and narrow blades 4–10 cm long, was most likely fitted to javelins and used in combat.

As military technology advanced, the Sintashta people's foresight led them to invest in metallurgy. They recognized the potential of copper and tin, which was the "oil of the Bronze Age," and capitalized on the rising demand for these metals. Each house served as a metalworking facility, with smelting ovens and copper slag found in the dwellings proving the intensity of metal manufacturing.

Most of the finished metal objects in Sintashta were made of arsenical bronze.[3] In Sintashta homes, archaeologists found tubular

3 Unlike regular bronze, the main alloy in arsenical bronze is arsenic, and manufacturing it was hazardous, hence grew less popular over time. Sintashta's arsenical bronze weapons contained 1–2.5 percent arsenic.

clay pipes used as bellows for the forges. Additionally, weapon moulds, copper ingots, and crucibles were also discovered.

Thanks to the unique location of the Sintashta culture at the eastern borders of the Pontic-Caspian steppe, they developed long-distance trade contacts with several civilizations. These contacts fuelled the metallurgical industry. One of the primary trade partners was the Central Asian Oxus Civilization, also known as BMAC, centered around the river Amu Darya. We will discuss Oxus in the next chapter. Central Asia served as the hub of Uralic copper. A text from Mesopotamia, dating to the reign of the Sumerian king Rim-Sin (1822 BCE to 1763 BCE), records the receipt of 18,333 kg of copper in a single shipment. A study from 2024 found that oxhide ingots discovered in Hagia Triada, Crete, dated to the fifteenth century BCE, contained copper traced to the Southern Urals.

You may be wondering why the Sintashta exported vast quantities of metals. The goal of the trade was to boost the wealth of the local chieftains, who were involved in endemic warfare.

Ritual warfare wasn't new in the region. We find proof of clashes between tribes in the Abashevo cemetery of Pepkino, on the lower Sura River Valley, where a grave pit dated 2200 BCE was found with the bodies of 28 young men. Eighteen of them were decapitated with axe wounds to their heads and arms. The absence of women and children in the grave suggests the men fell in battle. Settlement massacres include victims of all ages and genders. The men were buried under a single kurgan, which indicates that they likely died during a single event, possibly a battle with a rival tribe.

The Sintashta people continued the tradition of warfare of their Abashevo ancestors, but also introduced additional technologies. They invented the war chariot and bred a new type of horse to gain an advantage in battle. Each warlord had a cohort of chariot-driving warriors supported by foot soldiers.

While the spoked wheel chariot and horse breed were initially designed for war, their invention significantly transformed mobility for the next 4,000 years.

THE DAWN OF WAR ON WHEELS

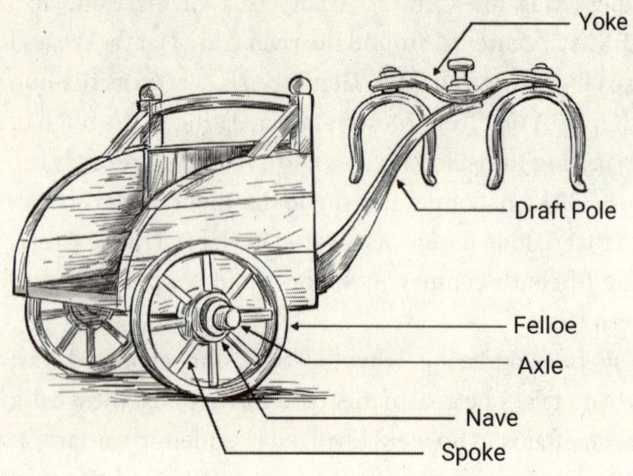

Reconstruction of the Sintashta chariot.

Until the 1990s, researchers attributed the invention of the war chariot to the civilizations of the Near East. They used examples from Sumerian reliefs, such as the Standard of Ur war panel, depicting kungas[4] pulling war wagons.

Scholars theorized that the spoked wheel chariot must have emerged from the war wagons of Mesopotamia. But these war wagons were slow and not a chariot. There are records of people abandoning them and fleeing on foot, as they were slow.

Speed defines a chariot.

---

4 Kungas were a hybrid between donkeys and the Syrian wild ass. Refer to Chapter 9.

Anthony and colleagues conducted radiocarbon dating in 1992, which revealed that the Sintashta chariots were at least two centuries older than their earliest depictions in the Near East.

The Sintashta chariots were the first of their kind in history. You may think, "What if the chariots weren't used for war?" If you examine the reconstructed chariot, it appears unstable. What if they were ceremonial and used by chieftains to strut around the settlement? These are valid questions.

However, a 2021 study by archaeologists Igor Chechushkov and Ivan Semyan revealed that the Sintashta employed chariots for warfare. The archaeologists used sinew, natural glues, and organic cheekpieces made from bones available to the Sintashta people and successfully tested their functionality in a military engagement.

Bridle cheek pieces of horses discovered in Sintashta burials offer further proof of chariotry. They were made from antler bones and are among the oldest artifacts found.

Chariot technology, born in a small society fighting for survival, quickly became a global phenomenon. By 1400 BCE, the Egyptians had mastered the technology, and images of chariots adorned imperial panels. By 1200 BCE, the first chariots were seen in China, marking the rapid spread of this revolutionary technology.

The remarkable spread of chariots across Eurasia was a game changer in ancient warfare. The Sintashta culture, with its early adoption and mastery of chariot technology, played a significant role in this spread. Speed became a key factor, and armies moved swiftly on their enemies.

Eventually, chariots paved the way for mounted warfare and cavalry, which became a mainstay of armies worldwide till the end of the First World War. The Sintashta culture played a pivotal role in the rise of cavalry and the widespread adoption of horses as a mode of transportation.

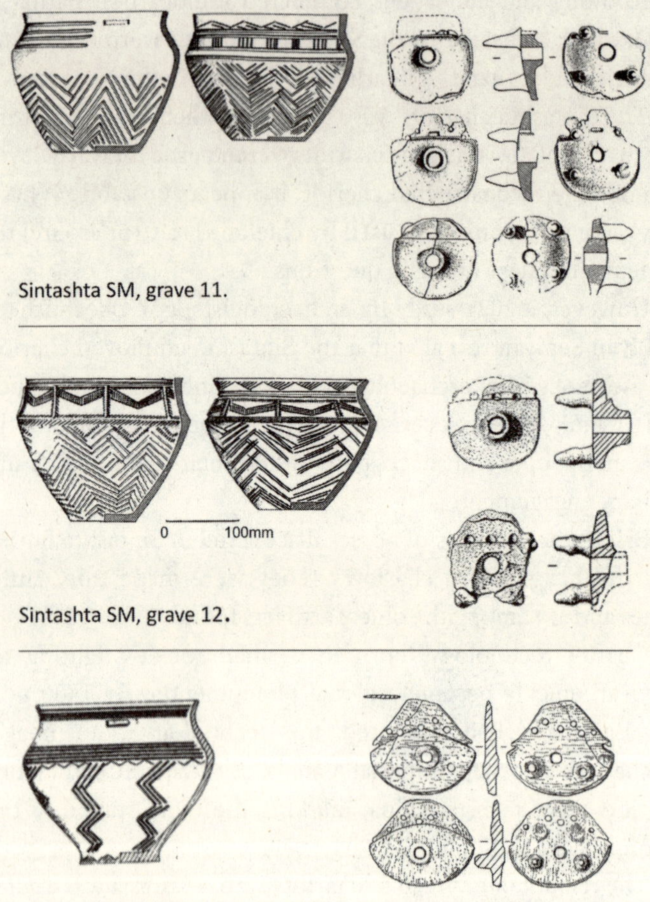

Ceramics and horse bridle cheek pieces found at Sintashta graves.

They were expert horse breeders. They developed horses that replaced all pre-existing domestic horse breeds. Today, we can trace all domestic horses to the ones bred by the Sintashta people.

ORIGINS OF THE MODERN DOMESTICATED HORSE

Wild horses were common worldwide during the Upper Paleolithic era, spanning from approximately 50,000 to 12,000 years ago. Among the 6,000 paintings of animals in the 17,000-year-old Lascaux Cave in France, horses are the most frequently depicted. Scientists say human predation and competition with other species caused the wild horse's extinction in most regions by the sixth millennium BCE.

But there was one place on Earth where this animal thrived: the Eurasian Steppes.

Humans first domesticated horses for milk and meat, not for transportation. They tamed the creatures in the Western Eurasian Steppes around the fourth millennium BCE. Horses are well-adapted to the harsh Steppe winters, and their powerful hooves can break up frozen streams, allowing them access to water. They thrive in environments where livestock can't, making them the ideal candidate for domestication.

In 2009, archaeologists discovered milk residue from a mare in pottery dating back to a 6,000-year-old site in northern Kazakhstan. The findings altered our understanding of early horse riding. The site we're talking about is called Botai. Excavations revealed that 99.9 percent of all animal remains were horse bones. The people of the Botai culture, who lived from 3700 BCE to 3100 BCE, subsisted solely on horse meat.

Was there any evidence from Botai that hinted at horse riding?

Anthony conducted a landmark study in 2011. He noticed deterioration in the molars of the horses found at the site and compared the patterns of tooth degradation to those of a modern domestic horse. The results were comparable. According to Anthony, bit wear caused the erosion in the teeth of the Botai horses.[5]

The dental erosion suggests that the people of Botai were horse riders. Early bits were usually made of bones or animal antlers, unlike the metal ones we use now. Hence, the bits from Botai didn't survive. We have evidence of artifacts made from antler bones at other archaeological sites in the Steppes, although they are dated after 2500 BCE.

The Przewalski's horse is a descendant of the horses domesticated in the Botai culture.

The study was a watershed moment in history since, for the first time, researchers pinpointed the location and timeline of horse domestication. However, subsequent studies painted a different picture about horse domestication. A 2018 DNA analysis discovered that the Botai horses were the ancestors of the Przewalski's horse (*Equus przewalskii*), a species distinct from the domestic horse

5 A bit is a horse's mouthpiece that applies pressure to the horse's tongue when the rider pulls the attached reins.

(*Equus caballus*). The short and stocky Przewalski's horse is a feral creature, similar to a mustang. According to researchers, the Botai horse contributed only 2.7 percent of the DNA of the present-day horse. Hence, horse domestication must have happened elsewhere. Anthony's evidence was indirect. Archaeologists didn't find any significant wear on the bits in Botai. A 2021 study by William Timothy Treal Taylor and Christina Isabelle Barrón-Ortiz found that the erosion observed in the teeth of Botai horses was natural rather than caused by bit wear. Another 2021 study of the dental remains of individuals buried at Botai found no milk proteins in their teeth. Although Botai had a horse-subsistence–based economy, there is little evidence that they used the creatures for long-distance riding.

A 2021 study by zooarchaeologist Ludovic Orlando examined 273 ancient horse genomes and discovered that horses raised by Sintashta herders replaced all existing horse breeds. Today's domesticated horses, known as DOM2, can be traced back to the Sintashta culture.

Though horse breeders at Sintashta may have contributed to increasing the availability of the DOM2, we can trace its rise to earlier horse populations in the third millennium BCE.

A 2024 study led by Pablo Librado Sanz, an evolutionary biologist, along with an international cross-disciplinary team of biologists, anthropologists, archaeologists, and geneticists, analyzed 475 ancient horse genomes, spanning over 50,000 years and covering a wide geographic range. They combined this data with 77 modern horse genomes to trace the genetic evolution of horses and identify key events in their domestication.

The study reveals the modern domestic horse lineage (DOM2) emerging around 2200 BCE in the western Eurasian Steppes. This lineage became dominant due to advanced reproductive control practices, such as close-kin mating and shortened generation times. Horse breeders want to replicate desirable traits, such as endurance, and eliminate undesirable ones, like aggressiveness. Close-kin mating, or inbreeding, is a practice to achieve this.

Inbreeding and smaller generation gaps enabled humans to selectively breed horses with desirable traits, such as strength, speed, and docility. Thanks to their new utilitarian characteristics, the DOM2 lineage eventually replaced nearly all local horse populations across Eurasia, beginning widespread horse-based mobility.

How can we be sure that the Sintashta people played a vital role in spreading the DOM2 horses? Librado and colleagues identified a severe domestication bottleneck around 2700 BCE, during which the horse population experienced a drastic decline. This bottleneck was followed by a rapid expansion of the DOM2 lineage, coinciding with the rise of spoke-wheeled chariots associated with the Sintashta culture and the increased demand for horses for transport and warfare. Hence, it is fair to say that the people of Sintashta played a vital role in breeding desirable traits in horses and helped popularize their use, along with chariots.

END OF SINTASHTA AND THE FIRST ARYANS

Intense competition for resources, loss of grasslands, climate change, and increased warfare all contributed to the decline of the Sintashta culture. Its residents moved to greener pastures.

The Sintashta culture gave rise to the Andronovo cultural horizon, a vast area spanning the Eurasian Steppes with varying regional expressions. Migrations of the Andronovo people resulted in the spread of the Indo-Iranian languages. Their shared Indo-Iranian linguistic identity was known as Aryan, as the speakers referred to those who practiced rituals, performed sacrifices correctly, and lived a virtuous life as *Arya*. Arya means noble in Sanskrit and Avestan. In contrast, a *dasyu* was a person who interrupted the ritual cycles between gods and humans.

Unfortunately, in the nineteenth century, these terms were interpreted and given a racial connotation. But, since then, there has been a wealth of evidence that "Aryan" was a linguistic term applicable to the speakers of Indo-Iranian languages and not a racial or ethnic group.

The importance of horse sacrifice, or the *ashwamedha*, in the Rigveda is also evident in the archaeological evidence from Arkaim and Sintashta, where ritual horse sacrifice occurred. Although horse bones comprised only 13 percent of the total animal bones found, they were the largest group in the cemeteries, accounting for 39 percent of all bones discovered. There is a close connection between the weapons and horses, indicating that the graves of the warrior elite contained both. Two-thirds of the graves containing horse sacrifices had weapons, and 83 percent of graves with multiple horses sacrificed contained weapons. However, as we shall see in the next chapter, ritual horse sacrifice was not unique to the Indo-Iranians, and horse burials in Central Asia predate those of the Sintashta. However, the ritual in Central Asia could have resulted from the intermingling of local cultures with the people of the Eurasian Steppes, since horses were not native to the region.

The oldest texts of the Indo-Iranians were mandalas (or books) 2–7 of the Rigveda. They were likely composed between 1500 BCE and 1200 BCE, and the *Avesta*, the earliest Iranian text, dates from 1200 BCE to 1000 BCE. The earliest recorded evidence of Vedic gods and a language similar to Vedic Sanskrit was discovered in Syria in the fifteenth century BCE during a peace deal between the Hittites and the Mitanni Aryans. Linguists refer to this language as Old Indic, a precursor to Vedic Sanskrit.

The ruling class of Mitanni, the *Maryannu*, is said to be closely related to Indo-Aryans because they worshipped the same pantheon of deities. However, Vedic Sanskrit contains loanwords that linguists believe may have originated in the Oxus Civilization (BMAC), which we will discuss in the next chapter. These loanwords are missing in the language of the Mitanni elite. At some point, the Mitanni Aryans and Indo-Aryans split, resulting in minor differences in their languages. Between 1800 BCE and 1600 BCE, Old Indic most likely evolved as a distinct language from ancient Indo-Iranian and was spoken by Indo-Aryans and Mitanni Aryans. A common Indo-Iranian language was possibly spoken before the emergence of Old Indic between 2100 BCE and 1800 BCE in the Sintashta and allied cultural zones.

Indo-Iranian migrants split into two directions. Indo-Aryans went east, whereas Iranians migrated west.[6] With the arrival of the Indo-Iranians, South and Central Asia entered a new historical era, introducing new faiths, languages, and sacred texts.

The Sintashta people lived in fortified settlements and practiced sedentary pastoralism, depending on livestock for survival. They invented the spoked-wheel chariot, which revolutionized warfare and mobility. The horses bred by Sintashta had better stress tolerance, endurance, and ability to carry heavy weights, and were easier to control. The animals eventually replaced all other horse breeds by 2000 BCE and changed long-distance transportation for the next 4,000 years.

The Sintashta culture traded with major Bronze Age civilizations, but no written accounts of these mysterious Steppe dwellers have been found. Although not documented in historical records, the enigmatic people of Sintashta significantly influenced our mobility, changing the course of history.

---

6 A 2023 paper by Paul Heggarty, a linguist at Max Planck Institute, suggested that Indo-Iranian languages may have entered the Indian subcontinent through the Iranian Plateau, which could also explain why Mitanni language didn't have non-Indo-European loanwords.

8

Oxus: The Fifth River Valley Civilization

THE KARAKUM DESERT SPANS 350,000 SQUARE KILOMETERS, accounting for approximately 70 percent of Turkmenistan's territory. In 1974, as a sparrow fluttered by, an archaeologist with a luxuriant walrus-like mustache labored tirelessly in this barren landscape. Two years back, he had found pottery shards at the location where he was digging. Between 1974 and 2013, he worked in harsh conditions, sometimes barefoot, to uncover a vast city spanning 55 hectares. The scholar initially thought it was a medieval city based on its size and architecture. However, subsequent research revealed that the metropolis was over 4,000 years old, dating back to the Bronze Age. He named the city, Gonur Depe, and believed it to be the capital of a forgotten civilization.

The discovery of Gonur Depe was a significant breakthrough for Viktor Ivanovich Sarianidi, whose superhuman efforts helped us learn about a fifth river valley civilization of the Old World. This incredible yet lesser-known civilization is the Oxus Civilization, also known as the Bactria–Margiana Archaeological Complex (BMAC).[1]

1 In this chapter, I will use the terms Oxus and BMAC interchangeably to refer to the same civilization. Sarianidi coined the term BMAC.

Who were these mysterious people who built a metropolis in the heart of the desert? What shaped their society, beliefs, and culture? How did they impact the world? What led to their decline? To answer these questions, let's review the earliest discoveries from Central Asia that challenged the notion that the Indus, Mesopotamia, Egypt, and China were the only river valley civilizations in the Old World.

THE DISCOVERY OF THE OXUS CIVILIZATION

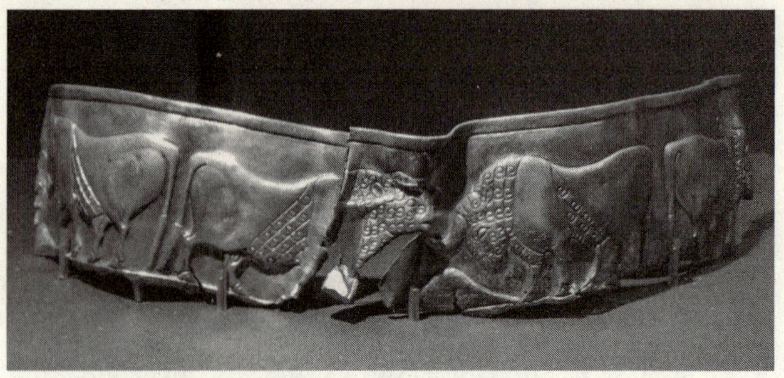

Fragment of a silver bowl found at Tepe Fullol.

In 1965, farmers near the village of Tepe Fullol in northern Afghanistan found a grave containing 20 gold and silver vessels. The treasure intrigued Sarianidi. The bowls' design and iconography resembled artifacts from ancient Mesopotamia and the Indus Valley. The finds at Tepe Fullol would be the earliest evidence of a Bronze Age civilization in Central Asia. However, we were still a decade away from knowing that a sophisticated culture existed in the region.

Sarianidi was born into a Pontic Greek family on September 23, 1929, in Tashkent, the capital of Uzbekistan. His parents, Ioannis and Athena, moved to Tashkent from Yalta in the 1920s. Initially, he aspired to be a lawyer, but later developed an interest in archaeology. He stated that "it (archaeology) was more free because it was more ancient." After graduating from Central Asia State University, in 1952, he earned a master's degree from the Institute of Archaeology in Moscow, in 1961. He completed his doctorate from the Soviet (now Russian) Academy of Sciences. His dissertation focused on Afghanistan during the Bronze and Iron Ages, and one of his career highlights was the unearthing of the renowned "Bactrian Gold" at the Tillya Tepe archaeological site in the country. The treasure has an interesting story. It vanished after the Taliban took authority in 1996, reappeared after their fall in 2001, and has again disappeared since 2021, when the Taliban reclaimed power.

Sarianidi's legacy is best associated with the Oxus Civilization. When the Afghan farmers told him they had discovered something, he began excavating various sites in the Dashly Oasis in northern Afghanistan. At the same time, his colleague A.A. Askarov investigated the Sapalli Tepe settlement in southern Uzbekistan.

The archaeologists carried out excavations on both sides of the Amu Darya, also known as the Oxus by the ancient Greeks, hence the term Oxus Civilization. In antiquity, Greeks named the region south of the Amu Darya and north of the Hindu Kush Mountains Bactria (*Bakhdi* in Old Persian and *Bāhlīka* in Sanskrit). Grave robbers looted the sites in northern Afghanistan, selling many relics to antique enthusiasts. Seeing the country's adverse political situation, Sarianidi and I.S. Masimov concentrated their research on the Murghab River Delta at the edge of the Karakum. This area was known as *Marghu* in Old Persian. The Greeks called it Margiana. Because Sarianidi and his colleagues discovered most of the sites in Bactria and Margiana, he dubbed the new civilization the "Bactria–Margiana Archaeological Complex."

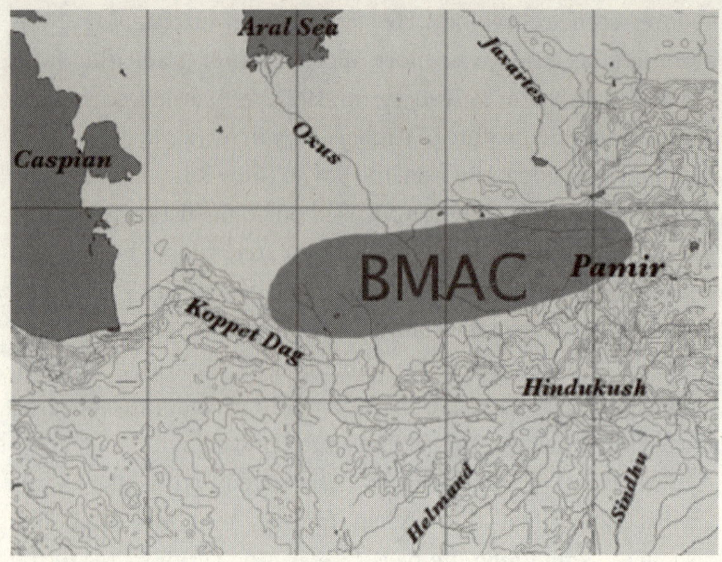

Location of the Oxus Civilization.

Soviet archaeologists discovered BMAC sites, such as Auchin or Takhirbaj 3, in the 1950s and 1960s, but their significance as part of a lost civilization was not yet understood. The discovery of megacities with monumental architecture, intricate jewelry, artifacts that hinted at long-distance trade, and sophisticated pottery led Sarianidi and his colleagues to conclude that they had found a Bronze Age civilization. However, as the Cold War was at its peak, news about BMAC's discovery barely made it beyond a few Russian archaeology and language journals.

Following the collapse of the Soviet Union, thanks to international collaboration and the diligent efforts of Sarianidi and his colleagues over the past three decades, we now have a clearer understanding of the Oxus Civilization, which coexisted with Mesopotamia, Egypt, China, and the Indus Valley.

WHO WERE THE PEOPLE OF THE OXUS?

The ruins of Gonur Depe.

The Oxus Civilization is bordered by the Kopet Dag Mountains to the southwest, the Hindu Kush Mountains to the southeast, and the Pamir Mountains to the east. To the north lie the vast grasslands of the Eurasian Steppes.

The oldest evidence of habitation in the Oxus area dates back to approximately 7200 BCE in the foothills of the Kopet Dag, where sites such as Namazga Depe, Ilgynly Depe, and Altyn Depe existed. The settlers were a mix of farmers from the Iranian Plateau and local hunter-gatherers. The burgeoning settlements at the foothills of the Kopet Dag were a part of the Namazga culture. There is evidence of domestication of goats and sheep, as well as the cultivation of wheat and barley.

The region transitioned into the Chalcolithic period[2] around 4000 BCE, which lasted until approximately 2800 BCE. Following

2 Chalcolithic era is also known as the Copper Age.

the Early Bronze Age (2800 BCE to 2400 BCE), BMAC emerged. Initially, archaeologists believed that an "urban crisis" prompted people to abandon settlements along the Kopet Dag and migrate to Margiana and then to Bactria, leading to the birth of the Oxus Civilization. The cities of BMAC share many similarities with the Namazga culture, especially in pottery and artifacts. Hence, the eastward migration theory was deemed a reasonable explanation. However, with improvements in radiocarbon dating, it became clear that the proposed migration theory does not match the chronology of the BMAC sites.

There were also noticeable differences between the burial practices and genetics of the BMAC and Namazga people. Hence, scholars consider the Oxus Civilization distinct from the Namazga culture, although the latter influenced its development. Around 3000 BCE, a cultural split occurred in the region, resulting in the formation of two groups. The first set of people, centered around Namazga Depe, Anau, and Kara Depe, had colorful pottery. The second group centered at Altyn Depe, in the east near the Geoksyur Oasis, had a more austere style. Migrants from Geoksyur moved into the Murghab Delta and expanded eastward, as evidenced by the rise of Shahr-i Sokhta, a city located on the banks of Afghanistan's Helmand River. We observe a continuation of the Geoksyur-style pottery in Margiana. This period in the history of the Oxus Civilization is known as the "regionalization era," a term derived from the chronology of the Indus Valley Civilization. The striking number of artifacts from Harappa and the Indus Valley trading outpost at Shortugai, Afghanistan, has led many archaeologists to draw comparisons between the two civilizations, resulting in a similar chronological classification.

During the "integration era," approximately 2250 BCE to 1700 BCE, the cities of Oxus rivaled those of the Indus Valley,

Elam, Mesopotamia, and Egypt. Located on the banks of the Murghab River in southern Turkmenistan, Gonur was the largest and most important settlement.

Who were the people of the Oxus Civilization? Were they related to the Indo-European (IE) people of the Steppes? This intriguing question has sparked a long-standing debate since the earliest finds.

The presence of several fire altars and temples led Sarianidi to conclude that the Indo-Iranians built BMAC. However, with further discoveries, archaeologists and linguists believe the Oxus was a separate culture from the people who lived in the Steppes.

Genetic studies play a crucial role in providing valuable insights into the origins and composition of the Oxus population. Geneticist Vagheesh Narasimhan and colleagues' landmark 2019 study of Bronze Age skeletons from the sites of Bustan, Dzharkutan, Gonur Depe, and Sapalli Tepe revealed that the BMAC people originated from preexisting Chalcolithic and Neolithic populations, with minor influences from Anatolian farmers and Siberian Hunter-Gatherers. BMAC residents lacked any ancestry associated with IE people.

Besides genetics, linguistics also helps us establish that the residents of the Oxus Civilization weren't IE people.

In our previous chapter, we discussed the Indo-Iranian languages and how the descendants of the Sintashta culture played a key role in spreading them. The Indo-Iranian language family is split into two branches: the Indo-Aryan languages, spoken in the Indian subcontinent, and the Iranian languages, spoken in Iran and Central Asia. The oldest hymns of the Rigveda contain 383 non-IE loanwords, accounting for roughly 4 percent of the Vedic Sanskrit vocabulary. These words are related to growing cereals, bread making, waterworks, tools or weapons (such as an axe or club), and seeds, including mustard and hemp, among others.

Among the non-IE loanwords of Vedic Sanskrit, 55 of them also appear in the earliest layers of the *Avesta*, composed around 1000 BCE. However, we don't find these loanwords in the Vedic Sanskrit-like language of the *Maryannu*, the Mitanni ruling elite. The absence of non-IE loanwords in the Maryannu language suggests they must have split from the Indo-Aryans sometime before 1500 BCE. The Indo-Aryans and Iranians likely adopted non-IE loanwords from a civilization with which they were in close contact. As the loanwords are closely related to cities, irrigation, and farming, many linguists believe they must have originated from the Oxus Civilization. This "ghost" language, which entered Vedic and early Avestan, was most likely the language of the BMAC people.

Unfortunately, due to a lack of written records and surviving inscriptions, we are not sure whether the people of the Oxus were literate. We have found only one seal, suggesting that they possessed a writing system similar to those in the Indus Valley, Mesopotamia, Egypt, and Elam. However, the evidence is insufficient to arrive at a definitive conclusion.

The inhabitants of Oxus were not isolated but were part of a vast, interconnected Bronze Age trade network. Much like the later civilizations of the Silk Road, BMAC was a melting pot of cultural influences from the Eurasian Steppes, Mesopotamian and Elamite cities, and the Indus Valley. The unprecedented intermingling of Central Asian cultures has led many archaeologists to suggest that the BMAC was an "interaction sphere" for different civilizations. Let us examine its chief trading partners and how they influenced the Oxus Civilization.

ECONOMY, ART, AND CULTURE

The two-humped Bactrian camel, late third to early second millennium BCE.

The Oxus people, like their contemporaries, had mastered the art of farming and irrigation. Wheat and barley served as the main crops, while they supplemented their diet with other foods. Grapes first appeared in Central Asia during the Bronze Age and may have been used to produce wine. Sheep and goats were the primary domesticated animals, providing wool, meat, and milk. The Oxus and its tributaries were a source of fish, and the nearby regions were ideal for hunting game, including ibex, gazelle, wild boar, and deer. The people of BMAC domesticated the two-humped Bactrian camel and used it for transportation and as a draft animal. We also have evidence of donkey bones, indicating that they complemented the camel as a beast of burden.

Archaeologists have discovered a model of a camel-drawn cart at Altyn Depe, dated to approximately 2200 BCE. They also found two-wheeled carts dating back to 3000 BCE at the site. These are the earliest pieces of evidence of wheeled transportation in Central Asia. The oxen-drawn carriages transported semi-precious stones, ceramics, and jewelry for trade. Horses were not native to the region and must have been introduced by the people of the Steppes through trade.

BMAC traded with Elam and Jiroft in Iran, the Indus Valley, China, and Mesopotamia. Being at the center of a vast exchange network made the residents of the Central Asian cities wealthy. Artifacts from the Oxus Civilization began to appear in the Indus Valley in the 1940s, long before anyone knew that a Bronze Age civilization had existed in Central Asia. At Altyn Depe, Gonur, Dzharkutan, and Dashly, several artifacts from the Indus Valley were unearthed, such as ivory items, etched carnelian beads, seated stone sculptures, and a glazed faience figurine of a monkey. The strong correlation between the two cultures is why archaeologist Henri-Paul Francfort used the term "Oxus Civilization," based on the "Indus Civilization." Though the Indus and Oxus Civilizations were interlinked, the Central Asian cities also had strong influences from Iran, particularly those of Jiroft and Elam. The Jiroft Civilization flourished in southeastern Iran between 2500 BCE and 2200 BCE. It was known for its advanced art, architecture, and artifacts, including intricate stone vessels and seals. It is a relatively newly discovered civilization, with the first artifacts emerging in 2001. Elam, centered in present-day southwestern Iran, thrived from around 2700 BCE to 539 BCE. It was a significant power in the ancient Near East, known for its unique language, monumental architecture, and often violent interactions with Mesopotamian civilizations like Sumer, Assyria, and Babylon.

The eagle-headed creature on an axe blade from Oxus, third to second millennium BCE.

The metal ceremonial axes with eagle-headed creatures found at BMAC bear a close resemblance to Elamite–Jiroft style artifacts, where eagle and snake iconography were popular. Oxus artisans may have adopted the design from Elam. In BMAC, we see the eagle-snake motif in axe heads and medallions. The discovery of several BMAC artifacts, such as a silver cup in Fars province near Persepolis in Iran, further supports the close connection between the civilizations of Iran and Central Asia during the Bronze Age. Excavations at the cities of Oxus revealed Iranian beads, stone vessels, and female figurines.

The Oxus residents were skilled metalworkers. They used tin, gold, and silver to produce intricately designed jewelry and objects adorned with unique geometric patterns and mythical figures. Notably, analyses of bronze artifacts from Dilmun[3] revealed that the tin used to make them originated from Central Asia, highlighting BMAC's advanced metallurgy and its key role in long-distance trade networks.

Bactrian Princess, a fertility deity worshiped in the Oxus.

The most recognizable figure from the Oxus is the "Bactrian Princess." She represented a fertility goddess popular in Bronze Age cultures.

The Oxus artisans made the idol from limestone, chlorite, and clay. She is seated, wearing a large dress and a headpiece that blends into her head. Archaeologists found statues of the

3 Dilmun is a trading center in present-day Bahrain that flourished between the later fourth millennium BCE and 538 BCE.

Bactrian Princess at various sites along the Oxus. The widespread availability of the figurine led scholars to believe she held special significance, and she was possibly connected to fertility and farming rituals.

Worshipping female deities was prevalent in the Oxus region. Unlike the disputed use of female figurines in the previous civilizations we discussed earlier in the book, the Bactrian Princess was found in the graves of Gonur and other cities, signifying a close relationship with life and death.

People in the area also had many bullhead figurines, which shows that they respected cattle, similar to the Mesopotamians and people of the Indus Valley, as bulls were vital for Bronze Age agrarian societies.

Monstrous male figure from the Oxus Civilization, dated third millennium BCE.

A unique statue made by the Oxus people is a humanoid figure with wide skirts, serpentine scales on its body, and a scarred face. The object was made with chlorite, calcite, gold, and iron; its height is 10.1 cm. Archaeologists have discovered this fascinating idol in the Steppes, the Persian Gulf, and the Indus Valley. While it is difficult to determine what the figure represents, finding the idol in distant places suggests that the Oxus people had a significant influence on their trading partners. The people of Oxus were talented and adventurous as they risked their lives to establish a global trade network.

But how did they live?

THE LIFESTYLE OF A LOST CIVILIZATION

Gold chalice with birds on the rim, Oxus third to second millennium BCE.

How do we determine the lifestyles of people who left no written records behind, save for one trading seal? It is a challenging task. However, we can get insights from cities and artifacts.

BMAC cities were well-planned, rectangular, and fortified, featuring an external, thick, plastered wall doubled by an inner, thin, plastered wall, separated by a corridor. These fortress cities initially featured rectangular or square towers, but later stages saw the development of round towers. Smaller settlements also exhibit this fortress-style architecture, a design that distinguishes them from their contemporary settlements in the Kopet Dag region. Although scholars debate the purpose of fortifications, their likely role was to deter enemies from attacking.

Sarianidi suggested that Gonur was the capital of BMAC. At its center was a gigantic palace measuring 150 m by 140 m, which served as the administrative headquarters. A massive temple complex of 140 m by 100 m was present. Like the other cities, Gonur was heavily fortified. The forts housed residential buildings, temples, and workshops. The city plan demonstrates that Oxus metropolises were equivalent to sophisticated Mesopotamian cities such as Ur, Uruk, and Eridu. Outside the city, there were mud-brick huts. Farmers most likely resided outside the city walls while the ruling class lived inside. The abundance of gold, bronze, and silver items shows that the Oxus elite lived in luxury, similar to their Middle Eastern counterparts.

Numerous tombs attest to the interment of human remains. In Gonur, archaeologists discovered a complete horse skeleton alongside bronze-rimmed wagons, dated to approximately 2200 BCE. The grave most likely belonged to a member of the city's elite, possibly a high-ranking noble. We encountered horse burials in the previous chapter on the Sintashta culture. However, the graves in Oxus were more than 100 to 150 years older than those in the Sintashta culture. In 2005, Sarianidi also unearthed parts of a stallion and interpreted horse sacrifice as a religious ritual of the Oxus people. The elaborate horse burials at BMAC challenge the popular notion that IE people were the only ones who practiced ritual horse sacrifices. The custom was widespread in Central Asia and not limited to IE societies.

We don't know what was the political organization at Oxus. However, some theories have emerged. During the regionalization era, multiple fortified villages were distributed across a vast region, indicating that an influential tribe leader owned each. During the integration era, Gonur experienced considerable growth, suggesting that power was centralized and a proto-state was emerging. For unclear reasons, the inhabitants abandoned Gonur and the minor settlements by 1900 BCE, and no other metropolis reached Gonur's size. The "localization era" between 1700 BCE and 1500 BCE, typically associated with the "collapse" of the Oxus Civilization, was a continuation of the abandonment of cities that began a few centuries earlier.

Academics interpret the religious beliefs of the Oxus people through the artifacts recovered, which are frequently subject to the personal opinions of the scholar investigating them. In Gonur, Sarianidi discovered a fire temple with four rectangular ovens. The layout was unusual for Mesopotamian fire temples, leading him to conclude that it was a kind of ancient Zoroastrian religious site. However, the temple predated the arrival of the Indo-Iranians in the region, suggesting that the worship of fire was an independent practice in BMAC. Many researchers believe that the religious rituals of the Oxus people may have influenced the development of Indo-Iranian religions.

A beaker constructed of electrum, a gold and silver alloy, dated to the late third to early second millennium BCE, may provide insight into how the people of the Oxus shaped the religious beliefs of the Indo-Iranians. The object, resting on a narrow base, expands gracefully upward into a wide, flared mouth. Eight birds of prey are intricately crafted and delicately carved with patterned lines around the rim. Each bird, positioned at equal intervals, spreads its wings wide and raises its head slightly above the vessel's edge.

What does this vessel represent?

The design suggests that this beaker was not for casual drinking. The placement of the birds, attached with round-headed rivets, would make sipping awkward. Instead, this masterpiece was most likely utilized for ceremonial purposes, such as libations to honor gods, spirits, or ancestors.

Many historians believe that this beaker was used in the *soma* drinking ritual described in the Rigveda, and the Indo-Aryans may have adopted this tradition during their migration through Central Asia.

Soma is a drink believed to have hallucinogenic qualities. It originated from the soma plant. The beverage was an essential part of Vedic rites and is known as *haoma* in the *Avesta*.

The legacy of the Oxus Civilization remains a subject of ongoing study, despite its numerous significant accomplishments and connections to other civilizations across Eurasia. As we move from its cultural highlights to its decline, the question arises: what circumstances led to the collapse of such an accomplished society?

END OF AN ERA

Unlike the more well-researched Bronze Age collapse in the Mediterranean region, the causes of the Oxus people's demise remain a mystery. There are no indications of large-scale warfare or conquest.

Some scholars have proposed that the people of Oxus abandoned their cities due to the migration of Indo-Iranian people from the Steppes, but how valid is this claim?

The romanticized belief that horse-and-chariot-driving warriors destroyed the cities of the Oxus persisted in the early

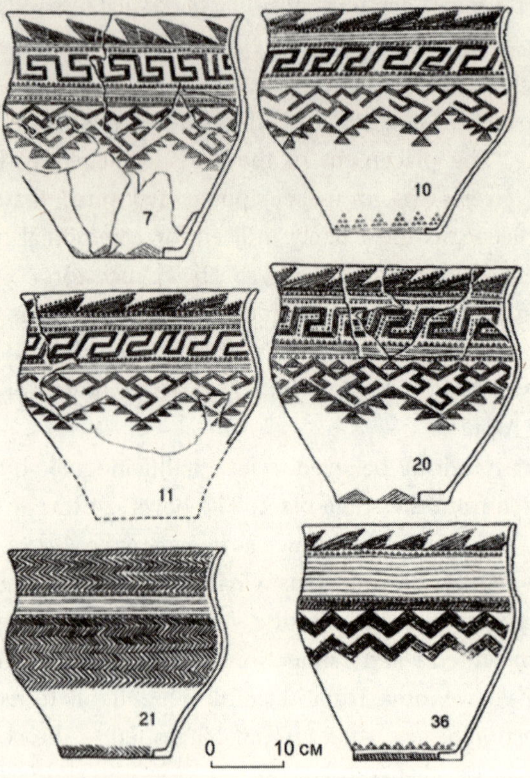

Andronovo-style incised pottery began showing up in the Oxus well before its decline.

days of research on the civilization. However, more recent finds show that Andronovo-style burial mounds, or *kurgans*, were present in the peripheral zone of the civilization during the regionalization period. Andronovo-style incised pottery began appearing well before the collapse of the BMAC, but its frequency increased after the abandonment of the Oxus cities.

We do not know for certain if the interactions between the Steppe pastoralists and the urban dwellers of Oxus were violent. Perhaps some of them were, but it wasn't black and white. They were also trading partners, and Indo-Iranian pastoralists may have mixed with the local people, giving rise to new cultures.

Many of the original inhabitants of the Oxus likely migrated south to India and Iran, where they intermingled with the local populations. Sadly, the cities collapsed after being abandoned, and the thriving urban culture vanished, leaving behind no legacy.

During the Achaemenid Persian invasion of the region (c. 540 BCE), Bactria was known for its militaristic and warlike inhabitants. Impressed with their fighting skills, the Persians recruited them into their army, and Bactria became a satrapy of the Achaemenid Empire, as mentioned in the Behistun inscription (c. 520 BCE). Later, Alexander faced much resistance but built a firm base in Bactria. He founded Alexandria Eschate,[4] which means "Alexandria beyond," the northernmost city of his empire. Central Asian civilizations continued to grow during Greek rule. The Han Empire of China would later conquer the Greek city, marking the beginning of the Silk Road. However, it would not be until the 1970s that we would learn about a Bronze Age civilization, which was a part of a global trade network that thrived in Central Asia. Their succeeding civilizations made no mention of BMAC, and unfortunately, thanks to grave robbers, a wealth of artifacts is lost forever. The inhospitable environment of the Karakum Desert poses significant challenges for excavations. The discovery of new sites in Eastern Iran, Afghanistan, and Tajikistan has changed our perception of BMAC. It was not restricted to the banks of the Oxus River and was widespread, with significant regional differences between the sites. As archaeologists continue to dig in Central Asia, we must realign our understanding of "Old World" civilizations to appreciate that a fifth river valley civilization flourished and was interconnected through a vast trade network long before the Silk Road.

---

4 For more details about Alexandria Eschate, refer to Chapter 16 on the Kushan Empire.

[illegible]

[illegible]

[illegible]

Section 3

Lost Cities

9

Tell Brak: The World's First City

FEBRUARY 28, 1934, *MURDER IN THE CALAIS COACH* HIT bookstores in Britain and the United States. You probably know it by its more well-known title, *Murder on the Orient Express*. The book by Agatha Christie is a classic among detective mysteries.

A few years later, from 1937 to 1938, archaeologist Max Mallowan led the excavation of a site in northern Syria. What he initially thought was a prehistoric settlement turned out to be something far more significant—one of the world's earliest cities, Tell Brak.

But why are we discussing Agatha Christie's works? What's the connection between her and possibly the world's first city? The unexpected relationship between two seemingly unrelated topics is fascinating.

Mallowan was famous not just for his archaeological skills, but also as Agatha Christie's spouse. Christie was a keen history enthusiast and was present at the initial excavation of Tell Brak alongside Mallowan. In her autobiographical memoir *Come, Tell Me How You Live*, she expertly combines her storytelling skills with her archaeological experiences. Her travels with Mallowan to various sites in the Middle East also inspired the novels *Murder in Mesopotamia* and *Appointment with Death*.

Christie and Mallowan had no idea they had discovered what may have been the world's first city.

Max Mallowan and Agatha Christie, 1950. Mallowan is credited with the first excavations of Tell Brak.

Tell Brak was the first of many townships to emerge in Mesopotamia, resulting in a cradle of civilization flourishing in what is known as the "Fertile Crescent." As agriculture spread, farming communes began transforming into urban centers. Mesopotamia became one of the world's leading civilizations, with its city-states driving human progress. Let us start our journey to the world of lost cities in Syria, where the ruins of Tell Brak lie in the Khabur Plain. Before we discuss Tell Brak, we must address a fundamental question: how do archaeologists decide if a site is a city? The question is key to understanding how we define a city and why Tell Brak might be the world's first city.

HOW TO TELL IF THE RUINS ARE AN ANCIENT CITY

Australian archaeologist V. Gordon Childe was one of the pioneers who devised a framework to identify a city.

We discussed Göbekli Tepe, Çatalhöyük, and Mehrgarh in the previous chapters. You may wonder why they weren't considered cities.

Imagine you are an archaeologist standing amidst the remnants of a bygone era. The task is daunting: how do you distinguish a city from a prehistoric farming settlement based on the ruins? This challenge has often led to misinterpretations, with archaeological finds mistakenly attributed to a city's antiquity. Many popular discussions suggest Jericho as the world's oldest city. While many present-day towns, such as Jericho, were occupied during the PPNA period, they underwent urbanization much later. Hence, we must clearly define and differentiate a metropolis from a Neolithic settlement.

In the 1950s, Australian archaeologist V. Gordon Childe made a list of rules for defining a city. They are:

1. In terms of size, the first cities must have been more extensive and densely populated than any previous settlements.
2. In composition and function, the urban population already differed from that of any village... full-time specialist craftsmen, transport workers, merchants, officials, and priests.
3. Each primary producer paid over the tiny surplus he could wring from the soil with his still very limited technical equipment as tithe or tax to an imaginary deity or a divine king who thus concentrated the surplus.
4. Truly monumental public buildings not only distinguish each known city from any village but also symbolize the concentration of the social surplus.
5. But naturally priests, civil and military leaders, and officials absorbed a major share of the concentrated surplus and thus formed a "ruling class."
6. Writing.

7. The elaboration of exact and predictive sciences—arithmetic, geometry, and astronomy.
8. Conceptualized and sophisticated styles.
9. Regular "foreign" trade over quite long distances.
10. A state organization based now on residence rather than kinship.

Childe's rules for defining a city are robust, but the knowledge of archaeology and the emergence of urban centers in different parts of the world have evolved since. I have seen many criticisms of Childe's definition of cities and civilizations as "Eurocentric." They probably are. But we must realize he lived between 1892 and 1957, when many of the civilizations and cultures discussed in this book were unknown. Hence, we should give Childe the benefit of the doubt, as he was working with the information available at the time. Childe did his best to define a city, but there were a few factors that he overlooked. Let us take, for example, criterion number 8. The presence of conceptualized complex art genres is not limited to cities. In Neolithic settlements, there is evidence of high-quality art. Even Paleolithic art is advanced, as seen in the Lascaux Cave in France or the Bhimbetka Caves in India. Recent dating of the 66,000-year-old cave paintings at the Maltravieso Cave in Spain suggests that the earliest artists were Neanderthals.

Art predates urbanization.

Point 7, the existence of sciences, maths, and astronomy, is another problematic requirement. Astronomy and sciences developed before the urban revolution. They don't require established cities to thrive. We encountered complex metallurgical processes in the Balkans in the chapter on the Vinča culture. The Indigenous people of North America living near the Great Lakes knew smelting and cold-working copper long before they began farming. Human progress is seldom linear.

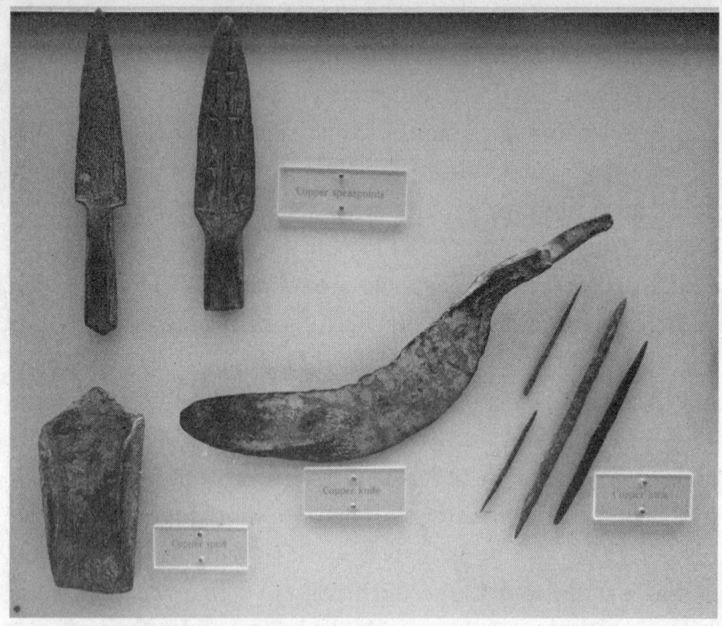

Copper tools and weapons dated 3000 BCE to 1000 BCE, found in Wisconsin, USA.

What about the monuments and public structures mentioned in point 4?

Göbekli Tepe has altered the perception that colossal structures are exclusive to cities. In Chapter 13, we'll explore how the Indigenous people of North America began building impressive earthwork mounds before farming. Several other megalithic structures, such as Ġgantija in Malta (c. 3600 BCE–2500 BCE), Stonehenge in Britain, and the Hopewell Mounds in the United States, predate cities.

Is a writing system required for a city, as Childe says in point 6? Cities have a long history of sophisticated record-keeping. However, there is little evidence of a writing system in the cities of the Oxus Civilization (BMAC), which were as culturally advanced as those of Mesopotamia or the Indus Valley. Archaeologists have found one seal, which suggests that the BMAC people may have been aware of writing.[1] However, there is no evidence of comprehensive record-keeping similar to that found in Egypt, Canaan, or Mesopotamia. In Varanasi, full-fledged urbanization is visible before the proof of writing. We should remember that many previous civilizations had oral traditions of recording their history. It is also possible that inflammable materials, such as grass and paper, were commonly used for writing and did not survive the test of time. I cannot imagine that cities of the Oxus Civilization and Varanasi would not have had a record-keeping system, given the evidence of their involvement in long-distance trade.

Hence, Childe's definition of a city has some limitations. But they shouldn't be dismissed entirely, as the list still serves as a handy guide for archaeologists. Except for points 7, 8, and, to a lesser extent, point 4, Childe's definition of a city is still valid.

Modern definitions of a city focus on the size of the settlement, large population, monumental architecture, and socio-economic complexity, such as specialized craft, trade goods, materials, distinct variable-sized houses, and burials. In his book, *The City Shaped* (1991), architectural historian Spiro Kostof proposed the concept of "energized crowding," a primary characteristic of ancient cities. Social activities, independent of ruling authorities, occur in densely populated settlements. These energized crowds drive a city's growth.

Our understanding of ancient cities evolves with the discovery of new evidence. We have broadly defined a city using Childe's and Kostof's guidelines. Based on the criteria we discussed and radiocarbon dating, archaeologists propose that Tell Brak is the world's earliest completely urbanized center. We'll begin our journey to the world of lost cities on the banks of the Khabur River, the Euphrates's largest tributary.

---

1 Refer to Chapter 8.

THE RISE OF TELL BRAK

A general view of Tell Brak.

Tell Brak was one of the earliest sites photographed aerially. Antoine Poidebard[2] spotted it in 1928 while looking for Roman irrigation systems in the region.

Although Mallowan began excavations at Tell Brak in the 1930s, a modern study of the site was not conducted until 1976. David Oates and Joan Oates from the University of Cambridge led the study, making significant contributions to our understanding of the world's earliest known city.

Initially, the archaeological team aimed to construct a chronological framework for examining the site's occupational history in the third millennium BCE and wanted to investigate the Akkadian influence[3] at Tell Brak.

2 Antoine Poidebard was a pioneer in aerial photography for archaeological surveys.

3 The Akkadian Empire conquered Tell Brak around 2300 BCE.

The antiquity of Tell Brak was far from determined in the 1970s. It wasn't until 2006, when Augusta McMahon took over the fieldwork, that the growth and sustainability of the early city, dating back to the end of the fifth millennium BCE and the beginning of the fourth millennium BCE, were thoroughly researched.

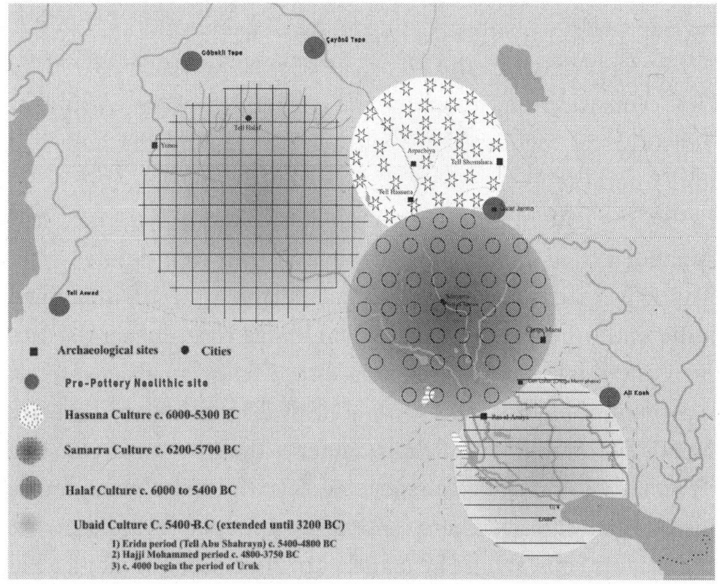

Location of Halaf (checkered) and Ubaid (striped) Cultures.

Tell Brak began as a tiny village in the seventh millennium BCE. The community belonged to the proto-Halaf culture, named after the site of Tell Halaf in the Khabur River Valley. Halaf culture was a Pottery Neolithic culture that thrived between 6100 BCE and 5100 BCE.[4] Artifacts from the Halaf period were discovered at Tell Brak.

4 Pottery Neolithic period began in the Near East at the end of the PPNB in late seventh millennium BCE.

Towards the end of the Halaf era, a transition to pottery typical of the Ubaid culture is observed at Tell Brak. The Ubaid culture was a Neolithic culture based in southern Iraq, spread across a vast region between approximately 5500 BCE and 3700 BCE.

The Ubaid period laid the foundation for the rise of later Mesopotamian city-states, such as Uruk, Eridu, Kish, Nippur, Ur, and Shuruppak. Excavations and surface surveys at Tell Brak revealed a large platform dating to the Ubaid period.

Though much of the city's early levels were destroyed by later construction, monumental structures were visible at Tell Brak throughout the Ubaid period (around the mid-fifth millennium BCE).

By the end of the fifth millennium BCE, Tell Brak had expanded to a 55-acre city surrounded by a well-defined wall. There is evidence of continuous inhabitation till the third millennium BCE. Several public buildings rose during the late fifth and early fourth millennia BCE. Mallowan discovered a massive temple complex with solid walls, dating to the early fourth millennium BCE. Scholars refer to the structure as the Eye Temple. Several alabaster socketed "eye figurines" were found inside the building. There is some uncertainty regarding what these idols represent. The statues are considered to depict the divinity Belet Nagar, which means "Lady of Nagar." Tell Brak was later renamed Nagar.

Mesopotamian sources show that Belet Nagar worship and pilgrimages to Tell Brak were popular. Some experts believe the eye figures are statues of Inanna, a prominent goddess in southern Mesopotamia. One text refers to Belet Nagar as Inanna Ḫabūrītum, with Ḫabūrītum being the goddess of the Khabur River, a perennial tributary of the Euphrates. This theory could be an example of religious syncretism at the time, and recent scholarship does not support the claim that Belet Nagar is identical to Inanna. The Belet Nagar cult elevated Tell Brak to a

Figurines from the Eye Temple, Tell Brak.

significant religious center in the ancient Near East, as evidenced by records of pilgrimages to the city.

By 3800 BCE to 3600 BCE, Tell Brak had expanded to a city of 130 hectares. Long-distance trade with Southern Mesopotamia may have begun as early as 3600 BCE. Uruk established a trading colony in Tell Brak during this period. We don't know what the original inhabitants called the city that archaeologists refer to as Tell Brak. But the city entered historical records around the third millennium BCE as Nagar.

THE DAWN OF A NEW ERA: NAGAR, AKKADIAN, AND MITANNI PERIODS

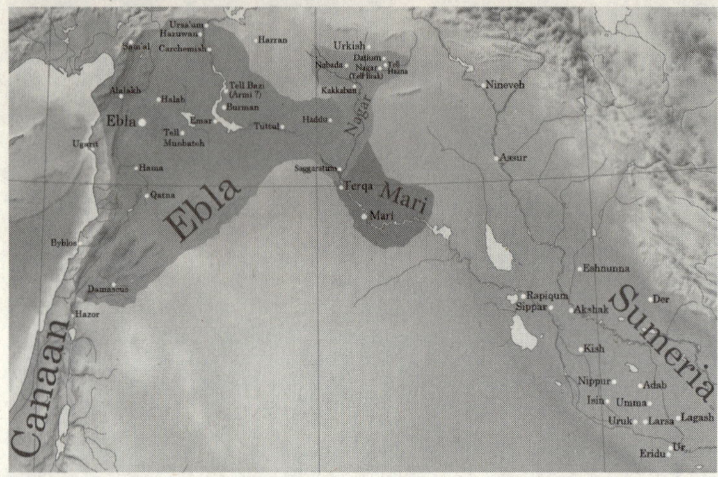

The Kingdoms of Ebla, Nagar, and Mari in the ancient Near East c. 2340 BCE.

Around 3000 BCE, the Urukeans abandoned their colony at Tell Brak. Despite ongoing trade with southern Mesopotamia, the size of the central city declined, and it was restricted to a small settlement with a temple. But then there was a significant revival. Around 2600 BCE, Tell Brak became a key commercial hub and began flourishing anew. The city was now known as Nagar.

We have evidence of a prominent administrative center from this era, the Brak Oval, with a curved exterior wall.

Tell Brak is referenced in the Ebla tablets, one of the ancient world's most extensive collections of texts. The tablets were discovered in the ancient Syrian city of Ebla,[5] with the collection comprising 1,800 whole clay tablets and 4,700 fragmentary ones. They date between 2500 BCE and 2250 BCE. Most of the tablets were in Sumerian and the city's local language, which, due to

5 Ebla was a key trading partner of Tell Brak.

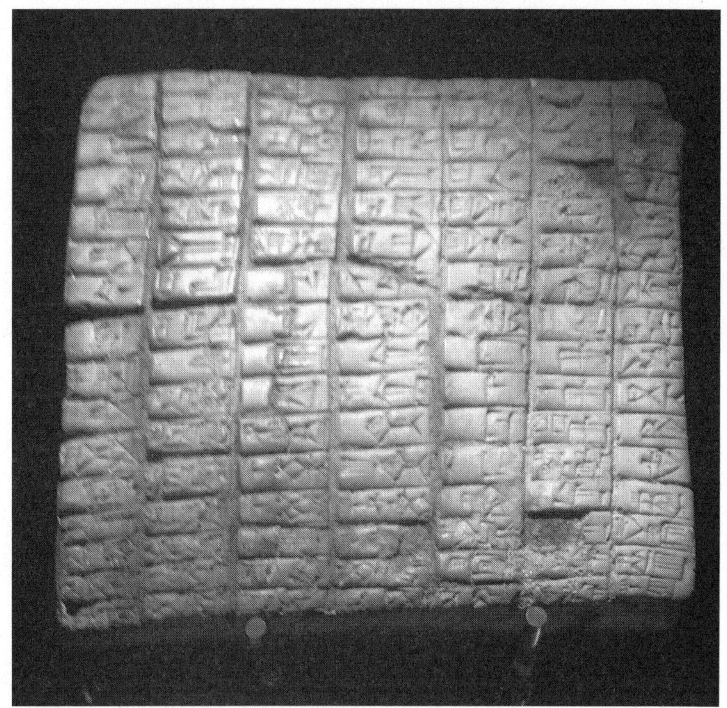

A tablet from Ebla's archive.

the lack of a better term, is referred to as "Ebalite." One of the tablets mentions the ruler of Tell Brak as "En," but it does not give us any further details about the monarch. Another tablet discusses Mari-II, the king of Nagar. He is the only known ruler of Tell Brak.

Ebla and Nagar had strong diplomatic and trade contacts, but their relationship wasn't always rosy. According to the Ebla texts, the two kingdoms engaged in a conflict with each other. One tablet recounts the victory of the Ebalite ruler Irkab-Damu over Nagar.

The famous "Mask of Sargon" is a bronze cast depicting Sargon. More recent scholarship suggests the representation may be based on Naram-Sin, his grandson, rather than Sargon.

The Akkadians destroyed Nagar around 2300 BCE with the rise of Sargon of Akkad and the Akkadian Empire centered in the city of Akkad.[6]

The Akkadian Empire was the world's first empire, encompassing modern-day Iraq and Northern Syria while also wielding power in Anatolia, the Levant, and the Persian Gulf. Sargon, the dynasty's founder and first ruler, served as the cupbearer to Ur-Zababa, ruler of the Kingdom of Kish. After deposing him, Sargon was crowned king in 2334 BCE. Soon after, he began conquering Sumerian city-states, before moving on to the northern Syrian kingdoms of Nagar and Ebla. Sargon's dynasty lasted until 2154 BCE, leaving an enduring legacy. The Sargonid influence impacted many future regional powers, including the Assyrians, whom we will cover in depth in Chapter 14.

According to Akkadian records, Tell Brak was rebuilt following its destruction. Although the Sargonid conquest diminished the city's political prominence, it remained the provincial administrative seat of the Akkadians. Two massive

6 Akkad is romanized from Akkade or Agade. Akkad's exact location is unknown, but it is assumed to be in central Iraq.

buildings date back to the Akkadian period. One was a temple built to worship the Akkadian deity Šumugan, associated with animals.

The ruins of the Palace of Naram-Sin at Tell Brak.

Perhaps the most prominent remnant of Akkadian rule in Tell Brak is the Palace of Naram-Sin,[7] which was built over a part of the Eye Temple. Before building Naram-Sin's Palace, the Akkadians temporarily abandoned Tell Brak. The monumental buildings were deliberately burned down and filled in with dirt. The city's prominent buildings were intentionally set on fire and then filled with dirt. According to Joan Oates, the residents may have burnt these enormous structures in response to a climate shift that led to desertification in the region. As a result, Tell Brak became uninhabitable between the time of the first Akkadian occupation and the construction of Naram-Sin's Palace.

7 Naram-Sin was the grandson of Sargon.

After the demise of the Akkadian Empire, Nagar experienced a power vacuum. The Hurrians, a people from northern Syria based in Urkesh, took over Tell Brak.

A tablet dedicated to the Hurrian deity Nergal by Atalshen, king of Urkesh and Nawar, c. 2000 BCE.

Akkadian documents suggest the Hurrians were initially allied with them, but by the time of Naram-Sin's reign, they had been established as a power in the Khabur River Valley. After occupying Nagar, the city was renamed Nawar, and the Hurrian king was referred to as "the king of Urkesh and Nawar." Towards the end of the Hurrian–Akkadian era, Tell Brak was destroyed around 2193 BCE, possibly by the Gutians, who were enemies of the Akkadians and operated from the Zagros Mountains. The Hurrians later rebuilt the city, and archaeological evidence suggests they also reconstructed Naram-Sin's palace.

During the Middle Bronze Age (1820 BCE–1550 BCE), Tell Brak was under the rule of Mari, as Yahdun-Lim, the ruler of Mari, conquered Nagar. But the Hurrian rule returned to the city.

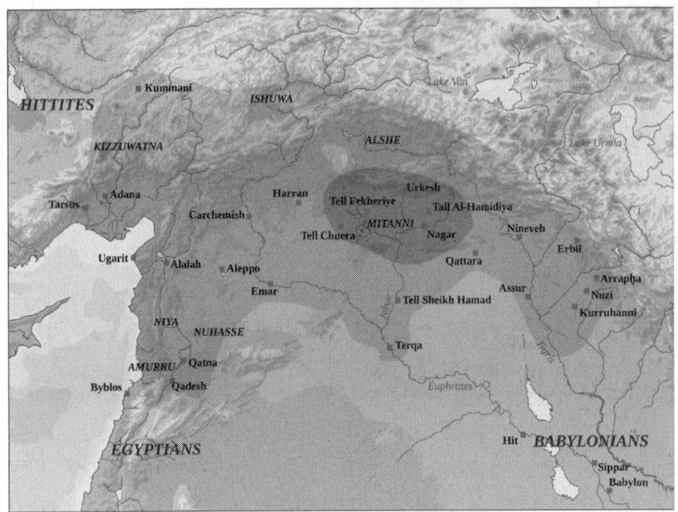

The Mitanni at the peak of their powers in 1490 BCE under Barattarna.

During the Late Bronze Age, around 1500 BCE, the city was a part of the Mitanni Kingdom, the most well-known Hurrian dynasty. We have encountered the Mitanni, along with their elite, the *Maryannu*, who spoke a language similar to Vedic Sanskrit, in Chapter 7. The Mitanni ruled from Washukanni. They defeated the Assyrians and formed a marital alliance with Egypt's mighty pharaohs. Some historians speculate that the Egyptian queen Nefertiti,[8] who was Pharaoh Akhenaten's wife and Tutankhamun's mother, might have been a Mitanni princess.

8 Nefertiti's name translates to "the beautiful woman has come," indicating a foreign origin, which has led to the hypothesis that she was a Mitanni princess. She also didn't have the usual titles of "King's Daughter" or "King's Sister," which indicates that she was not a relative of the pharaoh. Typically, pharaohs married their sisters or cousins, to preserve their bloodline.

Mitanni palace at Tell Brak.

The Mitanni built a two-storey palace in Tell Brak's northern section. Two Mitanni documents belonging to Kings Artashumara and Tushratta were found in the city. In the fourteenth century BCE, the Assyrians deposed the Mitanni from Tell Brak. Political turbulence marred Nagar's magnificence, as the Assyrians twice sacked the city.

The once glorious city would become a shadow of its former self. Before we discuss what happened in the town before its eventual abandonment, let's learn a bit about its unique set-up and a special creature bred by the city, which would be in great demand across the region.

A UNIQUE MESOPOTAMIAN CITY

Excavations at Tell Brak revealed that the city was densely populated in the center but less so on the periphery. The

Area TW of Tell Brak.

outskirts of the town had areas of high but uneven population density, mainly due to people working in storage and waste disposal activities rather than permanent residents living there. Brak's changing population contrasts with that of typical Mesopotamian cities, which have a consistent population density and well-defined city boundaries. Low-density urbanism is typical in Mesoamerican cities and Cahokia in present-day United States. Tell Brak fell halfway in the middle, with portions of the town resembling Mesoamerican cities, characterized by lower population density, and others densely packed, like a typical Mesopotamian metropolis. Thus, Tell Brak is classified as a city with variable-density urbanism.

Brak had two administrative centres. One was a massive structure with 2 m-thick walls in area TW (see image) at the city's northern edge. This power center monitored the city's industrial and manufacturing operations. Archaeologists discovered two cooking facilities in area TW: a large, dome-shaped oven, barbecue pits, grain storage rooms, and the remains of slaughtered animals. The finds reveal that this portion of the city was a vital administrative hub, thriving with economic activity and supporting a large population.

The second public institution was near the Eye Temple, and it galvanized citizens' religious and social demands. McMahon suggests that the two administrative units worked together to ensure the city's smooth functioning.

During the Chalcolithic period, Brak served as a prominent obsidian trading center. Several obsidian, white marble, and faience chalices, as well as flint tools, were discovered on site. Tell Brak had a well-developed domestic manufacturing sector and also worked with imported commodities. Following the establishment of the Uruk colony, we see a shift towards the production of goods desired in southern Mesopotamia.

Before the Akkadian conquest, Tell Brak was well known for its acrobats. Brak was a common training ground for Ebalite performers. Aside from entertainers, Brak was the source of the *kunga*, a prestigious animal given as a gift throughout Mesopotamia.

In 2022, Eva-Maria Geigl, a geneticist at the Institut Jacques Monod in Paris, made a remarkable discovery while researching animal bones from a burial site in northern Syria. She had stumbled on what appeared to be equine bones. However, the bones bore little resemblance to existing equids.[9]

Geigl's team initially assumed that it belonged to an extinct species known as the Syrian wild ass. However, the bones were larger than those of the ordinary Syrian wild ass. The scientists examined the bones of 25 equids from a royal burial site at Umm el-Marra, near Aleppo. The animals were sacrificed and buried with their owners.

---

9 Equids are horse-like animals such as horses, mules, and donkeys.

The bones were from an ancient Mesopotamian equid that lived 4,500 years ago. The Sumerians called them kungas, a creature bred using a male Syrian wild ass with a domesticated female donkey. Geigl had uncovered the first known example of human-made animal hybrids in history.

Sumerian writings mention kunga-breeding, though the specifics of the technique are obscure. The kunga was a highly prized animal in ancient Mesopotamia before the arrival of the horse, possibly due to the challenges involved in breeding them. Taming the Syrian wild ass was challenging because of its speed.

The Sumerians used the kungas in battle and as gifts for the privileged. Ebla's king was famous for distributing kungas as gifts to other states. Nagar was the region's top kunga supplier.

Though archaeologists have not yet found kunga skeletons at Tell Brak, Ebla tablets indicate that Nagar monopolized kunga production. Officers in charge of Ebla's kunga herd traveled to Nagar to collect the creatures. Archaeologists discovered war wagons and carriages at Tell Brak, likely driven by kungas. The Standard of Ur, a Sumerian artifact, shows the deployment of these carts driven by kungas.

The war panel from the Standard of Ur depicting wagons pulled by *kungas*.

Kungas were not the only valuable objects recovered from Tell Brak. Excavations between 1993 and 2004 revealed a large cache of carnelian, a range of pottery, an alabaster statue of a bear, stone maceheads, lapis lazuli beads, gold, and silver.

Besides material wealth, Tell Brak was also a center for educational excellence. Among the Uruk materials from the third millennium BCE was a standard text for educating scribes, a part of the training material for scribes in Mesopotamia. The document tells us that writing was present in Tell Brak, and the site meets all the criteria listed by Childe for a city.

THE FALL OF TELL BRAK

Tell Brak fell into decline after the Assyrians destroyed it. Small settlements flourished in the town's lower area throughout the Assyrian period. A satellite township emerged in the town's northern area during the Hellenistic period (400 BCE to 30 BCE). But digs have not revealed any pottery from the Roman–Parthian or Byzantine–Sassanian periods.

Tell Brak was abandoned during the early years of the Abbasid Caliphate in the eighth century and never reoccupied. The city's last recorded inhabitants were the Abbasids, who created a canal to bring water to the settlement and connect it to the nearby Jaghjagh River.

Historians and archaeologists have long considered Uruk the world's oldest metropolis. However, the recent excavations at Tell Brak compel us to reassess our previous conclusions.

The beauty of archaeology is that it helps us rewrite history based on evidence. We should remember that much of Tell Brak remains unexcavated. What secrets lie beneath the layers? Was it even older than what we know?

Time will tell.

10

The City of the Hawk

I HAVE DEDICATED THIS BOOK TO HIGHLIGHTING THE LIVES of people who didn't leave written records but gave us hints about who they were through their material culture. However, our objects do not necessarily define us. If the world were to end tomorrow and all that remains of me were my porcelain teapots and gold-plated pen, archaeologists would have to use

Horus as a falcon, wearing the double crown of Egypt, c. 500 BCE.

their best judgment to determine what I was like based on those artifacts and the location where they found them. My material possessions don't tell you who I am, but if that is what remains, we must work with it.

Even in civilizations with thorough record-keeping systems, it is impossible to determine precisely when they originated. Who was the very first ruler? We typically follow a list of kings compiled centuries later, whose accuracy is questionable.

But what if people wrote the story of a civilization's origins as it happened? What if they left jigsaw pieces for us to fit together, revealing the picture?

In 1894, archaeologists James Quibell and Frederick Green uncovered a temple 100 km south of modern-day Luxor, Egypt. The remains were unimpressive from a distance, yet beneath them lay the narrative of one of the most astonishing civilizations in ancient history. The English scholars stumbled upon the City of the Hawk, also known as Hierakonpolis in Greek and Nekhen in Egyptian. The structure they discovered was the Temple of Horus, the city's tutelary deity and one of the most respected gods in ancient Egypt. Unlike the other cities covered in this book, Nekhen is unusual because it preserves the story of Egypt's origins for millennia, as documented in the world's first known historical record.

Egypt is unique compared to the civilizations of Asia and Europe. Within 2,500 years of the first farming settlements, the Egyptians built the Great Pyramid of Giza, the tallest human-made structure for the next 4,000 years. Compared to Mesopotamia, India, and China, the shift from hunter-gatherer to sophisticated civilization occurred rapidly.

Before we begin our journey down the Nile, let us review the river's geography. The lush river valley gave rise to several cities, many of which evolved into significant political entities. These city-states were divided into Upper and Lower Egypt. Upper

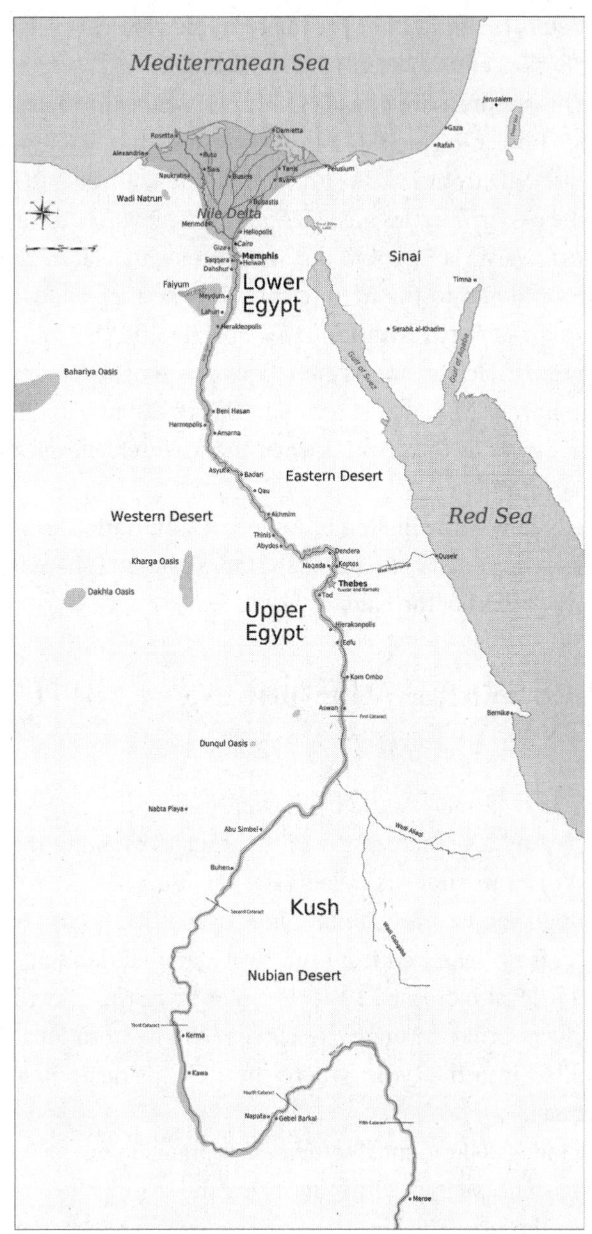

Map of Egypt showing Upper and Lower Egypt.

Egypt refers to the southern segment of the Nile Valley, whereas Lower Egypt refers to its northern section.

Why is southern Egypt called "Upper" while northern Egypt is called "Lower"? The Blue Nile, from Lake Tana, Ethiopia, and the White Nile from Lake Victoria in Uganda, nourish the River Nile. The two tributaries meet at Sudan's capital, Khartoum, and flow northward via Egypt to the Mediterranean Sea. As the Nile runs from Sudan to the Mediterranean Sea, ancient Egyptians associated the north with the river's origin and the south with its terminus. Hence, the region between the 30th parallel N and the border of Sudan is termed "Upper Egypt." In contrast, "Lower Egypt" is the area between the Mediterranean Sea and the same latitude.

The Nile was the lifeline of Egyptian Civilization. However, Egypt's extraordinary rise began in an oasis in the Sahara Desert, not on the banks of the Nile.

BEFORE NEKHEN: THE ORIGINS OF SETTLED LIFE IN EGYPT

Egypt's first farmers settled in a depression 100 km south of Cairo, fed by a branch of the Nile rather than along the river valley. This water body is called Lake Faiyum.

Though the Faiyum communities didn't live on the bank of the Nile, they benefited from the river's annual flooding, when the water level increased 12 to 14 times its normal flow. These rising rivers broke through the cliffs of the western Nile Valley and spilled into the oasis, where the rich silt made it suitable for farming.

Around 5000 BCE, small settlements sprang up on the banks of this oasis, with people cultivating crops and storing them in grain bins near the lake. The bins were circular woven reed baskets.

Arrowheads found at Faiyum dating to the fifth millennium BCE.

Near the grain storage, intact hearths were discovered, containing cooking pots with fish and animal bones, dated to around 4300 BCE. Archaeologists found 300 similar grain bins around Faiyum, which suggests villages surrounding the lake were sparsely populated, with only a few families.

In addition to grain cultivation, Faiyum farmers reared cattle, goats, and sheep, and supplemented their diet with catfish, turtles, crocodiles, and game such as gazelles and wild boars. Butchered hippopotamus bones indicated hunting and processing of the animals, a tradition that persisted in later Egyptian cultures and during the rule of the pharaohs.

Many of the crops grown by Faiyum farmers, such as wheat, barley, and emmer, as well as their livestock, were not indigenous to Egypt or Africa, indicating that migrants from the Levant must have introduced them. The designs of their grain bins and sickles were also imported. The Levantine influence at Faiyum suggests that Egypt had an established commercial network with the rest of the Near East by the middle of the fifth millennium BCE, long before the rise of the pharaohs.

The seed of a new civilization sown at Faiyum began to germinate, and cultures emerged across Egypt along the Nile River Valley. We won't delve into all the cultures to grasp Nekhen's story, but let us sail down the Nile to learn more about the Naqada culture, from which the cities of Upper Egypt emerged. But first, a quick pit stop at el-Badari in Central Egypt.

Badarian pottery with a distinctive gloss and black top.

The Nile River Valley is flanked by steep, rocky limestone cliffs, especially in Upper Egypt. In this cliff-lined valley, the Badarian culture was the first farming community that arose around 4400 BCE. It began a few centuries after Faiyum, but there was an overlap between the two cultures. The first excavations, led by English archaeologist Guy Brunton, in 1923, revealed shining, nut-brown pots with a ripple effect over their surfaces. Since the early days of Brunton's digs, this glossy pottery, known as Badarian pottery, was found in a vast area along the Nile Valley and the Sahara Desert. Unlike contemporary prehistoric Egyptian societies at Faiyum and Merimde in Lower Egypt, Badarian pottery was distinct and had advanced craftsmanship. The Badarians were renowned for their lifelike sculptures, which laid the foundation for later Egyptian artwork.

A hippopotamus-shaped vase from the Badarian culture, fifth millennium BCE.

Badarian culture was peaceful, with minimal traces of violence. Their farming practices were comparable to those of the Faiyum people, with cereals supplemented by livestock, fish, and game. When the area around el-Badari flooded in the autumn, the Badarians relocated to the dry plains above the valley. The Badarians enjoyed traveling more than the Faiyum and Merimde

Mortuary figurine of a woman from the Badarian culture
c. 4500 BCE–3600 BCE.

settlers. During the flooding of the Nile, some people journeyed up the valley, while others went south, starting temporary settlements. One such site, Mahgar Dendera, located about 240 km south of el-Badari, was only occupied during autumn when the Nile swelled. Egyptologists believe the continual travel up and down the Nile River Valley explains why the Badarian villages were sparsely populated.

The Badarians were approximately 5 feet tall, with a few slightly taller. The men were clean-shaven, strong, and wore long hair. The women's fringes and plaits were fastened using bone combs. Their hair ranged from light to dark brown and could be straight or curly. According to Egyptologist John Romer, the Badarians shared the same ethnic mix as the ancient Egyptians who would follow them.

The descendants of the Badarians played a significant role in shaping Egypt's cultural heritage, but the foundation for the civilization that most of us recognize today is found farther up the Nile River Valley at Naqada.

NAQADA CULTURE: THE ROOTS OF NEKHEN

The site of Naqada is about 225 km south of el-Badari. Around 4000 BCE, the first seeds of civilization were planted in this region, which later became the foundation for Egypt's Old Kingdom (2700 BCE to 2200 BCE). We can classify the Naqada culture into three chronological eras based on pottery sequences. Naqada I, or the early phase of the culture, lasted from 4000 BCE to 3500 BCE. Naqada II, or the middle phase, lasted between 3600 BCE and 3300 BCE. Naqada III, the immediate precursor to Egyptian Civilization, lasted between 3300 BCE and 3000 BCE.

Figure of a woman from the Naqada culture c. 3500 BCE to 3400 BCE.

The early Naqadan settlements bore a resemblance to those of the Badarians. They lived in wattle and daub[1] dwellings, traveled with their livestock, and collected crops.

Naqadan pottery was notable for its vibrant iconography, which contrasted sharply with the Badarian style. From the beginning of the culture, pots featured ornate images in their bowls and vases, characterized by thin white lines, which became Egypt's earliest form of graphic art. The imagery established the groundwork for the illustration tradition and the hieroglyphic script, which later became associated with Pharaonic Egypt. The paintings on Naqadan pots portrayed animals, nature, and human activities from everyday life, including hunting, fishing, and scenes of people, boats, mountains, donkeys, and hippopotamuses.

A white-cross-lined Naqada vase depicting a hippo hunt.

One of the most iconic images was a hippopotamus hunting scene on a white-cross-lined Naqada vase. Hunting hippopotamuses

1 Wattle and daub was a common ancient house-building technique in which a lattice of wood sticks, known as the wattle, was plastered over with a mixture of wet mud, clay, and straw, known as the daub.

in ancient Egypt was considered brave because the beasts were known to be hostile and would attack boats on the Nile. The ceramic depicts a man in hunting attire, sporting an animal tail and penis sheath and clutching two cords with harpoons lodged in the creature's face. Hippopotamus hunts were intertwined with rituals and stories about the king's authority. As a result, the tradition endured after the pharaohs rose to power. Copper harpoons discovered at Naqada and other prehistoric Egyptian settlements suggest the early Egyptians possibly used them to hunt hippopotamuses.

Archaeologists uncovered 60 Naqadan settlements, some of which have yet to be excavated. Much of our knowledge comes from British Egyptologist Flinders Petrie's initial digs, which yielded over 16,000 burials. In the graves of three Naqada sites — Naqada, Abydos, and Nekhen—lies the story of the birth of Egyptian Civilization.

The Naqada culture had three distinct centers of production, marked by differences in flint tools and pottery. The largest was the type site Naqada, where Petrie discovered 3,000 burials. Approximately 112 km, downstream from Naqada was Abydos, the resting place of Egypt's first pharaohs. Near a similar distance upstream from Naqada is Nekhen, the City of the Hawk.

THE RISE OF NEKHEN

Nekhen was a different place in 3800 BCE from the arid, dusty ruins you will encounter today. Back then, intense rainfall during storms lashed the ravines connecting the desert to the Nile, resulting in greenery on the Sahara's edge. This vegetation attracted the Naqadans to settle down. In the 1970s, American archaeologist Michael Hoffman began excavations at Nekhen, which had been overlooked since its discovery. In 1985, he discovered a vast, oval-shaped courtyard at the site, measuring over 100 feet in length, with a sloping, mud-plastered floor and brick and stone walls. Hoffman dated the courtyard to 3500 BCE. Several workshops were spread across the courtyard, filled with flint tools, gemstones, carnelian beads, obsidian, and rock crystals (a type of quartz). These objects were imported from Nubia, the Levant, and the Sahara Desert oases, indicating long-distance trade. The archaeologists also discovered lapis lazuli, ivory, and malachite, which were also vital during the later Pharaonic period.

Along with the materials and pottery shreds, the excavators discovered animal bones, including cattle, sheep, goats, gazelles, crocodiles, turtles, catfish, and Nile perch.

Hoffman saw parallels between the later Pharaonic Egyptian architecture and the bustling Oval Courtyard of Nekhen. He discovered four massive postholes in front of the courtyard, each 3 feet wide and 5 feet deep, which must have been part of a building tradition, as comparable pillars were discovered in the courtyard of the first pyramid over a millennium later.

Painted tomb of Nekhen, the earliest example of an Egyptian tomb mural.

Near the Oval Courtyard of Nekhen is the oldest tomb painting in Egypt, a practice that would persist for countless generations. The tomb was discovered in 1898 but was sadly plundered, and the original mural did not survive. Though we know little about

A man holding two animals from the tomb mural, believed to be a drawing inspired by Mesopotamian art. At the bottom, the handle of the Gebel-el Arak knife has a distinct Mesopotamian-style "Master of Animals" iconography.

the lives of the Naqadans, the remains of the wall painting can offer some insight.

A watercolor reproduction of the original depicts six boats on the tomb's wall, five of which are white and one black, delivering goods down the Nile. There is a definite Mesopotamian-style "Master of Animals"[2] scenario featuring a man holding two lions.

Another scene depicts a man striking a group of prisoners, assumed to be enemy warriors, marking the first known portrayal of this type in Egyptian history. Later, in Egyptian paintings, we see pharaohs glorified as they assault captured enemies. There were obvious signs of violence in Naqadan society. Archaeological sites revealed graves of people decapitated or bludgeoned to death. Aside from the representations on the tomb, the Battlefield Palette, dated around 3300 BCE to 3100 BCE, depicts violent scenes. According to one theory, Naqada's rulers clashed with the Buto-Maadi culture[3] of Lower Egypt and imprisoned their people. Another hypothesis suggests the depiction was a clash with the Libyans. A guy dressed in a leopard-skin robe appears before the naked prisoners, presumably as the king or his envoy. On the upper portion, we observe two birds: a falcon, which most likely represents Horus, and a pelican. The Battlefield Palette isn't the only portrayal of violence we will encounter. But it is essential to remember that the events shown on the palette hint at a potential conflict between Upper and Lower Egypt, a concept we'll explore later in the Narmer Palette and the story of Egypt's unification.

---

2 Master or Mistress of Animals motifs date back to the Ubaid period of Mesopotamia, and were found throughout the Near East. The iconography depicts a man or a woman holding animals or birds with both hands.

3 Buto-Maadi or Maadi culture is named after the sides of Maadi, near Cairo and Buto. The culture thrived between 4000 BCE to 3500 BCE and was a contemporary of Naqada I and II.

Battlefield Palette shows the clash between Naqada and possibly the people of Lower Egypt.

Narmer or Menes was Egypt's first pharaoh, and records say he unified the nation. However, before his rise, one more king may have attempted to bring the city-states of Lower and Upper Egypt under one banner.

BEFORE THE PHARAOHS: KING SCORPION

Do you recall the 2002 movie *The Scorpion King*, starring Dwayne "The Rock" Johnson and Kelly Hu? Set in pre-dynastic Egypt, the film is a spinoff of the worldwide successful Mummy franchise. In it, The Rock portrays a paid Akkadian assassin tasked with killing a royal sorceress played by Kelly Hu. Though the claim of "Scorpion King" may appear fictional, the film's title refers to King Scorpion, a mighty ruler from pre-dynastic Egypt.

Quibell and Green unearthed a macehead[4] in the Temple of Horus, in 1897, while excavating at Nekhen. But this macehead was no ordinary weapon; it was a ceremonial piece. Dated to around 3200 BCE, the 19.8-cm-long, with a maximum diameter of 18.7 cm, the pear-shaped limestone artifact depicted events from that period.

On the macehead, we see a man sporting a bull's tail, wearing the White Crown of Upper Egypt, and clutching a hoe. He is standing next to a canal, accompanied by two fan bearers, facing a man holding a basket. You can see a scorpion next to his face on the right. The moniker "King Scorpion" comes from the creature's image on the relic.

Behind the King Scorpion are papyrus clumps arranged in a linear formation. Facing away from the monarch are women clapping their hands and a group of people. Around the top of

4 Maceheads were used as weapons in ancient Egypt, but they also had ceremonial purposes.

The Scorpion macehead found at Nekhen.

the macehead are seven standards, each on a pole. From every pole hangs a lapwing bird with a rope around its neck.

The lapwing represented subjects over whom the king ruled. Who could these people be? If you recall the Battlefield Palette, there was a possible depiction of a ruler subjugating the inhabitants of Lower Egypt. One interpretation of the dangling lapwing is that it symbolized the people of Lower Egypt, whom King Scorpion subdued. The standards feature a row of hills; Set, Lower Egypt's primary deity; the sign of the god Min; and a jackal.

What was the incident shown on the macehead?

Close-up of King Scorpion.

There are various interpretations, the most common being that King Scorpion prepared the land to plant a new crop. Another possibility is that the monarch breached a dike to flood the field, which was now ready for seeding. The lapwings on the standards may represent events from a victory ceremony against Lower Egypt.

Egyptologists believe the events depicted on the macehead were an early form of hieroglyphic writing, before the invention of formal writing systems. Can we learn anything else about this enigmatic ruler who left behind such few records?

In 1989, German archaeologist Günter Dreyer uncovered a tomb in Abydos dated 3200 BCE. The burial, named "U-j" (tomb j in cemetery U), had been plundered, with the owner's mummy missing. Once upon a time, the 10-chambered tomb had cellars that stored up to 4,500 liters of wine, with several intact wine jars discovered during its excavation. Despite the burial missing some of its original contents, the archaeologists, in addition to the wine, found a few grave goods, including fragments of rare stones, ivory, obsidian, and gold. They also found storage jars

Details of the Scorpion macehead, showing an important event connected to agriculture or a royal triumph.

filled with food, ointments, perfumes, oils, and animal fat. There were several drawings on these jars, including a dozen depictions of bull heads on posts and 60 drawings of scorpions.

In the tomb's largest room, ivory fragments and a staff, comparable to the scepter of later pharaohs, were discovered, along with a man's remains associated with the scorpion emblem.

Was this King Scorpion's grave?

Several archaeologists think so. However, another grave in Nekhen, Tomb HK6-1, was discovered, which included multiple ivory tags with scorpion motifs and could have been the resting place of King Scorpion. The exact tomb of King Scorpion is disputed, but the finds at Abydos and Nekhen indicate that he was indeed a real person. Burials and the macehead are not our only proof of King Scorpion.

Illustration of the Scorpion Tableau at Gebel Tjauti showing a victory procession of a ruler associated with the scorpion symbol.

In 1995, Yale Egyptologists John Coleman Darnell and Deborah Darnell, his wife, made an important discovery at Gebel Tjauti, in the Sahara Desert, between Abydos and Nekhen. They found a rock graffiti depicting the victory procession of a king over his defeated rival. They termed it the Scorpion Tableau. The scribblings at Gebel Tjauti were not as sophisticated as Egyptian art of the time, and they appear to be etchings of passersby rather than the work of skilled artists. They show a man with a mace and a line of prisoners. There are 16 separate representations of birds, snakes, scorpions, a bull's skull on a post, and human figures shown as prisoners of a powerful individual. Gebel Sheikh Suleiman in Upper Nubia (present-day Sudan) has a similar rock graffiti depicting a scorpion attacking two chained men and an archer aiming his arrow at the victims. The drawings were relatively far from Nekhen or Abydos and may represent people's memories of a conquest in the region. The common scorpion signs in the graffiti could reference King Scorpion.

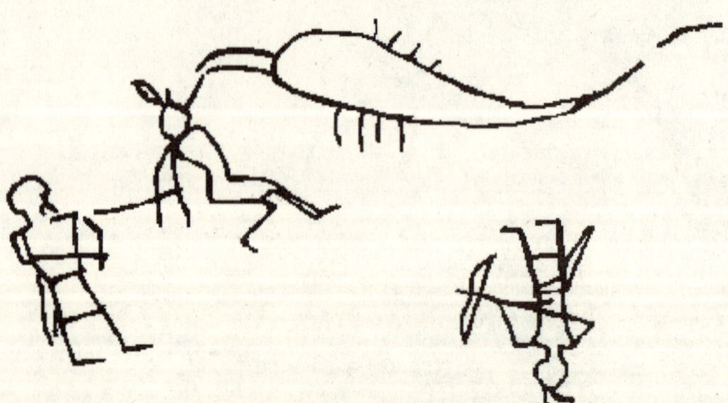

Scorpion relief at Gebel Sheikh Suleiman.

The extent of Scorpion's conquests is uncertain. Some historians believe his dominion extended to Lower Egypt, citing the Scorpion macehead as evidence. Others claim he consolidated Upper Egypt's petty kingdoms, which explains why we see scorpion symbols as far south as Sudan. Some Egyptologists believe Scorpion and Narmer were the same person. However, the adoption of different symbols for the two (scorpion for King Scorpion and catfish for Narmer) shows that they were distinct rulers. We can admire Scorpion for being a visionary king who saw that Upper Egypt would reach its maximum potential under one ruler, even though the extent of his rule is debatable. Trade expanded between Upper Egypt and Mesopotamia during his reign, enhancing the kingdom's prosperity. Scorpion paved the way for Narmer, possibly his son, to fulfill Egypt's destiny of unification.

A well-preserved siltstone palette in Nekhen reveals the story of Egypt's unification, from the limits of Nubia to the Nile River Delta, located on the Mediterranean Sea.

THE BIRTH OF A CIVILIZATION

Around 3100 BCE, Narmer, the ruler of Upper Egypt, had a vision for his people. He sought to unify Upper and Lower Egypt into a single, powerful kingdom that would become an exemplary civilization. As we will see from his subsequent acts, his purpose was more than just conquest.

Narmer's soldiers marched up the Nile, conquering the city-states of Lower Egypt and brutally crushing his enemies. Modern archaeologists believe that Egypt had multiple smaller kingdoms rather than two, and the unification process may have begun during King Scorpion's rule.

After unifying Egypt, Narmer sought to ensure that his people would accept him from the heart, rather than out of fear. He married a Lower Egyptian princess to win over his new subjects and made her his lawful queen.

The Narmer Palette.

After declaring himself the Pharaoh of Egypt, he merged the Hedjet, the White Crown of Upper Egypt, with the Deshret, the Red Crown of Lower Egypt, to produce the Pschent. Pschent was the united Egyptian crown, later becoming the Pharaonic regal symbol.

How do we know this?

The Narmer Palette, unearthed by Quibell and Green in the Temple of Horus, tells the story of Egypt's unification. It is the best preserved of the palettes discovered in Nekhen. Let us examine the artifact and understand its contents.

One of the most intriguing aspects of Narmer is that we know his name, unlike many of his predecessors, who were known as Bull, Elephant, and Scorpion.

The recto, or front side, of the Narmer Palette depicts the king as a towering figure wearing the traditional Hedjet and wielding a mace, about to strike a captive. He stands over two

Drawing of the front of the Narmer Palette depicts the pharaoh slaying his enemies.

more people who are also presumed to be prisoners. Attached to his belt are four beaded tassels, and he's seen wearing a bull's tail similar to King Scorpion's.

A serekh[5] is visible at the palette's top, immediately above the king's crown. A closer look at the serekh reveals a catfish and a chisel. In Egyptian, a catfish is called "nar" and a chisel is called "mer." Thus, King Narmer's name translates to "raging catfish."

Serekh showing a catfish and a chisel, which translates to Narmer.

Flanking the serekh on either side are two human-faced bovine heads, believed to represent the cow goddess, Bat. Another school of thought believes the human–bovine representations were of Hathor, Horus's mother. If you look closely at Narmer's belt, you'll see that the tassels also have the same human-headed cow goddess.

The upper right corner of the palette shows a falcon perched on papyrus blossoms. The bird is pulling a man's skull using a

5 A serekh is a rectangular enclosure containing a royal text.

rope hooked to his nose. The papyrus blossoms are a symbol of Lower Egypt, and the falcon represents Horus, the tutelary deity of Upper Egypt. The scene represents a subjugation of Lower Egypt by Upper Egypt.

The verso of the Narmer Palette.

Narmer is wearing the Deshret on the palette's verso, or backside, making it the first time in history that an Egyptian monarch wore both crowns. The pharaoh wields a mace and a flail, the symbols of kingship. In front of Narmer stands a tall, long-haired man, followed by four standard bearers. The standards include an animal skin, a dog, and two falcons. On the far right, a line of corpses is visible. They have been beheaded, with severed heads between their knees, and castrated, with genitals placed on top of their heads.

The Deshret and a row of dead bodies of his enemies represent a blood-soaked yet triumphant exhibition of Narmer's power.

Below Narmer, in the middle of the palette, you can see a fascinating picture of two men pulling mythical creatures with lion-like faces and snake-like necks. The braiding of their necks represents the unity of Upper and Lower Egypt.

At the bottom of the tablet, you will see a bull destroying the enemy's defenses and crushing a man. There is some controversy about the bull's symbolism. Most Egyptologists believe it depicts Narmer crushing his opponents, as subsequent Egyptian rulers were known as the "Bull of his Mother," and royalty was associated with the sacred cow, whose symbols appear on both sides of the palette.

Although the unification of Egypt may have started before Narmer, he was the final arbiter. Among the artifacts discovered at Nekhen's Temple of Horus is a stone macehead that Narmer used to record the specifics of his triumphs.

In the macehead, on the left, Narmer can be seen sitting under a canopy, wearing the Deshret and wielding a flail. A vulture, possibly the goddess Nekhbet,[6] hovers over him with extended wings. Below the pharaoh are his fan bearers. He sits

---

6 Nekhbet was one of the key goddesses of pre-dynastic Egypt, and was the tutelary deity of the city of Nekheb, in Upper Egypt. Her name translates to "of Nekheb."

The Narmer macehead and its drawing. Narmer is shown as a ruler of all Egypt receiving tribute.

across a veiled woman, probably a princess offered to him for marriage. Three attendants stand behind the princess. At the top, diagonally across the pharaoh, we see an enclosure with a cow and its calf, possibly representing the goddess Hathor and her son Horus. At the bottom is a chronicle of the plunder. Narmer received 400,000 livestock, 1.422 million goats, and 120,000 captives as war booty.

Narmer's unification of Egypt marked a watershed moment in the country's history. Thanks to the well-preserved palettes and maceheads, we know how Egyptian Civilization was born. Nekhen holds more secrets than stories about great monarchs; it also houses the world's oldest known zoo.

In 2009, researchers discovered the remains of a baboon, an elephant, cats, dogs, a leopard, two crocodiles, an aurochs, hippopotamuses, and gazelles near an elite burial site in Nekhen. The bones were dated around 3500 BCE. The remains bore no traces of sacrifice or butchery, indicating that these animals were not utilized in religious ceremonies or feasts. Some academics believe this was the world's oldest zoo due to the enormous number of animals in such a small area. The zookeeper kept the animals confined and didn't handle them with care. The baboon had broken arm and foot bones. A hippopotamus calf, cows, and antelopes were also injured due to being tied. Scholars have provided different explanations for the captive animals. One popular idea suggests that a wealthy person owned them, and they were sacrificial offerings. The owner might have kept them as pets or revered them as mighty spiritual beings. Sacrificing animals connected the human world with that of the divine.

Nekhen tells the story of Egypt's rise as a globally admired civilization. Long before an institutionalized record-keeping culture existed, its rulers and people documented history as it unfolded. The city is not as well known as other in Egypt's New Kingdom (1550 BCE to 1070 BCE), such as Thebes and Memphis.

Yet it remained an important religious center throughout the civilization's history.

Nekheb,[7] a city across the Nile from Nekhen, grew economically during the New Kingdom, while the once-famous City of the Hawk faded from prominence. Discoveries in the nineteenth, twentieth, and twenty-first centuries have helped us piece together the brilliant story of Egypt's rise.

7 Nekheb, now known as El-Kab, eclipsed Nekhen during the New Kingdom period and became the capital of the third nome, of the Shrine Land, of Upper Egypt. A nome is an ancient Egyptian territorial division.

11

Lost Cities of the Amazon

In 1541, a Spanish priest named Gaspar de Carvajal set out from Quito, Ecuador, on an expedition to find El Dorado.

Carvajal was born in Extremadura, Spain, and joined the Dominican Order to convert the people of South America. When he arrived in Peru, in 1536, he discovered a chaotic society reeling from the aftermath of the Inca Empire's Francisco Pizarro, the conquistador[1] who captured and executed Atahualpa, the last ruler of a united Inca Empire, wanted his brother, Gonzalo, out of sight. In addition to being a troublemaker, Gonzalo Pizarro perpetrated atrocities against the Incas that were intolerable even for the conquistadors.

Back then, the Spanish were obsessed with finding the mythical city of El Dorado, where legends of a local ruler with so much gold that he bathed in rivers of the metal were common. Francisco saw this as an opportunity to get rid of his brother and sent Gonzalo off on a voyage with 200–280 Spanish troops, 2,000 pigs, and 4,000 Indigenous people. Carvajal accompanied them as the chaplain.

---

1 Conquistadors or conquistadores were Spanish and Portuguese conquerors who colonized the Americas, Africa, Oceania, and Asia between the fifteenth and seventeenth centuries CE.

Nobody knew where El Dorado was. The arduous voyage depleted their supplies, and the Spanish lost their way. They stumbled upon the Napo River, an upper tributary of the Amazon that originates in Ecuador in the Eastern Andes. The expedition was running dangerously short of food. Due to a lack of information about the Amazon Rainforest's vegetation, the Spanish resorted to eating their pigs before turning to dogs and lizards to survive. The conquistadors had heard stories about a prosperous nation along the Napo. The Spanish mission's second-in-command, Francisco de Orellana,[2] split from Pizarro's group and decided to venture on another route down the Amazon in search of supplies. Carvajal joined Orellana's party.

Portrait of Francisco Orellana.

2 Orellana was Gonzalo Pizarro's cousin.

After nine days of journey, the Spanish finally found villages with food, a society called the Omagua.[3] Orellana refused to unite with Gonzalo and spent the following five months cruising around the Amazon. Friar Carvajal maintained a logbook of his experiences, recording every detail. He described witnessing "huge cities" with over 4,000 people near the mouth of the Tapajós River in Brazil, one of Amazon's largest tributaries.

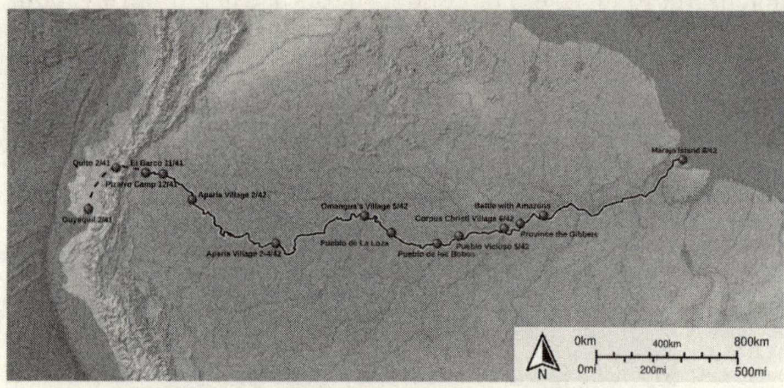

The route taken by Carvajal and Orellana along the Amazon.

For over four centuries, most historians believed Carvajal had lost his marbles or fabricated stories. The Amazon's soils were too acidic to support the agriculture necessary to feed such large cities. Moreover, there was no evidence of monumental architecture. Amazonian tribes relied on hunting and foraging.

How could there be a civilization in the Amazon?

In 1920, British geographer Percy Fawcett discovered a document titled "Manuscript 512" at the National Library of Brazil in Rio de Janeiro. The book, dated 1753 and written by an unknown author, stated that ruins of an ancient city with massive arches and a temple with hieroglyphs had been discovered in the Amazon. Fawcett dubbed it the Lost City of Z. After

3 Omagua, also known as Umana, Cambeba, and Kambeba, was indigenous to Brazil's Amazon River basin.

Percy Fawcett, the British explorer who set out in search of the Lost City of Z, never to be seen again.

becoming convinced of the existence of a sophisticated culture in the Amazon River basin, Fawcett embarked on a mission, in 1925, with his son and his son's friend to locate the Lost City of Z. The explorers vanished without a trace. Questions about the viability of large urban communities in the Amazon River basin resurfaced.

Archaeologists were staring at a dead end.

However, new findings in Brazil, Ecuador, and Bolivia have revealed that the Amazon Rainforest were home to cities over 2,500 years old and had vibrant agricultural societies.

Was Carvajal speaking the truth?

The Amazonian Indigenous people, who have been the focus of numerous documentaries, are not descended from ancient hunter-gatherers who have maintained their lifestyle since the Paleolithic period. Their ancestors might have lived in sophisticated cities. How did archaeologists find evidence of urbanization in the Amazon? Let us start with the last place Fawcett was spotted before he went missing: near the Xingu River Valley in Brazil.

TERRA PRETA AND THE GARDEN CITIES OF XINGU

After Fawcett disappeared, the Amazon received little attention from archaeologists for decades. In 1992, Michael Heckenberger, an anthropologist from the University of Florida, arrived at the Xingu River Valley's headwaters with a Kuikuro[4] chieftain. He and other experts began intensively studying the area's soil.

According to conventional wisdom, farming along the edges of the Amazon wasn't feasible as the soil was too acidic. Without agriculture, a thriving civilization couldn't have arisen on the Amazon's banks. The lack of farming communities in the Amazon basin was in sharp contrast to the civilizations of the Old

4 Kuikuro are Indigenous people of Brazil's Mato Grosso region, who speak Kuikuro, a Cariban language. They live in the Xingu National Park.

Kuikuro people, who are indigenous to the Xingu River Valley, helped in the discovery of a previously unknown civilization in the region.

World, which blossomed along river valleys. However, a closer examination of the Amazonian dark earth, known as *terra preta*,[5] tells a different story. A 2010 study by US-Brazilian scientists revealed that terra preta was rich in microorganisms, including bacteria usually found in tropical rice fields. How did such fertile land form on the banks of the Amazon? The Indigenous people of the river basin had a clever way of handling the soil. They practiced a form of agriculture known as "slash-and-char." The farmers physically mixed the activated carbon produced by partially burning organic debris from the forest, such as fallen trees, branches, and leaves, into the soil, thereby improving its nutrition. According to research conducted by the Kansai Environmental Engineering Center near Kyoto, Japan, charcoal can remain in soil for up to 50,000 years, binding nutrients and retaining minerals. This farming approach was unique to the Amazon River basin and was not found anywhere in the Old World.

5 *Terra preta* means black soil in Portuguese.

Slash-and-char agriculture created a vibrant farming community in the Xingu River basin. Heckenberger, with the assistance of the Kuikuro, discovered 28 towns, villages, and hamlets spanning 20,000 sq. km that may have supported up to 50,000 people. The largest "cities"[6] featured defensive ditches 3 m deep and 33 m wide, fortified with wooden palisades. Archaeologists also discovered enormous plazas, some 150 m wide. Residents designed their settlements to blend into the rainforest and not disrupt its nature. He found earthen dams and noted that the ancient inhabitants made artificial lakes to farm fish, which is still common among the Kuikoro.

Mandioca (Portuguese for cassava), a seventeenth-century painting by Albert Eckhout in Dutch Brazil.

6 Unlike the cities of Amazon in Ecuador and Bolivia, there is still much debate about whether Xingu Valley's settlements can be classified as cities.

Cassava was the primary starch grown in the region; roads and canals connected communities and surrounding areas. The region's earliest residents settled around 3000 BCE, while the first evidence of urbanization appeared between 400 and 500 CE. As we discussed in Chapter 9, the cities of the Americas exhibit low-density urbanism compared to the metropolises of Mesopotamia and Egypt. Heckenberger coined the phrase "garden cities" to describe the urban centers of the Xingu River Valley. However, the archaeologists remained skeptical because, while the elements of a city were present, a critical component was missing: monumental architecture.

Heckenberger was on the right trail. Though a "city" described by Carvajal and in the dubious "Manuscript 512" remained elusive, there were clear signs of a sophisticated society previously dismissed as implausible.

THE CASARABE CULTURE

In the 1960s, geographer William Denevan spotted earthworks in northern Bolivia's vast Moxos Plains (Llanos de Moxos). The Moxos Plains are a tropical savanna region, occupying the southwestern corner of the Amazon River basin. Several rivers from the Andes drain into the area. Like most tropical regions, the Moxos receive seasonal rainfalls, which, coupled with the Andean snowmelt, result in annual flooding of the low-lying plains. Like most of the Amazon River basin, the region appears like an undisturbed ecological zone. However, the "pristine myth"[7] of the Amazon was challenged when Denevan noticed

7 The myth of the pristine Amazon rainforests assumes that before the Spanish arrived in the region in the sixteenth century the area was untouched by humans.

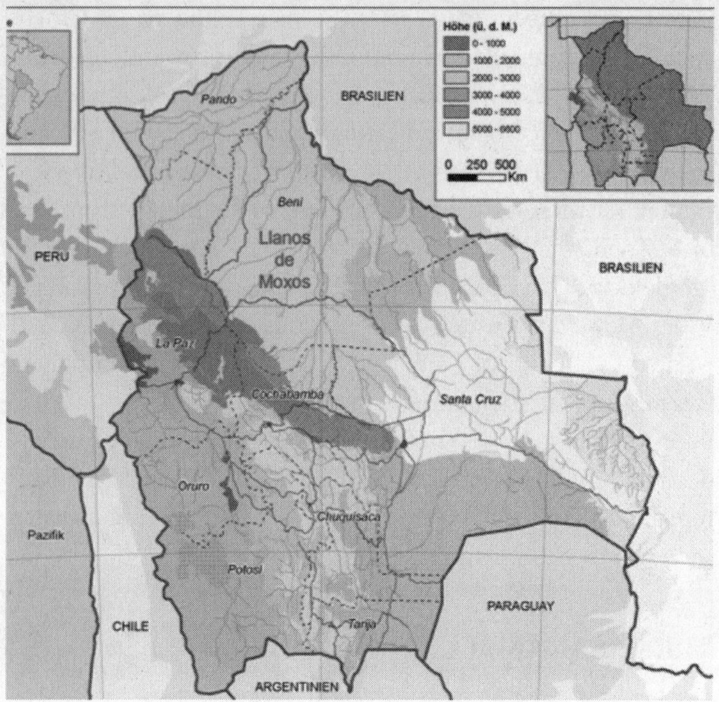

Map of Bolivia highlighting Llanos de Moxos.

roads and canals in the Moxos Plains, which were similar to their counterparts in the Xingu Valley.

Findings of Heiko Prümers from the German Archaeological Institute further supported Denevan's studies. Prümers conducted a LiDAR survey of the Moxos Plains, in 2022, revealing that once upon a time, widespread low-density urban settlements thrived in the region.

LiDAR stands for "Light Detection and Ranging." Laser beams aim at a surface, providing archaeologists with a 3D view of the area without the need for digging. A drone, helicopter, or airplane flies above the surveyed region. The airborne instrument then delivers a laser pulse onto a surface. The surface reflects the

Vast wet plains surrounded by forests characterize Llanos de Moxos.

laser, which travels back to the pulse source and is detected by sensors. The time it takes for the laser to travel is computed, and the distance traversed by the beam is determined. The time and distance reveal the characteristics of the scanned surface, making LiDAR a helpful tool where excavations are not possible.

Prümers and his team deployed a helicopter from approximately 200 m above ground level to scan the Moxos Plains, revealing a sprawling urban settlement called the Casarabe culture, which thrived between 500 CE and 1400 CE. The Casarabe cities had large platforms, pyramid architecture, and causeways linking multiple suburban communities. Reservoirs and canals controlled water distribution, resulting in an effective irrigation system.

The layouts of the cities of the Casarabe culture were comparable to those of the Upper Xingu River Valley. However, unlike the finds in Brazil, the Moxos Plains show substantial evidence of monumental architecture, including U-shaped temples and platform mounds. Heckenberger described the discovery at Moxos Plains as "the clearest case of a fully urbanized Amazonian landscape."

LiDAR found 26 unique Casarabe culture sites, including 11 previously unknown ones. The two largest urban centers, Landívar and Cotoca, were known before the survey, but LiDAR revealed that their actual size was much bigger. Rings of moats

A prehistoric causeway connecting two islands in the Moxos Plains.

and rampart fortifications surrounded each city. Landívar and Cotoca had artificial terraces, massive earthen platforms, and conical pyramids over 21 m tall. The buildings were made of mud brick, so they were not as durable as the enormous limestone monuments of Mesoamerica.

Causeways extending from the urban centers, like the spokes in a wheel, linked the two cities to a vast regional network of settlements.

Prümers argues that the Indigenous people of the Amazon established this complex culture. There is little evidence of influence from the Andean civilizations, such as the Moche, Wari, Tiwanaku, and Inca.

In January 2025, researchers provided further insights into the farming methods of the Casarabe people that enabled them to sustain a large population. An international team of archaeologists used LiDAR to discover an advanced irrigation network of drainage canals and water-storing ponds, which enabled residents to grow maize during both dry and rainy spells, allowing for two harvests annually. During the rainy season, canals drain excess water from the fields, while in the dry season, ponds that store water serve as reservoirs.

The Casarabe culture was an advanced society in the Amazon River basin that respected the forest and established a sustainable agricultural system, as well as a complex urban civilization. However, they were not the only ones. Our next clue for the lost cities of the Amazon comes from Ecuador's Upano Valley, home to the region's earliest urban centers.

THE VALLEY OF LOST CITIES

In the 1970s, Juan Bottasso, an Ecuadorian priest, stumbled upon an unusual mound atop a platform in the Upano Valley, in Morona Santiago province in eastern Ecuador. He brought this

The Upano River, Ecuador.

to the attention of Pedro Porras, a fellow clergyman from Quito. The priests rode to the mountain on horseback and organized an amateur excavation, publishing their report in an Ecuadorian paper. Over 15 years later, their findings caught the eye of Stéphen Rostain, a French archaeologist excavating a Mayan site in Guatemala.

Rostain set out for the Upano Valley in 1996 and began excavating the mounds first observed by Bottasso and Porras. He concentrated on the archaeological sites of Sangay and Kilamope, which revealed beautiful pottery with painted designs and lines created by skilled incisions. Several large jars were found that stored maize beer, known as *chicha*.

Rostain's team saw plazas built around mounds. Radiocarbon dating shows that the culture in the Upano Valley flourished between 500 BCE and 600 CE. The archaeologists didn't have sufficient evidence to conclude that a long-lost civilization existed, although there were signs that one had.

Unfortunately for Rostain, not everyone was thrilled with his discoveries. Two years later, his colleague abandoned the

A model tray for making *chicha* from the Peruvian Chancay culture, c. 1400 CE.

project. But the archaeologist pushed through the rainforests, uncovering hundreds of mounds.

Fate smiled on Rostain, and his determination paid off in 2015, when Ecuador's National Institute for Cultural Heritage funded a LiDAR survey of the valley. Little did anyone expect what the laser beams would disclose in the rainforests of the Upano River Valley. A vibrant civilization spanning over 300 sq. km was found, with ten small settlements and five large ones. Rostain termed the discovery a "lost valley of cities."

Earthen platforms and plazas were the most frequently detected features in the LiDAR survey. Approximately 6,000 mounds were discovered within a 300 sq. km area. The conventional shape was 20 m × 10 m, with a height of 2–3 m. The mounds were arranged in groupings of six to ten around a plaza with a central platform. The LiDAR scans revealed colossal structures that could have served to conduct public functions and manage civic activities, promoting communal well-being. Kilamope's most visible structure spans 10 hectares and measures 140 m × 40 m in size, with a height of 4.5 m.

To understand the enormity of these settlements, the primary area of Kilamope is comparable in size to Egypt's Giza Plateau. That is not a tiny region!

Rostain and his team divided the fifteen communities they discovered using LiDAR into two categories: five central, heavily populated locations and ten peripheral ones. The density was calculated based on the number of platforms per square km. Sangay was the largest, with 125 platforms per sq. km. A 2.5-km route connected the town center to the cliff's highest point, which overlooks the Upano Valley. Kilamope and Copueno both had vast ceremonial complexes. Archaeologists also discovered several truncated hills artificially flattened to facilitate access.

Agricultural fields on hillside terraces surrounded the cities in the Upano Valley. The villagers grew corn, cassava, and sweet potatoes. Canals and drainage ditches supplied water to the farms. Scholars believe that the adjacent Sangay volcano provided fertile soil for agricultural production.

Broad, straight highways connected the cities. Roads linked the city's communities and homes. One of the mysteries Rostain and his team had to solve was why these enigmatic people built 5-m-deep straight roads across the mountains when it would have been quicker to stroll through the gaps between hills. Rostain believes the answer lies in the Inca Civilization's legendary 30,000-km-long Qhapaq Ñan road network, which connected the Andes to the Amazon. For the people of the Upano Valley, roads may have been symbolic, and they wanted to leave their mark on the land. Qhapaq Ñan is still regarded as a "living road" today by the descendants of the Incas, and perhaps the people of Upano Valley felt the same way about their roadways.

The population of cities in the Upano Valley is a hotly debated topic, with the most conservative estimates suggesting that about 10,000 people once lived there. Antoine Dorison, the coauthor of the LiDAR study, believes the peak population ranged between 15,000 and 30,000 people.

The Upano Valley cities differ from the other Amazonian sites we covered, which were built more recently, had fewer urban structures, and lacked an extensive network of highways. The Lost Valley of Cities is the oldest and most prominent example of low-density urbanism in the Amazon. Unlike the other Amazonian cities, there are hints of bilateral relations with the contemporary Andean civilization of the Chavín culture.[8]

We have a robust urban civilization in the Amazon that dates back centuries, predating the Mayans and Aztecs. Yet by 600 CE, the cities of the Upano Valley declined. What led to their downfall?

How did the Amazon River basin people, who once built complex societies, turn to foraging and hunting?

THE GREAT AMAZONIAN COLLAPSE

The astonishing engineering feats at Upano Valley, Moxos Plains, and Xingu Valley call into question several long-held beliefs about Amazonian societies that have been neglected in discussions of civilizations. The people weren't foragers who subsisted on whatever the forests provided. They were skilled farmers who built roads, canals, and sacred monuments.

Carvajal was onto something when he wrote about cities in the Amazon Rainforest. After decades of ridicule, he stands vindicated, thanks to improved technology that allows us to find civilizations without risky excavations that could harm delicate ecosystems.

---

8 Chavín culture was a civilization that thrived along the Peruvian coast between 900 BCE to 250 BCE, and is named after the typesite Chavín de Huántar.

Why did the cities that Spanish explorers may have encountered crumble and vanish from our collective memory? Though we are far from certain, a few theories exist. Let us return to where we started, the Upper Xingu River Valley.

After the arrival of Europeans in the early sixteenth century, diseases such as smallpox and measles rapidly spread among the Indigenous people of Brazil, wiping out almost two-thirds or more of the populace. The decaying cities were abandoned and swallowed up by the forest. It is quite likely that early Spanish explorers didn't encounter the original inhabitants who lived in the Upper Xingu Valley.

Several severe droughts have occurred throughout the Amazon River basin in history, which could have affected the civilizations that flourished in the region. A prolonged dry spell also affected the water management systems, which depended on annual floods.

Sangay Volcano, Ecuador.

Much of what we see today in the Amazon Rainforest is much younger than we believe. In ancient times, large tracts of land were savanna grasslands, and the shifting climate may have affected agriculture, thereby disrupting the food supply that sustained large populations.

Rostain claims that the Sangay Volcano eruption caused the demise of Upano Valley cities, though it is too soon to say for sure. He suggests that a series of eruptions may have resulted in the cities' abandonment.

Scientists have yet to discover a "Pompeii-like" event, but the spread of hazardous gases from the volcano and resulting diseases could force residents to flee their towns. The survivors began foraging and retired to the forests.

Can the native Amazonians trace their ancestry back to these advanced cultures? Was the collapse of their cities so traumatic that they abandoned urbanism?

Native American tribes such as the Comanche abandoned farming after the introduction of horses in the Americas and subsisted by hunting. A lifestyle change for entire communities, from sedentary to mobile, isn't unheard of. It boils down to food security. We are programmed to gravitate towards a system that offers the best chances of survival.

Did the forests provide greater food security to the Indigenous people of the Amazon? Additional research can answer these questions.

We have uncovered the tip of the iceberg. As new findings challenge our understanding of ancient Amazonia, more excavations, LiDAR scans, and genetic tests may reveal information about the societies that built these sophisticated cities and whether their descendants are survivors of a post-apocalyptic world.

The Amazons are the lungs of the earth and home to diverse flora and fauna. The discovery of ancient cities in this delicate ecosystem using non-invasive technologies is a pivotal moment in history. It challenges the preconceived notion that the Indigenous people of the Amazon weren't adept at building a sophisticated civilization.

Explorers like Gaspar de Carvajal, who took immense risks only to be mocked for centuries, may have witnessed the last days of glorious civilizations that once thrived in the region.

12

Center of the Universe on the Silk Road: Balasagun

A TOWER STANDS IN BARREN GRASSLANDS AROUND 80 KM EAST of Kyrgyzstan's capital, Bishkek, near the town of Tokmok. Locals call it the Burana Tower. According to legend, a tenth century CE Khan who governed the region built the monument. He had a daughter and hosted a big party when she was born. The ruler invited prominent fortune tellers of the land to join the celebrations.

He wanted to know what the future held for his baby girl. The soothsayers were unanimous: she would have a long, healthy life and do great things. Among them, one elderly man disagreed. The old fortune teller predicted that the girl would die at 16 from a spider bite.

Shocked, the Khan immediately ordered the construction of a tall tower for the princess that no spider could reach.

When she turned sixteen, convinced that his security measures kept his daughter safe, the Khan presented her with a basket of the choicest fruits of the land on her birthday. Unfortunately, a spider lurked in the basket and bit the princess,

The Burana Tower is all that survives of the bustling Silk Road city of Balasagun.

resulting in her death. Unable to cope with the shock, the Khan died as well, and a portion of the tower collapsed.

When I first heard about this tragic legend, I assumed it was a moral lesson for kids: no matter how hard they try, they can't escape their fate. The message wasn't positive. However, viewed through a historical lens, the tower's fate symbolizes the rise and fall of the once-thriving Silk Road city of Balasagun, which once stood nearby.

Mahmud al-Kashgari, a polymath and cartographer from the eleventh century CE, included Balasagun at the center of his map, suggesting that the city had a rich history and was significant during his time. But now, only a tower remains. What happened to this enigmatic metropolis in the Eurasian Steppes? To understand Balasagun's importance during the Middle Ages, let us learn about its discovery in modern times.

IN SEARCH OF BALASAGUN

According to medieval Islamic texts, Balasagun was in the Chüy River Valley of present-day Kyrgyzstan. The city was an essential stop on the Silk Road and part of the Chang'an-Tianshan Corridor. This trade route spanned over 5,000 km, running from Chang'an (present-day Xian) in central China, the capital of the Han and Tang dynasties, to the Zhetysu area in Central Asia (present-day southeastern Kazakhstan). The route was active from the second century BCE until the sixteenth century CE and functioned as a vital link for commerce and the diffusion of religious and cultural ideas.

Fascinated by the history of the Turkic peoples, in the late nineteenth century, Vasily Vladimirovich Bartold (born Wilhelm Barthold), a German-origin Russian orientalist and historian, set out to discover the lost cities along the Silk Road, among them Balasagun. He says that the Sogdians,[1] an Iranian-speaking people from Central Asia, built the legendary city. Barthold was correct in identifying who built the city; he didn't get the location right, though he was close. Barthold had mistakenly associated Balasagun with Suyab, another Sogdian city near Tokmok in present-day Ak-Beshim, Kyrgyzstan. Suyab was a settlement of Sogdian merchants that sprang up as an urban center between the fifth and sixth centuries CE. The First Turkic Khaganate governed the city, and during the tenure of

1 Refer to Chapter 17 on the Göktürks for more information on the Sogdians.

Tong Yabgu (618 CE–628 CE), Suyab served as the capital of the western portion of the empire.

Later, Soviet scholars supported Barthold's claims and linked Balasagun to Suyab.

Hence, for a long time, everyone assumed Suyab was the lost city of Balasagun. Only recently has Balasagun been correctly identified with the Burana archaeological site.

Barthold didn't intentionally mislead us about Balasagun's location, and thanks to his correctly identifying the city's Sogdian roots, researchers could trace parts of its early history. The residents of Balasagun spoke Sogdian till the eleventh century CE, and Turkic complemented it, eventually becoming the city's primary language.

Wilhelm Barthold discovered Balasagun but wrongly identified it as Suyab, a nearby city.

The Turks called the city *Quz-Ordu*. *Quz* translates to "northern side of the mountain," while *Ordu* means "the ruler's camp." Thus, the Turkic etymology tells us that the city was a northern capital.

Whose capital are we talking about?

Tenth-century CE Islamic records mention that "infidel" Turks conquered Balasagun, and its Muslim residents appealed to the city of Bukhara in modern Uzbekistan for help. Historians believe the Turks discussed in the writings were Karluks, a Turkic tribe who later converted to Islam and established the Qara-Khanid Khanate. They made Balasagun their capital. The Qara-Khanids are crucial to our quest to uncover the city's history because Balasagun reached its peak during their reign.

THE RISE AND FALL OF BALASAGUN

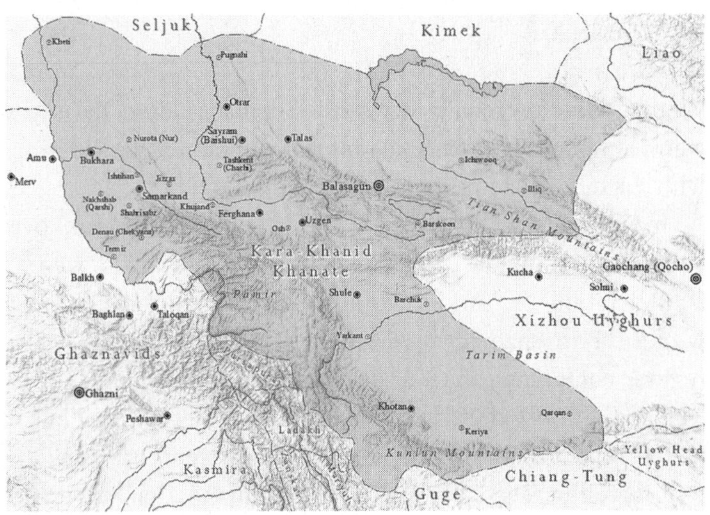

Map of the Qara-Khanid Khanate in the early eleventh century CE.

We know very little about Balasagun during the Sogdian era. However, we can get an idea of what life was like from neighboring Suyab.

Seventh-century CE Chinese traveler Xuanzang describes Suyab and the adjacent region as follows:

> "Traveling 500 li to the north west of Great Qing Lake, we arrive at the city of the Suye River. The city is 6 or 7 li in circuit; various Hu ("barbarian") merchants here came from surrounding nations (reference to Sogdian traders) congregate and dwell. The soil is favorable for red millet and for grapes; the woods are not thick, the climate is windy and cold; the people wear garments of twilled wool. Traveling from Suye westward, there are a great number of isolated towns; in each there is a chieftain; these are not dependent on one another, but all are in submission to the Tujue (*Khagan* of the Göktürks)."

We don't have any records of who the Sogdian rulers of Balasagun were, although we have some information about the Göktürks who ruled the region.

In the mid-tenth century, the Qara-Khanids took over Balasagun from the Sogdians. The Qara-Khanids were a confederation of Turkic peoples living in western Xinjiang, western Tian Shan (in modern Kyrgyzstan), and the Zhetysu region, comprising the Karluks, Yagmas, Chigils, and Tuhsis. The epithet *Qara* translates to black, which was the regal hue of many nomadic tribes, but the term also represents bravery.

The Karluk Turks originally hailed from the Altai Mountains. In 742 CE, they were part of an alliance that revolted against the Göktürks, leading to the eventual collapse of the Second Turkic Khaganate. The Karluks collaborated with the Tang dynasty to fight the Umayyad Caliphate's advances into Central Asia. However, later the Karluks defected to the Abbasid Caliphate at the historic Battle of the Talas River in 751 CE, resulting in a decisive loss for the Tang army. The fight was a crucial turning point in history, as captured Chinese troops and officers helped disseminate papermaking technology across the Islamic world, from which it eventually reached Europe, revolutionizing the spread of knowledge. By 766 CE, the Qara-Qhanids had captured Suyab, making it their capital.

The Persian Samanid dynasty, based in eastern Iran's Khorasan province, ruled Central Asia during the ninth century CE. After 990 CE, the Samanids's power began to diminish. The Qara-Khanids, led by Harun Bughra Khan, seized the opportunity and conquered Samarkand, Fergana, Ilaq, and Bukhara, the capital of the Samanids. By 999 CE, Balasagun came under the Qara-Khanid rule. They controlled the prosperous Silk Road cities and established Balasagun as their primary capital. Kashgar and, later, Samarkand served as their other capitals.

Balasagun thrived under the Qara-Khanid rule, prompting Mahmud al-Kashgari, a native of nearby Barsaghan, to refer to it as the center of the universe. Between 1072 CE and 1074 CE, al-Kashgari compiled the first dictionary of Turkic languages, *Diwan lughat al-Turk* (Compendium of the Turkic Dialects). The seminal work featured the first map of the world of Turkic origin, depicting Balasagun at the center. Kashgar, in the present-day Xinjiang region of China, is shown as a learning hub. The scholar's birthplace, Barsaghan, is likewise described as a city where Turks reside. A vital feature of the map is that it was the first to depict Japan.[2]

---

2 Japan is mentioned as "Jabarqa" on Mahmud al-Kashgari's map of the world.

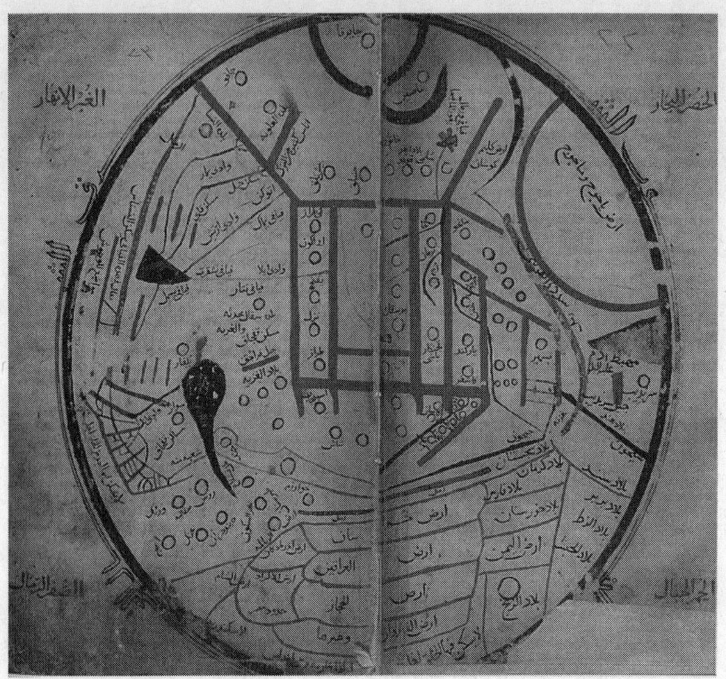

A map of the world by Mahmud al-Kasghari.

A copy of the map was available at Baghdad's House of Wisdom. Though al-Kashgari is remembered for his works in Turkic languages and for highlighting Balasagun on a world map, the city's most well-known son was Yusuf Khass Hajib, also known as Yusuf Balasaguni, a vizier, poet, philosopher, and theologian.

Balasaguni was born in either 1018 CE or 1019 CE. His father was a prominent figure in the city, ensuring his son had access to a top-notch education. The works of renowned Islamic thinkers such as Ibn Sina, Ferdowsi, and al-Farabi influenced a young Balasaguni. A contemporary of al-Kashgari, Balasaguni, at the age of fifty-four, published his iconic work *Kutadgu Bilig* (Blessed Knowledge) in Turkic. The language, also known as the Karluk language or Qara-Khanid Turkic, was comparable to Old Turkic. However, it incorporated a substantial amount of Persian vocabulary because Persian was the lingua franca of Central Asia. Despite being fluent in Persian and Arabic, Yusuf Balasaguni authored *Kutadgu Bilig* in Turkic, popularizing his native tongue in written form.

He finished the book in Kashgar and handed it to the Qara-Khanid monarch, Hasan ibn Sulayman, who bestowed upon him the title of *Khass Hajib* (roughly equivalent to a special chamberlain).

Kutadgu Bilig describes life during the Qara-Khanid Khanate period. The poet instructs the ruler on how to run the land and urges him to appreciate his farmers, cattle herders, and artisans.

The Qara-Khanid rule ended in 1137 CE when the Khan of the Qara-Khitai, also known as the Western Liao dynasty, defeated the Turks and captured Balasagun. The Khitai, or Khitans,[3] were a para-Mongolic people who played a crucial role in the politics of the Eurasian Steppes from the twelfth century CE until the rise of Chinggis Khan in the early thirteenth century CE. You may have heard the name "Cathay," which Marco Polo used to refer to China. Cathay is derived from Khitai.

Enraged and humiliated by losing their eastern capital, the Qara-Khanids appealed to the Seljuk sultan, Ahmed Sanjar, for help. In 1141 CE, the Seljuk–Qara-Khanid alliance clashed with the Qara-Khitai, led by Yelü Dashi, at Qatwan, just outside Samarkand. The Qara-Khitai triumphed over the Islamic coalition, ending the Qara-Khanid influence in Central Asia. Christendom celebrated the victory of a non-Islamic army over a powerful Muslim alliance as the Crusades reached their peak.

---

3 Khitans descended from the proto-Mongolic Xianbei. We use the term "para-Mongolic" to describe them, as they spoke a Mongolian-like language.

According to rumors, many Christians associated Yelü Dashi with Prester John, a mythical Christian king from the East who people during the Middle Ages thought would save Christianity and free the Holy Land from the Muslims. The legend of Prester John was eventually proven false, as he was a fictitious character created to bolster the confidence of the Crusaders. However, rumor suggests that the decline of the Qara-Khanids had a profound impact, felt thousands of miles away.

The Qara-Khitai predominantly practiced Buddhism and Nestorian Christianity, a branch of Christianity popular among the Assyrians and the nomads of the Eurasian Steppes. Nestorian Christians and Buddhists had lived in Balasagun since the Sogdian era, and the city had a tolerant religious atmosphere, a tradition that continued under the Khitans.

In 1208 CE, Kuchlug, a Naiman prince, fled Chinggis Khan's rising Mongols and sought safety in the Qara-Khitai Khanate. The Naimans were a Mongolian tribe that initially opposed the Mongols but later joined them when Chinggis Khan unified Mongolia.

Kuchlug was ambitious. He seized power and toppled the last Khitan ruler, Yelü Zhilugu, who was also his father-in-law.

From 1211 CE to 1218 CE, Kuchlug and the Naimans ruled Balasagun. Unlike the city's previous governors, Kuchlug didn't believe in religious tolerance. He began harassing Muslims, demanding they convert to Buddhism or Nestorian Christianity. His usurpation of power and upsetting of the kingdom's culture of coexistence didn't go well with the citizens, who begged Chinggis to intervene.

The Great Khan didn't need much convincing to pursue his former adversary, so he dispatched one of his best generals, Jebe, to track down Kuchlug. The Mongols overcame the Naiman usurper, seized Balasagun, and annexed the remainder of the Qara-Khitai Khanate into their expanding empire.

A Nestorian Christian silver plate depicting the Battle of Jericho, made by Sogdian merchants under Qara-Khanid rule, ninth to tenth centuries CE.

Some recent sources indicate the Mongols destroyed Balasagun. However, historical evidence contradicts this. The Mongols renamed Balasagun, *Gobaliq*, meaning "beautiful city," implying that it continued as a vibrant cultural and trading center following the Mongol takeover.

We know little about Balasagun during the Mongol rule, and by the fourteenth century CE, the city had vanished from historical sources. We're left with a lone tower to remind us of its glorious past.

THE BURANA TOWER AND BALASAGUN'S LEGACY

The Burana Tower was probably built in the late tenth and early eleventh centuries CE during the Qara-Khanid era. The archaeological complex at Burana includes a tomb, mosque, church, Christian and Muslim cemeteries, and a bathhouse. Although legend holds that a local Khan built the tower to protect his daughter, inscriptions near the tower suggest it was erected in honor of a lawmaker named Imam Muhammad. Usto Bako, who constructed the Kalyan Minaret in Bukhara, is the likely architect of the Burana Tower. Both minarets are similar in appearance and could have been built during the same period, under the rule of the Qara-Khanid ruler Mohammad Arslan Khan. The actual date of the construction of Burana is unknown, but since Kalyan was built in 1127 CE, we may assume that the tower at Balasagun was erected a few years earlier or later. While we may never

Decorative details at the base of the Burana Tower.

know the true significance of the Burana Tower, there is a clear difference between its purpose and that of Kalyan's. The Kalyan Minaret was designed primarily for religious prayers, whereas the Burana was a memorial.

The Burana Tower is made of red bricks. It is 25 m tall, 9 m in diameter at the base, and 6 m at the top. The original tower was 45 m tall, but earthquakes have damaged the structure significantly over the years. In the fifteenth century, a major earthquake destroyed the top half of the tower, reducing its height to its current 25 meters.

Archaeologists N.M. Bachinski and M.M. Loginov started the first restoration work in 1927–28. Additional restoration was completed in 1973–74, and the tower survived thanks to conservation efforts. Unfortunately, its artistic appearance was compromised in the preservation process. Plain bricks replaced the original ornate foundation, and the tower's top got distorted during the repairs.

Strong winds blowing from the west have caused significant degradation on the western part of Burana, and the tower leans slightly towards the southwest. The restorers decided not to correct this deformation as substantial alterations to the pedestal would be needed, which could damage the structure permanently.

Tourists access the tower using newly built metal stairs at the back. They can climb the tower's summit and enjoy a fantastic view of the Tian Shan Mountains.

Near the tower is a field of *balbals*, or stelae, of ancient Turks who resided in the area during the sixth and ninth centuries. The balbals have engraved faces, which might be those of the deceased. Erecting stelae to commemorate one's ancestors was a prevalent practice throughout Eurasia, and such stones have been discovered in locations ranging from Ukraine to Mongolia.

Balbals found near the Burana Tower.

The Burana site contained gravestones with crosses belonging to the Nestorian Christian community. An archaeological dig revealed a Buddhist deity, highlighting the influence of Buddhism and the tolerant religious culture that thrived in Balasagun.

We have little information regarding what happened to Balasagun or why it vanished. A prosperous metropolis where people traded, composed poetry, and built monuments disappeared from the face of the Earth. Warfare, hunger, and the disintegration of trade networks may have all contributed to the city's eventual abandonment.

All that remains is a magnificent tower, reminding us of the glory days of Balasagun.

In 2014, UNESCO added the ruins of Balasagun at the Burana archaeological complex to its list of World Heritage Sites. The Kyrgyz government collaborates with UNESCO and

Winding staircase inside the Burana Tower.

the local community to actively involve them in conserving the Burana Tower and the remnants of one of the most significant Silk Road cities.

13

Cahokia: The Forgotten Mississippian Metropolis

Congressman Henry M. Brackenridge, an amateur historian, lawyer, and friend of Thomas Jefferson, visited St. Louis, USA, in 1811, and discovered over a hundred large mounds on the city's outskirts.

The magnificent view filled Brackenridge's heart with awe, as he commented:

> "I was struck with a degree of astonishment, not unlike that which is experienced in contemplating the Egyptian pyramids. What a stupendous pile of earth! To heap up such a mass must have required years and the labors of thousands."

In a letter to Jefferson, Brackenridge was the first Euro-American to acknowledge the existence of an enormous city, rivaling those of the Aztecs and Mayans, near St. Louis. The Congressman had stumbled upon the remnants of a colossal pre-Columbian city.

Centuries before Christopher Columbus arrived on America's shores, a vast metropolis thrived near modern-day

Henry M. Brackenridge was the first Euro-American to describe Cahokia.

St. Louis, Missouri. On the eastern banks of the Mississippi River in southern Illinois lie the ruins of Cahokia,[1] the largest city built north of the Rio Grande River.[2] In its heyday, it boasted a population of 10,000 to 20,000 inhabitants, comparable to those of London and Paris during that era.

1 Cahokia is pronounced as *ka-ho-kia*.

2 Cahokia was the largest city north of Mexico till the rise of Philadelphia in the eighteenth century.

The media astonishingly ignored Brackenridge's report. The lack of awareness about the existence of a grand ancient city built by the Indigenous people of America resulted in unchecked construction, causing damage to many of Cahokia's structures. Early European-origin American scholars were uninterested in researching the constructions at Cahokia. Some even denied that Indigenous people could have built such a grand metropolis, instead attributing the city's construction to a mythical race of Atlanteans. The Phoenicians, Romans, and Chinese were also touted as the builders of Cahokia.

Jefferson was the first Euro-American to recognize that Indigenous people built the mounds that enchanted Brackenridge. Thanks to excavations since the 1960s, we know that Cahokia was home to a bustling city with plazas, causeways, and 120 large mounds, some covering an area greater than the Pyramids of Giza.

What did these enigmatic structures represent? How did a city rise on Mississippi's floodplains?

To get the answers, let us discover who built Cahokia and what attracted them to the city. We will briefly explore the history of mound-building in America to gain a deeper understanding of the communities that constructed them.

AMERICA'S FIRST MOUNDBUILDERS

Before we search for the moundbuilders of Cahokia, it is vital to remember that the city we call Cahokia is named after the Cahokian tribe. These Algonquian-speaking Native Americans moved to the area in the seventeenth century, several centuries after the Mississippian metropolis collapsed. They were not related to the founders of Cahokia. Nobody knows what the mysterious moundbuilders called themselves because they did not leave any written records.

Artistic reconstruction of the Ouachita Mounds.

Our journey to the origins of mound-building in northeastern Louisiana begins on a hill overlooking the Ouachita River. Around 3500 BCE, Indigenous people built 11 irregularly shaped mounds connected by a ridge, the largest of which was roughly two stories tall. These earthworks, known as the Ouachita Mounds, were built long before the advent of agriculture in North America. Their discovery cast doubt on the idea that hunter-gatherers could not create elaborate structures and lacked social hierarchy.

Building a ring of mounds with baskets full of dirt, without the help of draft animals, is a labor-intensive and long-term project that involves the entire society. The workers' food security had to be guaranteed. Hence, a certain level of civic organization and leadership was required. At Göbekli Tepe,[3] we saw that charismatic leaders encouraged people to undertake massive construction projects even before humans began settling down permanently.

3 Refer to Chapter 2 for more details.

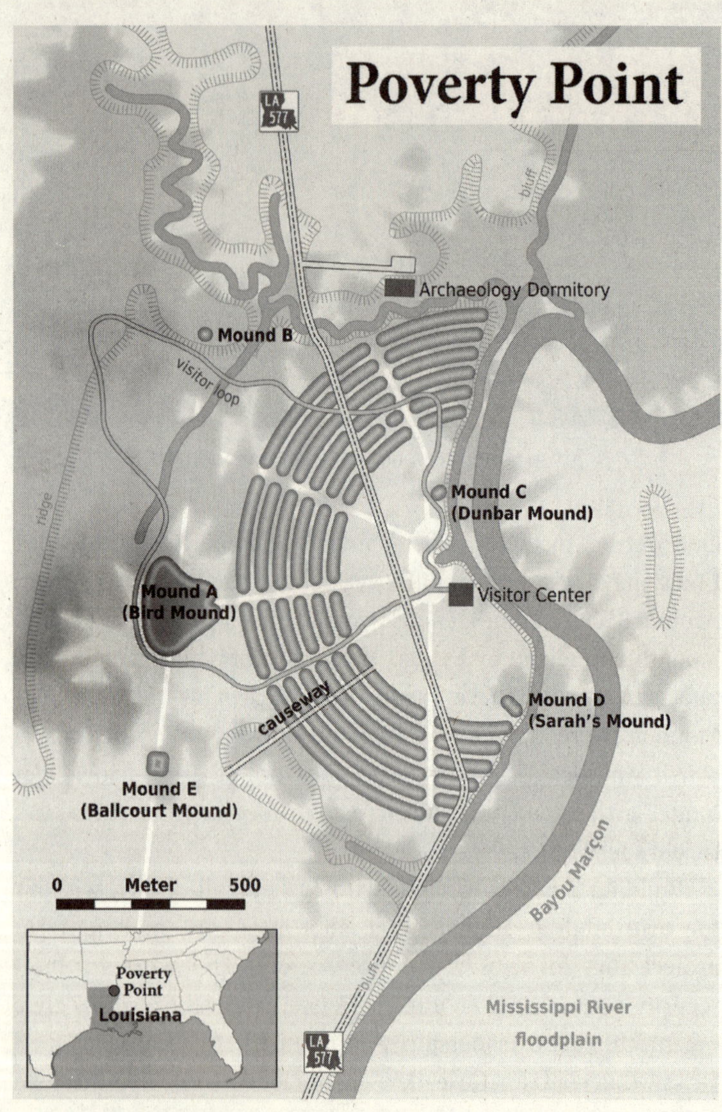

A map of the mounds at Poverty Point, Louisiana.

After the Ouachita, there is a millennia-long hiatus before mounds appear at Poverty Point, Louisiana.

Poverty Point, located 55 km from Ouachita, features earthen ridges and mounds erected between 1700 BCE and 1100 BCE. The construction resembles an amphitheater, with six concentric C-shaped ridges, each 5 feet tall. The ends of the widest ridge are 3,950 feet apart, and it wasn't until the 1950s that archaeologists discovered they were structures, thanks to aerial photography.

Criel Mound built by the Adena culture.

The subsequent evidence of mound-building appears 700 years later in the Ohio Valley, where the Adena culture flourished between 800 BCE and 100 BCE. The Adena mounds served as tombs, much like the *kurgans* of the Eurasian Steppes, and archaeologists found grave goods such as copper beads, bracelets, stone tablets, textiles, and stone tobacco pipes.

Agriculture flourished across America during the Adena period, spurring a cultural expansion that extended from the Midwest into Indiana and Kentucky, and to the east as far as Vermont. Initially considered a conquest, archaeologists now believe that the Adena people influenced other Indigenous communities through trade and cultural exchange.

Following the demise of the Adena culture, the Hopewell culture, also centered in Ohio, emerged as America's next prominent mound-building civilization.

Hopewell Mounds at the Hopewell Culture National Historical Park.

Hopewell may have been a later stage of the Adena culture, thriving between 100 BCE and 400 CE. The culture, named after the farmer on whose land the first site was unearthed, was one of North America's most prominent pre-Columbian civilizations. At its greatest extent, it stretched from the northern borders of Lake Ontario to the Crystal River, Florida, in the south.

The Hopewell culture was not a uniform tradition, but instead included diverse regional expressions. During the Hopewellian era, seashells from the Gulf of Mexico, shark teeth from Chesapeake Bay, and obsidian from Yellowstone were found in the American Midwest. In exchange for pottery, bows, and arrows, the Hopewellians traded their ceramics across the country.

The Hopewell culture's most notable characteristic was the construction of differently shaped earthwork mounds, with squares, rectangles, and circles being the most popular. The Hopewell Culture National Historical Park contains 23 mounds. Inside each mound is a charnel house[4] containing the deceased's remains. After someone died, Hopewellians cremated the body, torched the charnel house, and then constructed a mound over it.

Artifacts found in the mounds include copper figurines, mica, projectile points, tobacco pipes, and shells, which most likely belonged to the buried person.

During the Hopewell period, a crystallization of social hierarchies that originated during the Adena culture is evident. Some academics argue that a hereditary elite class evolved at Hopewell, dominating society and driving large-scale construction projects. According to author Charles Mann, the Hopewellian religion and the shamans associated with it played a vital role in attracting audiences and explaining where the gods wanted their mounds to be raised.

Mound-building was a joyous occasion that brought the community together. The elaborate procedures for decorating the tombs of the dead and creating complicated geometric designs for mounds necessitated a tremendous commitment

4 Charnel houses in pre-Columbian America stored bodies, like a crypt, but were large and offered room for mortuary services, such as cremation and removal of flesh before burial.

of time and resources, overseen by charismatic leaders. Mann proposes that the religious expressions of the Hopewellians spread to other parts of the country. Like Christianity, the new converts had a unique interpretation of the religion, differing from the beliefs of the original faith.

The spread of the Hopewellian religion, driven by an elite class, provided the necessary momentum, eventually laying the foundation for Cahokia's rise.

THE BIG BANG AND RISE OF CAHOKIA

A map of Mississipian and their allied cultures. Cahokia was a part of the Middle Mississipian culture.

St. Louis sits at the confluence of the Missouri and Mississippi Rivers. The area is a floodplain blessed with abundant natural resources, known as the American Bottom. The river system is ideal for the movement of people and goods.

Around 600 CE, several small agricultural settlements arose in the American Bottom. These communities supplemented their diet with hunting, fishing, and foraging. These groups were fairly insular, and there was little interaction among them.

Around 900 CE, maize was introduced into the region from Eastern America. A single maize kernel produces many seeds, which allows the farmer to grow enough corn to feed a family. On a large scale, maize production can sustain a city's food supply. The fertile land allowed the cultivation of maize, squash, gourds, and wild beans. Domesticated beans would not be grown before 1250 CE. Maize, squash, and beans are known as the "three sisters" of Indigenous agriculture and remain staples among the First Nations of North America.

By the tenth and early eleventh centuries CE, a few thousand people lived in small villages within a 6,500 square km area in the American Bottom. They grew crops during the summer and stored them for winter. The harvesting season sparked religious festivities. Neighboring communities gathered together to share common resources, resolve territorial disputes, and mourn the passing of village elders. The largest of the villages, which had a population of more than a thousand people by the beginning of eleventh century CE, was "Old Cahokia." Archaeologists debate whether this village was the site of a government or a ceremonial center for other neighboring communities.

Then, something unique happened in 1050 CE.

A new societal order emerged, with Cahokia growing from a few thousand individuals to a city of over 10,000 people in just a few decades. Archaeologist Timothy R. Pauketat of the University of Illinois refers to this sudden, unexplained population growth and the formation of a megapolis in the American Bottom as the "Big Bang of Cahokia."

What triggered this tumultuous transformation? Unfortunately, we can only speculate.

Perhaps a charismatic leader united the community, motivated by a desire to construct a flourishing metropolis. Possibly, people undertook large building projects because food was plentiful. A massive surplus of food freed people to undertake monumental construction. According to Pauketat, the supernova SN 1054, recorded in sources worldwide in 1054 CE, was interpreted by Cahokia's leadership as a divine cosmic sign, justifying the formation of a powerful central authority to oversee large-scale construction. The supernova can still be seen with a telescope, and, in the past, it was visible during the daytime.

Although the causes for the abrupt change will forever remain unknown, we know that Old Cahokia was abandoned and ultimately destroyed. In its stead, North America's largest city arose, complete with enormous mounds, plazas, and causeways.

In addition to Cahokia's mounds, the Big Bang created the St. Louis Mounds across the Mississippi and the East St. Louis Mound complex, the second biggest after Cahokia.

As a result of the Big Bang, Cahokia experienced a tremendous migration of people who were enamored with the new world order. The rapid arrival of new migrants is evident in the pottery found in Cahokia. The early pottery reflects styles from the Coles Creek culture (700 CE–1250 CE) in current Louisiana and the Plum Bayou culture (600 CE–1000 CE) in northern Arkansas. The diverse burial traditions found at Cahokia also support the theory that people of different backgrounds settled in the burgeoning metropolis. To study human migration, scientists examine strontium isotopes in bones and teeth. Strontium is an element that occurs naturally in rocks, soil, and water, and has several isotopes. Strontium enters our bodies through food and water, and, like calcium, it lodges in our teeth and bones. The strontium ratio varies by location, and the region's geology can influence the results. Cahokia inhabitants had 20–30 percent non-local strontium signatures. Though the strontium ratio doesn't tell us where they came from, we can confirm they were migrants to the burgeoning city. Cahokia was a true cosmopolitan metropolis, characterized by diverse ethnicities, cultures, and languages.

Why were so many people coming from all over America to Cahokia? What attracted them to this grand metropolis?

We have explored how increased food security, trade, and transportation may have contributed to the emergence of Cahokia's Big Bang. Other well-connected, fertile regions in America existed, but there was only one city on the banks of the Mississippi.

Scholars believe that the transition in Cahokia was as much a cultural and political movement as it was an economic one. The Cahokian polity differed from previous Indigenous cultures. Pauketat describes it as a "political vortex" that sucked people in. The culture was highly stratified, with a chiefdom centered

Ceramic beaker jar depicting the Woodhenge, found at Cahokia.

in Cahokia, the capital of a proto-state known by scholars as the Ramey state.

One of the city's distinguishing features was the Ramey incised pottery, unique to the new Cahokian polity. Shell tempering, or incorporating riverine or marine materials, such as mussels, into the clay paste, gave the pottery a distinct finish. It was in high demand as a commodity across America. These pots featured several cosmograms, which are flat geometric figures that represent cosmology. These pots served domestic and ritual purposes. Religion, lucrative commerce, and an organized polity were not the only attractions of Cahokia.

Illustration of a Mississippian Cahokian player.

Cahokia was home to a high-stakes, popular sport called chunkey, reminiscent of the gladiatorial contests at the Colosseum, minus the spectacle of death witnessed in ancient Rome.

Chunkey first appeared in the early stages of the Mississippian culture[5] around approximately 600 CE. The sport involved sliding polished discs, or chunkey stones, on a playing field. The player then tried to throw giant spears, several of which were larger than he was, as close to the chunkey stone as possible. The game drew large crowds, who cheered on their favorite players. It frequently

Clay figurine of a chunkey player found at Cahokia.

---

5 Cahokia was a part of the Mississippian culture, a widespread pre-Columbian culture spread across southeast and Midwest of the United States and thrived from 700 CE to 1500 CE. Chunkey appears before the Mississippian culture peaked, around 600 CE.

entailed gambling, with some players wagering everything they owned. Those who lost sometimes committed suicide after being unable to repay their debts.

Much like the gladiator games of ancient Rome, the Cahokian elite used chunkey to control the masses. Different game versions spread across the Great Plains and into the South. Pauketat suggests that emissaries from Cahokia visited tribes across the country with chunkey stones in one hand and war clubs in the other. Combining the threat of violence with sporting diplomacy, these ambassadors enforced a region-wide peace, known as Pax Cahokiana.

The long-lasting effects of chunkey among the Indigenous people were seen centuries after the collapse of Cahokia. The game continued to be popular among Native Americans well after European contact, with Euro-Americans mentioning chunkey games among the Choctaw, Muscogee, Chickasaw, and Mandan tribes. Chunkey served as a vital regional pacifier, but the main attraction of Cahokia was its gigantic mounds.

THE ENIGMATIC MOUNDS OF CAHOKIA

In 1100 CE, a massive mound of dirt, over 100 feet high, would greet visitors to Cahokia. The top of the mound, known as the Monks Mound, was flat, like a platform, and may have housed a powerful chieftain or priest. It was the largest structure ever created in the pre-Columbian United States.

I am sure you are wondering why "Monks Mound." When Brackenridge first visited Cahokia, he observed a group of Trappist monks living on the mound. They took advantage of the elevated platform and started a garden. Hence, Brackenridge termed the structure the "Monks Mound."

Work started on the mound around 950 CE, a century before Cahokia's rise, and was completed between 1100 CE and 1150 CE.

Present-day view of Monks Mound.

The structure is built on a slab that is 900 feet long, 650 feet wide, and more than 20 feet tall. The foundation covers 13.1 acres, nearly the size of the Great Pyramid of Giza (13 acres) and larger than the Pyramid of the Sun in Teotihuacán, Mexico. Monks Mound is a platform mound with four terraces.

The Cahokians built three types of mounds: platform, conical, and ridgetop. Platform mounds had flat tops with important buildings on their terraces. Conical mounds may have served as burials for the city's elite, as seen in earlier cultures such as the Hopewell. Ridgetop mounds were unique to Cahokia and featured a linear ridgetop. Their purpose is unclear, but some, such as Mound 72, contained multiple burials.

Each terrace of Monks Mound would have had buildings on top, most likely for ritual purposes. The structure was built by hauling heaps of earth in baskets. The builders chose specific soils and clays, serving both practical and aesthetic purposes.

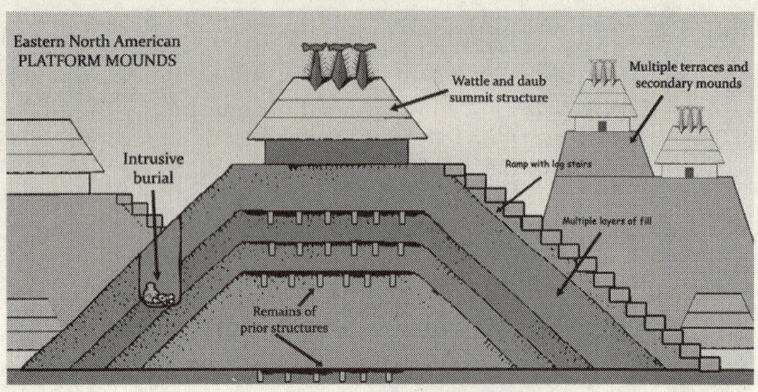

Platform-style multi-layered mound.

The foundation slab was kept wet but not overly damp. The builders alternated layers of sand and clay. Sand served as a moisture-retaining safeguard for the slab, while clay allowed rainwater to run off the mound's surface quickly. The mound's volume was 26 million cubic feet (740,000 cubic meters approximately), so you can visualize the massive amount of earth used to build the construction. In front of the Monks Mound lies a massive 59-acre plaza. The city's planners leveled and smoothed the area with sand. The plaza hosted public events, including ceremonies of faith, feasts, and chunkey contests.

The Cahokian aristocracy ruled from the tops of the mounds, which provided them with a panoramic view of the city and its surroundings, enabling them to oversee construction projects and organize festivities.

The next largest mound at Cahokia, the Powell Mound, suffered a tragedy. The mound was a ridgetop mound and remained in place until December 1930. The State of Illinois was unable to reach a financial agreement with the Powell family, on whose property the mound was located. Sadly, the structure had to be removed, resulting in a colossal loss of understanding of Cahokia's history.

Though the loss of Powell Mound is irreplaceable, in the 1950s, archaeologist Gregory Perino uncovered Mound 34, another vital mound in Cahokia's history. This platform mound was noteworthy because it housed a big copper workshop, the only one found in Cahokia.

Copper was imported from the Great Lakes region[6] to make ritual objects or diplomatic gifts for neighboring Mississippian settlements. Mound 34 contained a variety of copper nuggets, copper fragments, and stone tools used to work with copper. The Mississippian copper plates with avian designs are the most remarkable items discovered.

In addition to copper items, Mississippian pottery, shell beads, a perforated shark tooth necklace, serrated flint arrowheads, and shell cups were uncovered.

Mississippian copper plate.

6 The area around Lakes Superior, Huron, Erie, Michigan, and Ontario was home to the Old Copper Complex (between 6500 BCE and 1000 BCE), and has some of the earliest known copper tools. Copper manufacturing continued well into the Cahokian era.

Monks Mound and Mound 34 provide essential insights regarding Cahokia's urban design and economy, but Mound 72 is perhaps the most significant archaeological discovery. It contains the graves of hundreds of people, revealing vital clues about the Cahokian society.

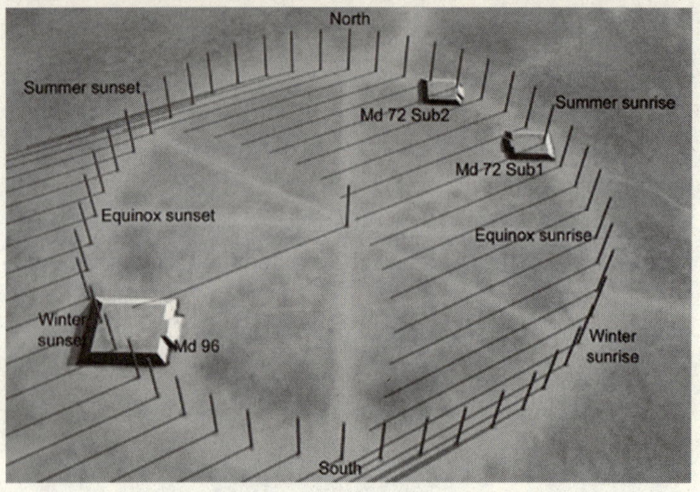

Woodhenge at Cahokia with Mound 72.

Mound 72, situated approximately 850 m south of Monks Mound, was part of Woodhenge, a ceremonial circular complex featuring 48 wooden pillars. The Woodhenge was constructed using red cedarwood poles placed strategically to represent the summer and winter solstices, as well as the spring and autumn equinoxes.

Mound 72 is one of six ridgetop mounds located in Cahokia. One explanation for the large number of graves found at Mound 72 is its intimate relationship with astronomy and religion.

Perhaps the most well-known burial was a man buried with more than 20,000 shell beads from the Gulf Coast. The beads were placed in the shape of a thunderbird or falcon and accompanied by copper objects, large stones, and arrowheads. The interment is called the "Birdman Burial" or "Beaded Burial."

Birdman tablet found at Cahokia.

The falcon warrior or birdman was a popular concept in Mississippian culture, and a tablet with a human-falcon figure was discovered in Cahokia. A woman, likely his wife or another prominent female figure from the city, was buried directly below the "birdman," and the burial was associated with the society's elite.

Excavations at Mound 72 revealed over 260 human skeletons. Archaeologists discovered the bodies of 53 young women aged 15 to 30 who had been strangled and buried neatly organized in rows in a pit adjacent to the grave of four men who were missing their hands. A human sacrifice of this scale was unprecedented in ancient America, north of Mexico. The women were malnourished, and strontium analysis revealed many of them were not local. We don't know if they were slaves, captives, or offered for sacrifice as tribute from adjacent populations, but the massacre displays the elite's control over the locals.

Were people willing to accept such a harsh exhibition of power? Building a metropolis on the magnitude of Cahokia, hosting festivals, chunkey contests, and large-scale human sacrifice may not have been acceptable to some of the city's and surrounding populations.

Another burial at Mound 72 tells us that 39 men and women were brutally murdered before being dumped in a pit. Their skulls and jawbones showed signs of fractures; some individuals were decapitated, while others were buried alive. Did the Cahokian elite ruthlessly punish a rebel group? Was it an invading tribe whose warriors were captured and killed? Was the society that built such magnificent mounds and carved intricate copper plates beginning to show signs of discord?

THE FALL OF CAHOKIA

Cahokia's collapse was as dramatic as its rise. Within 150 years of becoming North America's largest city and rivaling London and Paris in population, Cahokia experienced a severe decline. Perhaps the most ironic factor in Cahokia's population collapse

An artist's reconstruction of Cahokia at its peak.

was the very factor that led to its rise: maize. With the need to feed a massive population, residents began clearing forests and vegetation for more farmland. As the city continued to expand, workers cut down the trees and used them to produce timber without replanting. With the tree cover gone, heavy rains lashed the Mississippi Valley during the summer and seeped into the rivers and their tributaries rapidly, resulting in severe flooding. Around 1200 CE, massive floods destroyed the maize fields, cutting off people's access to their primary food source.

More recent research has indicated that the Cahokians fought floods by creating dikes, channels, and levees that protected most of the city, especially the central district. Agriculture was divided between the highlands and lowlands to prevent crop destruction in the event of a flood. A 2021 paper found very little evidence of flooding caused by human activities.

Reconstruction of the palisade at Cahokia's central district.

The ruling authority may have been a part of the problem. As Cahokia grew, land from smaller settlements was encroached upon. One can imagine that not everyone was happy with the new world order, having to bow down to a powerful elite, sacrificing their freedom. Fear may have kept them in check. But some of the more daring souls may have challenged the central authority. Though we haven't found direct evidence of warfare at Cahokia, the central district was surrounded by a 3.2-km palisade with protective bastions and L-shaped gates at regular intervals. The construction of the palisade incurred massive economic costs due to the wood and labor required, and the city rebuilt the structure four times throughout its history. Archaeologists aren't sure what caused the palisade to collapse, but if we were to make an educated guess, it would be that some Mississippians were dissatisfied with the ruling class and revolted against them.

Repeated attacks by rebels on the city may have caused damage to the palisade.

Another piece of indirect evidence supporting the idea that society at Cahokia was becoming increasingly violent is the fire that destroyed the town that once stood at the nearby East St. Louis site. The fire broke out around the same time when Cahokia's residents reinforced their defenses with palisades. However, we should keep in mind that at East St. Louis, we don't know what was behind the fire, as archaeologists have not found any evidence of warfare. But the coincidence is intriguing and raises the possibility of rising conflict. People may have lost faith in the political system that once attracted them to the city.

Diseases might have been another factor in the population drop. As the city grew, sanitation became a massive concern. Pellagra, a condition that arises from a deficiency of vitamin B3 and is common among societies with a maize-intensive diet, such as Cahokia, could have led to a less healthy populace. However, there is no conclusive evidence connecting nutritional deficiencies to a societal collapse.

By 1250 CE, Cahokia had been severely depopulated, with only 4,500 living in the city, down from a high of possibly 20,000 a century earlier.

The moundbuilders are still deeply ingrained in the ancestral psyches of many modern-day Native American tribes, including the Apalachee, Caddo, Cherokee, Chickasaw, Choctaw, Creek, Houma, Kansa, Missouri, Mobilian, Natchez, Osage, Quapaw, Seminole, Yamasee, and Yuchi.

Cahokia marked the pinnacle of America's mound-building tradition. The Cahokians produced unparalleled engineering feats, had extensive trade networks, made accurate predictions of the sun's and moon's movements, and were able to support North America's greatest pre-Columbian population center.

Though the metropolis was forgotten and overlooked until recently, today, we are a step closer to understanding the people who built this enormous city, which was not surpassed until the expansion of Philadelphia in the late eighteenth century.

Section 4

Forgotten Empires

14

Empire Building 101: The Assyrians

WHAT COMES TO MIND WHEN YOU THINK OF AN EMPIRE? IS IT the Roman Empire, with its impressive road network? Maybe you imagine the Mongol Empire, which spanned from Beijing

The lamassu, or the winged bull-man, is one of the monumental symbols of the Assyrian Empire.

in the east to Hungary in the west. What about the British Empire, driven by a vast railroad system? These empires pushed the boundaries of human progress while wreaking havoc on their enemies.

What was the secret to their success? Was it effective management? Superior military technology?

Empire-building is a paradox. How did the Mongols, nomads without formal education, defeat great civilizations such as China, Persia, and the Kyivan Rus? How did merchants from the tiny British Isles come to rule over a quarter of the world's population?

To answer these questions, we must travel back in time to a city in northern Iraq. The once-magnificent metropolis of Assur is now in ruins, but during antiquity it was the birthplace of the first true global empire, the Assyrian Empire. At its peak, the Assyrian domains included modern Iraq, Iran, Israel, Palestine, Syria, Lebanon, parts of Türkiye, and Egypt. The Assyrian Empire laid the blueprint for future world empires. Let us examine how this transcontinental power functioned to understand why small groups of people successfully govern vast territories and populations.

ASSYRIANS: THE ORIGINS

"Assyrian" comes from Assur, also known as Ashur. The city took its name from the warlike deity Ashur, the chief god of the Assyrian people. The Sumerians, who hailed from Southern Mesopotamia, occupied Assur during the Early Dynastic period (2900 BCE to 2350 BCE). The city became part of the Akkadian Empire, which existed from 2334 BCE to 2134 BCE, under Sargon of Akkad. Sargon may not have been his birth name; we don't know what it was. Sargon is the Romanized form of *Sharru-kin*,

A relief from the Assyrian capital of Nimrud showing the god Ashur. Assyrians derive their name from Ashur.

or "rightful king," the title used by the founder of the Akkadian Empire. The empire was centered in the city of Akkad in southern Mesopotamia. The Assyrians regarded Sargon as their direct ancestor.

During the early period of Assyrian history, Assur became a popular trading center for the Bronze Age's most valuable resource, tin. Assyrian history is classified into three eras. The Old Assyrian period is the first period of Assyrian history, spanning from 2025 BCE to 1364 BCE. The Middle Assyrian period lasted from 1363 BCE to 912 BCE. The Neo-Assyrian era (911 BCE to 609 BCE) is the period of Assyrian history when the empire reached its peak. In popular discussions, "Assyrian Empire" refers to the Neo-Assyrian Empire.

Under the rule of Shamshi-Adad I (reign 1808 BCE to 1776 BCE), Assur became a powerful city. He extended the city's influence beyond its borders. Assyrian merchants established trading colonies in Anatolia, and their risk-taking endeavors significantly contributed to Assyria's expansion across northern Mesopotamia. The burgeoning regional trade catalyzed Assur's transformation into a prosperous metropolis.

Unfortunately, in the early fourteenth century BCE, the Assyrians succumbed to a Mitanni[1] invasion. Assur was sacked, its temples destroyed, and its wealth looted. After the humiliating defeat by the Mitanni, the Assyrians learned the hard way that they needed a strong army. The honor and survival of the people of Assur depended on it.

Tablet from the reign of Ashur-uballit , who was responsible for the rise of the Assyrian Empire.

1 Refer to Chapters 7, 8, and 9 for more details about the Mitanni Kingdom.

In 1363 BCE, Ashur-uballit, a high priest of the temple of Assur, seized power, liberating the Assyrians from Mitanni's domination. He attacked and defeated the Mitanni ruler Shuttarna III. Ashur-uballit also interfered in Babylon's internal affairs and made direct contact with the pharaohs of Egypt. The Babylonians, angered by the decision to bypass them and send official communication to Egypt, declared war on Assyria. The Assyrian ruler defeated Babylon and installed a puppet, Kurigalzu II, on the Babylonian throne.

Assyria meant business. No longer would they be vassals of another power.

Since Shamshi-Adad, Ashur-uballit was the first Assyrian to adopt the title *Sar*, which means king. His coronation marked a pivotal moment in Assyrian history. Near Eastern kingdoms, such as Egypt and the Hittites, soon regarded Assyria as equals. Due to Ashur-uballit's policy of military expansion, Assyria expanded from a city-state to a regional power. The sword was only half the equation; the Assyrians spread their influence through diplomacy, alliances, and ruthless population transfer.

BUILDING AN EMPIRE: THE CONQUEST

Ashur-uballit conducted military expeditions against the tribes and kingdoms that had previously defeated the Assyrians. He also valued alliances with regional powers. Despite initial success, he didn't want to be drawn into a protracted war with the Babylonians. To secure long-term peace, Ashur-uballit married his daughter to the king of Babylon.

During Shalmaneser I's reign (1273 BCE to 1244 BCE), the Assyrians avenged their humiliation at the hands of Mitanni by conquering them and destroying the Mitanni capital, Washukanni.

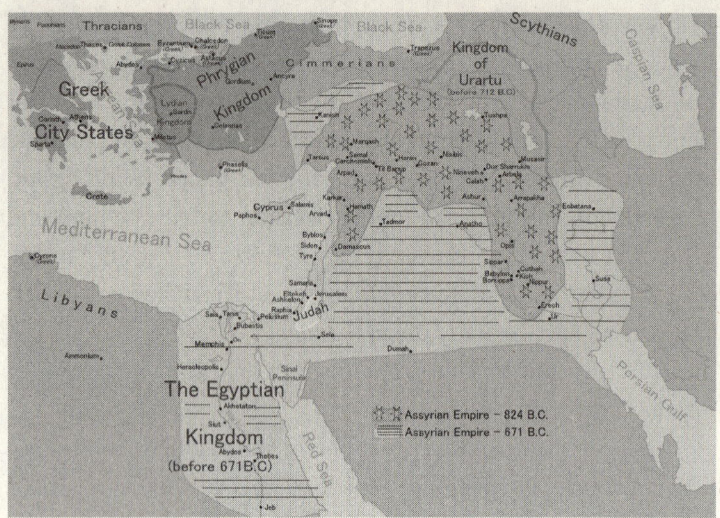

The Assyrian Empire at its peak, during the rule of Esarhaddon, making it the largest empire of its era.

Military conquest and diplomacy remained key strategies for future Assyrian leaders. The governors were required to have the resources to feed an army. They expected subjugated kingdoms to supply soldiers, and refusing to do so was seen as an act of rebellion.

Many of the world's later major empires, such as the Achaemenid Empire and the Roman Empire, relied heavily on the support of foreign troops from the conquered territories. Likewise, the Mongols depended on Muslims for siege engineering and the Chinese for expertise in gunpowder.

As the Assyrian Empire expanded, it became clear that relying solely on outsiders during times of conflict was a concern. Assembling soldiers required time. The delay often gave rebels a head start in executing their plans.

Emperor Tiglath-Pileser III (745 BCE to 727 BCE) established a full-time standing army, the first in Assyria's history. By the Late Bronze Age, professional armies had become the norm in the Near East. However, Assyria still maintained a seasonal army assembled using conscripts during the summer. Tiglath-Pileser replaced the draftees with highly trained and disciplined soldiers always ready for war. This new centralized army under the king's command was known as "kiṣir šarri" (or the king's unit). One of his significant additions to the army was the introduction of siege engines, which changed the course of warfare as the Assyrians stormed city after city in the Fertile Crescent with devastating effect.

An Assyrian siege engine, showing archers and a battering ram, dated 850 BCE.

The Assyrians introduced a complex system of roads to facilitate the rapid movement of their military and curb revolt. Communication, transportation, and army movement were all carried out via designated routes.

Assyrians were brilliant military innovators. They transported their war chariots across the Euphrates and the Tigris on inflated sheepskin.

The Assyrians understood that brute force was not the only way to win wars. Propaganda and psychological warfare were crucial. Assyrian monarchs used cruel methods of torture and execution to attain their military goals and instill terror in their foes. In a terrifying description, Emperor Ashurnasirpal II (883 BCE–859 BCE) was the first to leave detailed accounts of brutally torturing enemies. After conquering a city during his campaign against the Kingdom of Aram (in modern Syria), he inflicted atrocities on the city's defenders.

Ashurnasirpal says:

> "I flayed as many nobles as had rebelled against me (and) draped their skins over the pile (of corpses); some I spread out within the pile, some I erected on stakes upon the pile. I flayed many right through my land (and) draped their skins over the walls."

Later, Assyrian rulers stereotyped and repeated such depictions, suggesting their prime purpose was propaganda. Two centuries later, we find a similar account in Ashurbanipal's engravings, which uses almost the same language as Ashurnasirpal, but the victims of the emperor's wrath are different.

Brutal executions were the norm for the era. What was special about the Assyrians? Like the Egyptians, the Assyrians kept meticulous records of their military exploits, documenting every gruesome detail of their campaigns. The records served as propaganda.

Propaganda was crucial for later empires. During the Mongol campaigns, Chinggis Khan imported massive amounts of paper from China and Korea to feed his enemy scribes. The writers penned exaggerated images of the conqueror and the Mongol destruction of cities across Persia, Central Asia, and China.

Because of Chinggis's fearsome depictions, cities surrendered without a fight.

Tiglath-Pileser III introduced a widespread deportation strategy. He relocated conquered people to other parts of the empire. Uprooting people from their place of birth severed loyalties and family bonds and reduced the chances of revolts. Future Assyrian rulers continued to deport and relocate people throughout the empire. Migrants from Assyria colonized newly conquered lands, introducing new cultural practices and establishing settlements.

Almost every empire in world history, following the Assyrians, believed in colonization and mass deportations as a means to maintain peace, a cruel yet effective strategy. However, given the size of the conquered people, deporting and executing everyone wasn't possible. Keeping their subjects happy was as vital to the Assyrians as dominating them militarily.

LEGITIMIZING RULE PART 1: THE SPREAD OF KNOWLEDGE

Tablets from Ashurbanipal's Library, now displayed at the British Museum.

Every great empire has profited from keeping its people happy, especially the conquered. For the Assyrians, the well-being of their subjects was crucial in preventing revolts and ensuring a smooth revenue collection.

The Assyrians were brutal conquerors but also great seekers of knowledge. They believed the imperial strategy would be incomplete without an emphasis on education. We would be hard-pressed to find a civilization in the ancient Near East that promoted scholarship as much as the Assyrians.

Mesopotamia had a long history of maintaining tax documents and literary works in temples. Later, the storage of these texts shifted to libraries. Archaeologists found the oldest collection of documents, dated between 2500 BCE and 2250 BCE, in Ebla, Syria. The collection, known as the Ebla tablets, consisted of 1,800 whole clay tablets and 4,700 smaller, damaged fragments. Hattusa, the Hittite capital, was home to the world's first organized library. Located in Türkiye, the library had over 25,000 Hittite texts. Today, this collection is known as the Bogazkoy Archive.

The manuscripts included royal orders, laws, religious edicts, and mythological stories. Most texts were written in Hittite, but a few tablets were in Hurrian and Akkadian. The Library of Hattusa would have been the world's largest in the Late Bronze Age (1550 BCE–1200 BCE). Assyrians built on the tradition of collecting knowledge prevalent in the Near East.

A library's primary purpose was to store records and holy books. Today, we view a sacred book from a spiritual perspective, but in ancient times, they were more than just spiritual guides. In Mesopotamian society, divinity played a key role. Diviners convinced rulers and the people that they foretold the future. Everyone saw diviners as knowledgeable individuals who read the stars and understood patterns of human behavior. They were like astrologers but more influential. Divinity was more than a mystical exercise. The ancients taught it as a subject, like chemistry or mathematics. By the end of the third millennium BCE, divine scriptures in Sumerian and Akkadian languages were widely available in Mesopotamia. These writings had the value of a modern guidebook in any discipline.

Rulers used holy scriptures to justify their authority and gain people's trust. The king often represented a god, typically the city's deity. People believed that he was in power because the gods favored him.

The Assyrians ruled over diverse peoples. They conquered Mesopotamia, parts of neighboring Elam in Iran, the Levant and Egypt. When faced with rebellions, the Assyrians sought divine intervention. One way to do so was by keeping diviners and religious scriptures close to them.

Sargon II (722 BCE–705 BCE) may have built the empire's first library by collecting religious texts in his short-lived capital of Dur Sharrukin. His grandson Esarhaddon took Sargon's quest for knowledge to a whole new level. Scribes and religious leaders had to report to the scholars whom the king had chosen in Nineveh, the new Assyrian capital. It wasn't enough for Esarhaddon to collect texts. The reports had to be read to him daily by a trusted individual in his private gardens. From a correspondence between Ashurbanipal, Esarhaddon's son, and an Assyrian official, we learn about the custom of reading reports to the emperor.

Ashurbanipal expanded on his father's intellectual base. But unlike Esarhaddon, Ashurbanipal had a significant advantage. He was literate. Only a few people could read and write in ancient times, which didn't always include royalty. Esarhaddon educated his children, ensuring they were knowledgeable in topics such as governance, literature, magic, and divination.

The Assyrians sacked Babylon in 689 BCE, during the reign of King Sennacherib (Ashurbanipal's grandfather). The destruction of southern Mesopotamia's most influential city created an atmosphere of distrust between the Babylonians and the Assyrians. Though Esarhaddon rebuilt the Temple of Babylon and spent a fortune renovating the city, its priests and scholars were wary of the Assyrians. Spiteful Babylonian intellectuals deliberately misinterpreted holy texts. Esarhaddon knew the Babylonians were duping him, but he didn't know how to identify the truth because he was illiterate. To avoid being deceived, he taught his children, including his heir Ashurbanipal, to read and write.

When Ashurbanipal became king in 668 BCE, he didn't hesitate to take valuable texts by any means necessary. Esarhaddon was careful in how he dealt with his subjects. He knew the Babylonians had the most extensive collection of books and valued them dearly, so he requested copies rather than the originals. However, Ashurbanipal was less diplomatic. In a letter to Shadunu, possibly an Assyrian bureaucrat, Ashurbanipal commands that he wants all rare tablets and documents from the cities of southern Mesopotamia for his library in Nineveh. Withholding any manuscript meant dire consequences. Because he was well-read, Ashurbanipal could interpret religious writings without depending on diviners.

The astrologers and scribes could not mislead him. His library had over 30,000 tablets, making it the largest in the ancient world before the Library of Alexandria. We can group the library's collection into two types of texts.

The first category was legal and administrative documents. The second category comprised literary works, holy texts, medicinal, mathematical, and mythological works. *The Epic of Gilgamesh* is the best-known book in this group.

The Epic of Gilgamesh tells the story of Gilgamesh, the legendary king of Uruk. It revolves around his friendship with Enkidu, a part-animal, part-human creation whom the gods send to control Gilgamesh. The story inspired many popular tales and influenced later literary works, such as the Bible and the Iliad.

The Epic of Gilgamesh is the first ancient work to mention the Great Flood, a story later recounted in the Bible.

Most of the texts in the library were in Akkadian, a broad term for both the Babylonian and Assyrian languages. Assyrian librarians organized books in a systematic way resembling modern libraries. They categorized the collection into distinct sections for law, theology, astronomy, geography, and history, ensuring easier access to knowledge.

In 612 BCE, the Medes and Scythians sacked and destroyed Nineveh. A fire caused colossal damage to the library and burned it to the ground. However, the flames baked the clay tablets, preserving them forever.

The Assyrians weren't just book collectors; they also put their knowledge to practical use, as seen in their engineering marvels. I am sure you are familiar with the famous Hanging Gardens of Babylon, one of the Seven Wonders of the Ancient World. But did you know they were not in Babylon, but rather Nineveh?

LEGITIMIZING RULE PART 2: ENGINEERING MARVELS

Ashurbanipal and his wife in the Hanging Gardens.

Ancient sources claim that Nebuchadnezzar II, ruler of the Neo-Babylonian Empire (605 BCE–562 BCE), constructed the gardens.

However, Nebuchadnezzar, who left extensive records of his rule, does not mention building a world-class garden. Don't you think this is strange? Why would a king who was meticulous in documenting his reign omit such a remarkable engineering feat? The matter gets murkier because none of the Babylonian texts mentions a gigantic garden.

Archaeologists tried to solve the mystery of the missing Hanging Gardens of Babylon. Surprisingly, they found no evidence of the gardens described in the literature in the city of Babylon (near present-day Al-Hillah, Iraq).

Berossus, a Babylonian high priest of the deity Marduk, was the first to mention the Hanging Gardens in 290 BCE. Later, Roman historians such as Josephus, Quintus Rufus, and Strabo cite Berossus as the primary source of information about the gardens. Berossus claims Nebuchadnezzar built the gardens for his queen Amytis.

He describes the garden as a tiered square building with solid brick walls. The gardens featured waterfalls and imported exotic trees, including cedar, cypress, ebony, walnut, pine, willow, and rosewood, blooming with flowers and fruits such as quince, pomegranate, and plum.

Strabo says sophisticated screws transported water from the Euphrates to the gardens for watering the plants. The Babylonian kings gathered exotic creatures and kept them in the palace gardens.

Many centuries after Nebuchadnezzar's reign, authors who had no connection to the city penned the tales of Babylon's gardens. They had little knowledge of horticulture or engineering. There are questions about whether they had access to firsthand accounts.

Archaeological evidence uncovered along the Euphrates's banks does not support the existence of a spectacular multi-level garden with terraces watered by a complicated irrigation system.

Did the Greek and Roman authors create a fantasy version of an ideal Mesopotamian garden?

On the outskirts of Mosul, present-day Iraq, lies Nineveh, where we find evidence of the Hanging Gardens. The Assyrians had a long tradition of collecting exotic animals and creating elaborate gardens. In Nineveh, a magnificent palace garden was built by Sennacherib.

The first evidence of a magnificent garden in Assyria comes from Sargon II's (Sennacherib's father) reign, who built a gorgeous estate at Dur Sharrukin. Against the backdrop of a mountain, the garden also served as a hunting place for the royals. There was a lake for boating, although it is unclear if it was within or beyond the city walls.

Sennacherib continued his father's legacy by meticulously documenting the splendour of his new garden at Nineveh. He mentions using screws to transport water to the plants on the artificially raised slopes of the garden.

They were an early version of the Archimedes screw used in the Greco-Roman world to transfer water from a lower level to a higher level. Though we don't have exact details about how these screws worked, we can make an educated guess based on the functioning of the Archimedes screw.

Sennacherib says that his gardens were a "wonder for all people." His deployment of screws and advanced water engineering techniques must have made the garden famous in the ancient world. Sennacherib's grandson, Ashurbanipal, is depicted dining in this garden with his wife.

But why aren't the Assyrians credited with building the Hanging Gardens, and why "Babylon" rather than "Nineveh"?

There might be several reasons why ancient writers misidentified the real Hanging Gardens of Nineveh with a supposed one in Babylon. Most of them, like Roman authors, relied on the works of Greek historians. The Greeks relied on

Berossus, a Babylonian source. Because the Babylonians were bitter towards the Assyrians after the sack of Babylon, they weren't inclined to give their conquerors the due credit for building the gardens.

Classical texts often confuse the cities of Babylon and Nineveh. Quintus Curtius Rufus was the first Roman writer to identify an Assyrian king as the builder of the Hanging Gardens, but he mentions that the gardens were in Babylon. Another source of confusion might be the Hebrew Bible's mistaken identification of King Sennacherib with Nebuchadnezzar.

Both Sennacherib and Nebuchadnezzar sacked Jerusalem and burned it to the ground, so ancient Jewish sources frequently had them mixed up. We can see this in the *Book of Judith*, which says that Nebuchadnezzar was the king of the Assyrians and ruled from Nineveh, though he was a Babylonian. Modern historians argue that biblical scholars may have misidentified Nebuchadnezzar with Sennacherib.

Why did so many ancient authors confuse Nineveh in northern Mesopotamia with Babylon, in the country's south? To understand this, we need to determine what "Babylon" means. It translates to "God's Gate." By naming the gates of Nineveh after the gods, Sennacherib suggested that he wanted his city to be referred to as Babylon as well. We can find another critical clue in Arabic sources on astronomy. The latitude of "Old Babylon" was used to determine the longest day of the year. This latitude does not pass through Babylon but through Nineveh. Hence, it is likely that when ancient authors mentioned Babylon in their writings, they were likely referring to Nineveh.

Royal gardens and intellectuals played a vital role in the Assyrian Empire. Knowledge and engineering marvels helped legitimize the rule of the Assyrian elite, but ordinary citizens also had to view their monarchs as benevolent benefactors to prevent revolts. How did the Assyrian reign help regular people?

An extensive irrigation network built by the Assyrians in northern Mesopotamia revolutionized regional water distribution. Drawing water from the Tigris was a bigger challenge than taking water from the Euphrates. Assyrian engineers used hydraulics, canals, waterways, and aqueducts to transport water and build a state-of-the-art irrigation system.

Northern Mesopotamia relied on aqueducts for water distribution. Later empires, such as the Romans, realized the importance of building aqueducts for their citizens. A sophisticated irrigation network reduced the chances of drought, making the farmers happy.

Assyria was one of the few ancient empires where we saw progress in the status of women over time. Although the society was patriarchal, there is much more to the stories of women from Assyria than we usually think of.

WOMEN AND THE EMPIRE

In Assyrian society, women were primarily expected to focus on their families, which can sometimes be an oversimplified perspective. Some women found ways to carve out vibrant and dynamic roles within the palace. Female singers, musicians, and artists were part of the royal household and valued for their talents. These women combined traditional family roles with the special responsibilities of court life.

Among the royal women, the king's mother was a key figure, sometimes overshadowing the queen in influence. However, the queen was not merely a figurehead; she actively managed the royal household and supervised the women of the palace. Additionally, she had control over a substantial portion of the palace economy, particularly in textile production, which generated wealth for the empire.

The seal of Hama, an Assyrian queen. The scorpion is visible on the left.

The queen had her seal, which featured an image of a scorpion, signifying her authority. This choice may seem strange, but it was fitting. The scorpion symbolized a fiercely protective mother, willing to defend her young at all costs, making it an ideal emblem for a queen. Her seal was as crucial as the king's in matters of the palace.

After King Esarhaddon's conquest of Egypt in 671 BCE, he relocated Egyptian families to central Assyria. Despite being outsiders, they adapted and integrated into Assyrian society, carving out their own spaces within it. Egyptian women, in particular, stood out. They were far more visible in public life than Assyrian women, often running businesses and appearing in legal records. Egyptian women owned property, signed contracts, and held positions that demonstrated their independence and influence.

The status and rights of women of other ethnicities reveal something fascinating about the Assyrians. While they were ruthless conquerors, they refrained from interfering in the personal lives or customs of the people under their rule. Egyptians living in Assyria were allowed to maintain their traditions, showing a surprising degree of tolerance in a fiercely militaristic society.

LEGACY

The Assyrian Empire thrived because it understood the value of long-distance communication. Its merchants used an impressive road network, enabling trade to flourish across vast distances. The Assyrians started as a trading community and carried that spirit forward, protecting property rights and supporting small business owners at a time when most states controlled everything. They showed that private ownership and economic freedom could coexist with imperial power.

Their logistical genius was just as remarkable. The Assyrians developed techniques for moving massive loads, such as timber and giant stones, over vast distances. The development of siege warfare and construction techniques laid a blueprint for every empire that followed. Logistics would be a crucial factor in determining an empire's success. The Assyrians' legacy goes beyond war, roads, and trade. They knew that an empire couldn't run solely on conquest. Prosperity and stability were essential for maintaining control and achieving long-term peace. Yet their methods were often harsh. They ruled with as much fear as they did innovation. This duality, their dazzling achievements, and their brutal conquests defined them.

In the end, the Assyrians learned that might isn't always right. In 612 BCE, the Medes and Babylonians conquered Nineveh, the capital of the Assyrian Empire, and integrated it into the Neo-Babylonian Empire. The Assyrian impact, however, remained. They left lessons for future civilizations, for better or for worse.

15

The Scorned Son: Modu and the Rise of the Xiongnu

THE PRINCE MOUNTED HIS HORSE AND RODE OUT ON A HUNT across the expansive Steppes. The king, his father, joined him. A band of devoted followers trailed them as the prince spotted a stag. As was customary, he let his father do the honors and pursue the beast. The unsuspecting monarch chased the deer, isolating himself from the rest of the hunting party.

The prince took an arrow from his quiver. He pulled his bow and focused on his target. The arrow wasn't a normal arrow. He had a special whistling arrow that instructed his soldiers to fire in the same direction. If they didn't, the penalty was death. Just as the king was about to shoot the deer, he heard an arrow whistle. Before he knew what was going on, the sky darkened with arrows.

The king was dead.

The prince, who assassinated his father, established the largest empire in ancient history, surpassing the Achaemenid Persian Empire, Alexander's Macedonian Empire, and the Han Chinese Empire. He created a template for subsequent generations of powerful rulers, including Chinggis Khan and Attila, and laid a framework for future Steppe empires. But history has forgotten him. We know him as Modu *Chanyu* or Modun, the founder of the formidable Xiongnu Empire.

In the final section of *Forgotten Footprints*, we started with the Assyrian Empire, which was a pinnacle of civilization in the early Iron Age and laid the blueprint for future empires worldwide. However, the empires of the Eurasian Steppes are often viewed in a different light. People see them as brilliant military powers who contributed little to human progress beyond raids and conquests. In the book's remaining chapters, I'll present the Steppe empires from a different perspective than their popular imagery as ruthless raiders. We'll discuss their rise and clashes with settled civilizations, but also focus on their remarkable achievements, such as their administrative systems, writing, building cities, sponsoring sophisticated art, and controlling long-distance trade, which we seldom associate with nomads. Academic discussions have evolved beyond the traditional portrayal of Steppe empires as "barbarians," yet this image persists in popular discourse. I have rarely written an article about the people of the Steppes without receiving at least one comment that referred to them as "barbarians." Hence, we need a more nuanced view of these mighty powers that profoundly impacted our history.

THE ORIGINS OF THE XIONGNU

The Xiongnu[1] left no written records about their rule. Our knowledge of them comes from the writings of ancient China's grand historian, Sima Qian. In his monumental work, *Shiji,* the scholar says that before the third century BCE, the Xiongnu

1 The Xiongnu, meaning the "fierce slave," is a modern Mandarin rendition of the Old Chinese term *hoŋ-nâ* or *Huna* (Sanskrit). The term Xiongnu was considered disrespectful in Chinese accounts, hence the leader of the confederacy was addressed as "Xiongnu da chanyu," or the emperor of the Xiongnu in official communication.

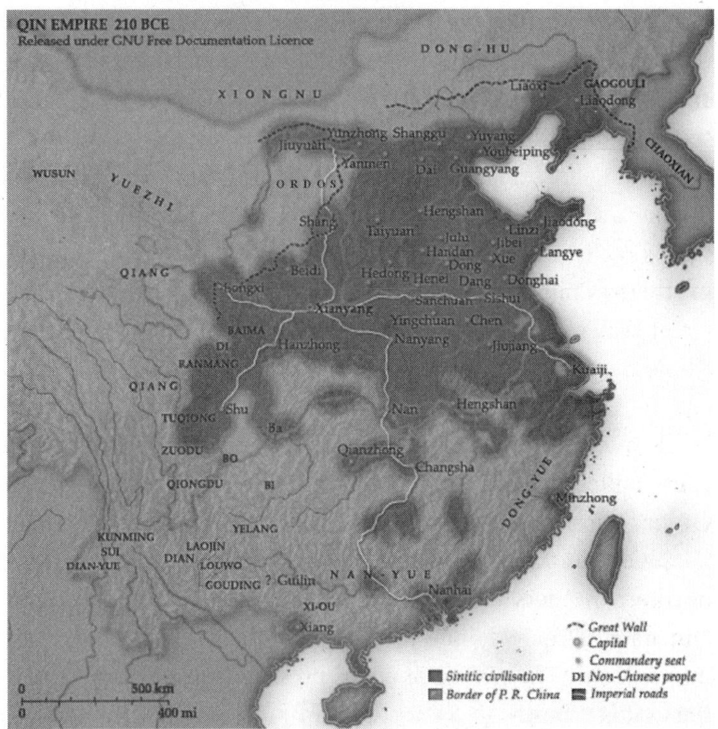

The political situation in China and its northern borders before the rise of the Xiongnu, during the Qin era.

were known by names such as Chunwei, Xunyu, Shanrong, and Xianyun. These adversaries of China were dubbed the Rongdi, which translates to "western and northern barbarians." Sima Qian mentions a group called Quanrong, who captured the Western Zhou dynasty around 770 BCE, forcing the Chinese to flee east. The Quanrong could have been the ancestors of the Xiongnu.

Sima Qian's account is the only source of the Xiongnu, but we must consider his account cautiously. Modern scholars have questioned Sima Qian's claims about the Xiongnu's origins, as he may not have had a complete understanding of events that occurred centuries before his time. Yet it's not unimaginable that the so-called "barbarian" tribes, who played an essential role in ancient China before the rise of the Xiongnu, may have had a strong connection with them.

In 221 BCE, the first Chinese emperor, Qin Shi Huangdi, fought and banished these tribes from their homeland in the Ordos region, which is now part of modern-day Mongolia and northern China. Huangdi is famous for commissioning the Great Wall of China[2] to keep out these warlike tribes. Countless Chinese citizens died during the wall's construction.

The Qin general, Meng Tian, was in charge of defending the borders from the barbarians collectively called "Hu." Historian Christopher Atwood argues that Hu referred to the tribes of the Ordos region, in present-day Inner Mongolia, and were the same people as the Xiongnu. Meng Tian's formidable army kept the northern invaders at bay. After the death of Qin Shi Huangdi, the Qin state fell quickly due to a rebellion, and China descended into anarchy. The period of chaos provided breathing space for the Ordos tribes.

Sima Qian then mentions Touman, the first known Xiongnu chanyu,[3] who reclaimed their homeland in the Ordos. The chanyu was the Xiongnu's equivalent of an emperor. Before Touman, the Xiongnu were not a significant force in the Steppes. Competing nomadic groups hemmed them in on both sides: the proto-Mongol Donghu to the east and the Indo-European Yuezhi to the west.

Contrary to popular belief, the chief rivals of Steppe confederacies like the Xiongnu were not the Chinese but other Steppe tribes.

---

2 What you see today as the Great Wall dates to constructions from the fourteenth-century CE Ming dynasty era.

3 *Chanyu* is pronounced as "shan-yu."

From underdogs fighting for survival, the Xiongnu became the largest empire in the ancient world within three decades. The architect of this success was Modu, Touman's successor and the most well-known Xiongnu ruler. He was the first great Steppe conqueror and inspired later empires such as the Huns, Göktürks, and Mongols.

Modu was born into a turbulent world of near-constant conflict. His name may have been something other than Modu, based on how early Chinese accounts describe him. *Baghatur*, meaning "hero" in Mongolian, was likely his real name. Baghatur later became an honorific meaning brave, and we can find different versions of it in several languages, including *Bátor* (Hungarian), *Bahadur* (Hindi), *Bahador* (Persian), *Bahadır* (Turkish), and *Bogatyr* (Russian). How did Modu's name become synonymous with bravery?

Touman was determined to get rid of Modu, who was his son from an unpopular wife. The chanyu wanted his favorite wife's son to succeed him. Some historians suggest that Modu may not have been Touman's son, but his nephew. Steppe confederacies often practiced lateral succession, in which a ruler's brother, rather than his son, inherited the throne. If that were the case, Touman may have wanted to eliminate Modu to secure the succession for his favored son. This interpretation, however, remains largely speculative.

Touman handed Modu over to the Yuezhi, a rival tribe, as a hostage. The Yuezhi were an Indo-European people who lived in the Gansu province of China. Later, one of their ruling clans, the Kushans, forged a vast empire in Central Asia and India, playing a crucial role in the Silk Road trade, as we'll see in the next chapter.

Touman attacked the Yuezhi, hoping they would kill Modu as payback. The young prince proved to be a tough survivor. He escaped by stealing a horse from the Yuezhi and returned to

Statue of Modu Chanyu, Chinggis Khan National Museum, Ulaanbaatar, Mongolia.

the Xiongnu court. Touman was pleased with Modu's bravery, though I doubt it was a happy reunion. Nevertheless, impressed with his abilities, he put Modu in charge of 10,000 soldiers and promoted him to a general.

After Touman's betrayal, Modu had much to contemplate. He realized his life would be in danger unless he gained a loyal following. For that, he needed the absolute obedience of his soldiers. He instructed his men to shoot at a target to test their loyalty, which became challenging over time.

First, Modu asked them to shoot his favorite horse. Some soldiers hesitated. Modu executed the ones who refused. Then he asked them to kill his favorite wife. The soldiers were shocked. Some hesitated. He put them to death. Lastly, he asked them to shoot down his father's favorite horse. By now, Modu had drilled into his soldiers that disobedience meant death. He cultivated a band of devoted warriors who would follow him no matter what.

Modu was patiently plotting his revenge. He hadn't forgotten Touman's plan to assassinate him and install his stepbrother on the throne. Having assembled a loyal following, he decided that the time had come to make his move.

One day, in 209 BCE, he invited Touman on a hunt. While Touman was chasing the prey, Modu shot an arrow at him, and his soldiers showered the unsuspecting king with arrows, killing him.

Modu then executed his stepbrother and stepmother, thus removing any potential rivals to the throne. A blood-soaked coup cemented his rise to power. Modu was now the chanyu of the Xiongnu.

THE RISE OF AN EMPIRE

Modu's first mission was to make the Xiongnu the most powerful Steppe confederacy. His chief opponents were the Yuezhi and the Donghu. The Donghu tested the new chanyu's authority.

A Donghu ambassador requested that Modu give up his father's battle horse. The offensive demand infuriated the

Gold tiger artifact, Xiongnu metalwork dated second century BCE.

Xiongnu ministers, but Modu gave away the horse without a second thought. Next, the Donghu pushed the new ruler's limits by asking for his favorite wife. Again, Modu answered yes without hesitation. His ministers protested, to no avail. The Donghu grew bolder and asked for a plot of barren land. The ministers, having realized that protesting was pointless, remained silent.

Modu was furious.

Land is the foundation of a nation; how could he give it away?

He was willing to sacrifice women and horses to maintain peace, not land. He executed the ministers who counseled him to relinquish control of the territory. Modu then assembled his forces and launched an attack on the Donghu. His ferocity and unpredictability surprised them. The Donghu were annihilated and forced to flee north.

Modu next turned his attention to the Yuezhi, who had held him hostage during his early life. He defeated and chased them westward, beyond the Tarim Basin, in modern-day Xinjiang.

Modu launched several campaigns against the Yuezhi throughout his military career, diminishing their power.

After that, he embarked on a conquering mission, crushing the Wusun, Dingling, Huyun, and 26 other tribal confederacies to establish a vast empire that reached modern-day Kazakhstan. For the first time, Inner Asia[4] was united under a single political banner.

Sima Qian notes that several confederacies voluntarily joined the Xiongnu and recognized Modu as their supreme leader.

Their army had 300,000 soldiers, and they were ready for their next big challenge. Modu's grandest prize was yet to come: the subjugation of Han China.

Following the collapse of the Qin dynasty in 206 BCE and a period of anarchy, Liu Bang seized power in China and established the Han dynasty in 202 BCE. He was known as Emperor Gaozu of Han. Gaozu sought to solidify the state's borders and expand the fortifications constructed during the Qin dynasty. Modu, meanwhile, had taken advantage of the chaos in China during the rise of the Han dynasty and captured several strategic bases in the southern Gobi Desert.

Gaozu sent a regional ruler named Han Xin[5] to defend the borders. In 201 BCE, Xin was shoring up the defenses of the Mai fortress when Modu launched a surprise attack, catching the Chinese off guard. The emperor's spies reported that Xin was negotiating a peace treaty with the Xiongnu without his approval.

---

4 Inner Asia refers to the landlocked region of North, East, and Central Asia, approximately from Buryatia province of Siberia in the west till western Kazakhstan, and Tuva Republic of Siberia in the north till Tibet in the south.

5 Han Xin is not to be confused with Gaozu's general by the same name, who was later executed on charges of plotting against the emperor.

A Ming-era (1368 CE to 1644 CE) portrait of Liu Bang, the prime adversary of Modu.

Enraged, Gaozu personally led a massive army, believed to number 320,000 men, to deal with the Xiongnu threat.

Modu displayed astute acumen and lured Emperor Gaozu into a trap at Baideng in 200 BCE. Gaozu, believing Modu's army was a bunch of ragged raiders, underestimated their strength and engaged with the Xiongnu, who raided in small batches till the favorable winter conditions set in. Frost-bitten and exhausted, the Chinese army got a glimmer of hope when they saw the Xiongnu cavalry retreat, and Gaozu decided to chase them.

At the Baideng Fortress, the retreating Xiongnu army suddenly turned around and started attacking the Han forces, with reserve forces joining and ensuring a rout. The classic feigned retreat technique was popular among later nomadic empires with the Mongols mastering the strategy, which played a key role in forging the largest land empire in human history.

The Han army suffered a devastating defeat at Baideng. Though Gaozu managed to bribe Modu's wife and escape, he recognized the Xiongnu's power and started diplomatic negotiations. In exchange for peace, the Chinese agreed to provide the Xiongnu

Portrait of Wang Zhaojun, one of China's legendary beauties who tried to unite the Xiongnu and the Han.

with silk, wine, food, money, and princesses. This policy, known as *heqin*, effectively ensured the Xiongnu's subjugation of China for the next six decades.

The policy of intermarriage wasn't always forceful. The Chinese believed it was an effective tool to "civilize" the Xiongnu and Sinicize them. The children of mixed Han and Xiongnu marriages would have a natural affinity towards the more sophisticated Chinese culture, thus reducing potential conflicts. The most famous example was Princess Wang Zhaojun, one of the legendary beauties of ancient China, who was sent to marry Huhanye Chanyu in 51 BCE. The Xiongnu appreciated her. She had two sons and two daughters with Huhanye. After he died in 31 BCE, Zhaojun wanted to return to China, but Han emperor Cheng rejected the proposal. As per Xiongnu custom, she married either the eldest brother or her husband's eldest stepson (from the first marriage). She had two more daughters and was honored in Chinese literature as a heroine who tried to unite two cultures. Today, her statue stands in a park south of Hohhot, in Inner Mongolia.

The cultural exchanges with the Chinese helped the Xiongnu learn much from their neighbors. Though they were adversaries of the Han, the nomads were happy to trade and adopt technologies from the Chinese.

REIMAGINING THE STEPPES: WRITING, AGRICULTURE, AND URBANIZATION

How do we tell the story of a people who left no written records?

Many books and movies portray the people who built Steppe empires as illiterate, but this view is not entirely accurate. Historian Kenneth Harl suggests Modu's officials devised a script based on Chinese ideograms popularized by Qin Shi Huangdi.

Modu appreciated the Chinese love for calligraphy and wanted the Xiongnu to embrace it.

Another theory is that the Xiongnu learned writing from Zhonghang Yue, a Chinese eunuch and Han official who defected to the Xiongnu. He resented the Han for sending him away with a princess, as per the heqin policy, and promised to be their worst enemy. He taught the Xiongnu many state secrets, including writing and bureaucracy, helping the nomads to design a successful imperial system that lasted for centuries, and their successor states, such as the Huns and Göktürks, adopted it.

The vengeful Yue encouraged the chanyu to use a "bigger board (wooden) and seal to reply to the Chinese emperor" to display the Xiongnu's dominance.

Ancient Chinese sources refer to the Xiongnu writing system as the Hu script. The script may have formed the basis of the later, more well-established Old Turkic script found in the Orkhon inscriptions, which we'll discuss in Chapter 17. Barring a few characters, written records from the Hu script didn't survive, but it is clear that the Xiongnu valued writing as a means of diplomatic correspondence.

Archaeology helps us understand the Xiongnu better. Our common perception of the people of the Steppes is that they were all horseback nomads roaming Eurasia in search of pastures. While the elite were indeed nomadic pastoralists, the Steppe empires supported agriculture. Farming was an essential part of the economy of Eurasia. According to a 2020 study by the Max Planck Institute, millet cultivation was the backbone of prosperity for the Xiongnu, the first Steppe empire. Agriculture was encouraged and grew significantly during the thirteenth-century CE Mongol Empire. The research produced some intriguing results. People who lived closer to the centers of power of the Mongolian empires, like the Xiongnu, ate more millet-based dishes than those who lived further away. The study shows that

Hun	Chinese	Hun	Chinese	Hun	Chinese
1	二	2	五	3	六
4	七	5	八	6	九
7	七六	8	甲	9	乙
10	丙	11	壬	12	丁
13	己	14	卯	15	午
16	化	17	公	18	朋
19	大	20	行	21	工
22	其	23	口	24	木
25	禾	26	少	27	羊
28	日	29	月	30	亭
31	老	32	父	33	魚
34	刀	35	鳥	36	城
37	丘	38	丘	39	丘

The Xiongnu characters (*left*) found in Noin Ula and their Chinese counterparts (*right*).

the governing class favored agriculture in the central regions. The researchers also found that over time, grain consumption increased, and a more diverse diet developed.

The aristocracy were pastoralists. But they lived in highly organized states. There were clear boundaries where a clan could and couldn't graze their animals. Crossing over into another clan's domain meant war.

Remains of the Southern Xiongnu city of Tongwancheng.

There were no pure nomadic zones. The Steppes have historically been home to a diverse mix of farmers, hunter-gatherers, urban dwellers, and nomadic pastoralists.

Sima Qian provides us with the necessary evidence of urban life in the Steppes. He starts by criticizing the Xiongnu for not living in towns. But his subsequent writings mention the Xiongnu's cities. This paradox leads us to infer that urban centers must have existed in the Xiongnu territory. So far archaeologists have found one city, Tongwancheng, which belongs to the Southern Xiongnu state of Da Xia.[6] The city dates back to the early fifth century CE, long after the power of Modu's Xiongnu Empire waned.

Historian Hyun Jin Kim suggests that the traditional Marxist human evolution model from hunter-gatherer to farmer and urban dweller doesn't apply to the Steppes. People were flexible. They could live in cities and abandon them to live on the plains as nomads, and vice versa. The Ordos region was home to the Xiongnu's cities and later Steppe metropolises such as Ötüken (capital of the Göktürks), Ordu-Baliq (capital of Uyghurs), and the well-known Mongol capital of Karakorum.

DECLINE AND LEGACY

After Modu's death, the Xiongnu Empire continued to prosper under his successors. However, internal conflicts, external pressures, and leadership crises ultimately marked its decline.

Laoshang Chanyu, Modu's successor, maintained the empire's dominance by defeating the Yuezhi again in 162 BCE. This battle drove the Yuezhi further west into Greco-Bactrian territory in modern Uzbekistan, firmly establishing Xiongnu authority over Inner Asia. The Wusun were given these freshly captured regions

---

6 Da Xia translates to the great Xia or the grand Xia.

Portrait of Emperor Wu of the Han dynasty, who led a punitive campaign against the Xiongnu.

as a prize for their loyalty during the struggle. For nearly 70 years, the Han Empire, awestruck by the Xiongnu's power, paid regular tribute to Laoshang and his successors under the heqin appeasement policy.

The accession of Emperor Wu of Han in 141 BCE marked a turning point. Abandoning appeasement, Wu initiated an aggressive campaign to challenge Xiongnu supremacy. By 129 BCE, full-scale war erupted. Despite the Han's initial struggle, they inflicted significant, costly, defeats on the Xiongnu. Internal strife among the Xiongnu, sparked by the death of Gunchen Chanyu in 126 BCE and a subsequent succession crisis, further weakened their resistance.

The usurper Ichise Chanyu's rise to power alienated key Xiongnu nobles, leading to defections to the Han court. Exploiting this division, the Chinese reclaimed the Ordos region and expanded their influence in the Steppes.

By 60 BCE, after decades of warfare, the Han achieved decisive victories, securing the Tarim Basin and triggering rebellions among the Xiongnu's vassal states, including the Wusun, Dingling, and Wuhuan. Internal leadership struggles further fragmented the empire. Between 114 BCE and 58 BCE, the Xiongnu cycled through eight chanyus, most of whom ruled briefly. The principle of primogeniture[7] clashed with the traditional Steppe practice of lateral succession, intensifying factional disputes.

By 54 BCE, the Xiongnu throne was split between two contenders: Zhizhi in the north and Huhanye in the south. Huhanye submitted to the Han, marking a stark reversal of fortune. In a display of subservience, he paid homage to the Han emperor in Chang'an (present-day Xian). Huhanye received military aid to defeat Zhizhi, culminating in the latter's death in 36 BCE.

Huhanye's allegiance signified the Xiongnu's diminished status as a tributary power. Humiliated by their crushing defeat against the Han, the Xiongnu briefly regained strength during the Han Civil War following the rise of the short-lived Xin dynasty (9 CE to 23 CE). Seizing the opportunity, the Xiongnu

---

7 Primogeniture is the tradition of the first born son succeeding his father.

restored their influence over former vassals and reclaimed the Tarim Basin. However, this revival was short-lived, as internal divisions resurfaced, leading to a permanent split between the Northern and Southern Xiongnu in 46 CE. The Southern Xiongnu aligned with the Han, integrating into Chinese society and securing their survival. In contrast, the Northern Xiongnu, who continued to lead a nomadic lifestyle, faced mounting pressure from their adversaries.

The Northern Xiongnu's decline accelerated after attacks from the resurgent Han Empire, rebellious vassals, and the rise of rival powers, such as the Xianbei, descendants of the Donghu whom Modu had vanquished. In 87 CE, the Xianbei inflicted a devastating defeat, killing the reigning chanyu and scattering Northern Xiongnu forces. Subsequent campaigns by Han generals, including Dou Xian in 89 CE, crushed the remaining Xiongnu resistance, culminating in their retreat to the Ili River Basin in present-day Kazakhstan by 91 CE. By the second century CE, the Xianbei replaced the Xiongnu as the dominant power in Mongolia and the eastern Steppes.

Though fragmented, the Xiongnu persisted in the Altai region for centuries. Surrounded by hostile powers like the Dingling, Kangju, and Xianbei, they remained in obscurity until their reemergence in history as the Huns.

During his thirty-five-year reign, Modu Chanyu transformed the Xiongnu into a formidable power, reorganized its administration, and established the world's largest empire of the era. Under his rule, the Xiongnu consolidated their authority over the Eurasian Steppes and forced the Han Empire to pay tribute. Popular discussions often draw parallels between Alexander and Modu, but the Xiongnu leader's exploits and lasting impact position him as a conqueror worthy of greater praise. As they gained power, both leaders were accused of patricide; Alexander with Philip and Modu with Touman. Yet, Modu was more effective as a politician and an administrator. Alexander's empire fragmented into warring states after his death. However, the Xiongnu Empire thrived for 400 years under the successors of Modu. His legacy endured, establishing him as one of history's most dominant rulers, and his empire became a model for future powers from the Eurasian Steppes.

16

Buddha Meets Hercules on the Silk Road: The Rise of the Kushans

IN 2008, DURING A TRIP TO WASHINGTON, DC, I HAD THE opportunity to visit the National Museum of Asian Art. There's a gallery on Buddhist iconography. One of the panels titled "The First Sermon at the Deer Park in Sarnath" shows the Buddha seated beneath a tree, surrounded by devotees. He wears a robe resembling a toga. Some of the people around him are wearing distinctive Greek attire.

This panel is unique. It is one of the earliest depictions of the Buddha in human form. The style is Gandhara art, which dates from the first century BCE to the fifth century CE, and incorporates elements of both Indian and Greco-Roman art.

There are reliefs of Gandhara art in museums and art galleries across the world. I've seen them in The Metropolitan Museum of Art, New York, and the Indian Museum, Kolkata. The patrons of this artwork were the Kushans. They were one of the five ruling clans of the Yuezhi,[1] a nomadic people whose origins we can trace to China's Gansu province.

---

1 Yuezhi, pronounced as "Ue-tsi" (i silent), means "moon clan" or "moon branch" in ancient Chinese.

"The First Sermon at the Deer Park in Sarnath," dated to the Kushan era, second to third century CE.

The Kushans ruled over a multiethnic empire in Central Asia, where cultural interactions brought together Eastern and Western art traditions. Their goal of making Buddhism appealing to the masses resulted in the religion becoming a global faith. They also played a pivotal role in expanding the Silk Road, facilitating the exchange of goods and knowledge between the East and the West.

The worlds of the Buddha and Hercules blended in this forgotten Central Asian power. Despite being one of the four prominent ruling dynasties in the world during their time, alongside the Romans, the Han, and the Parthians, the Kushan Empire remains largely a mystery.

In the previous chapter, we learned about the Xiongnu's rise and its domino effect on the ancient world. One group whose fortunes took a sharp turn was the Yuezhi.

ORIGINS: THE YUEZHI MIGRATIONS

Yuezhi prince from Khalchayan archaeological site, Uzbekistan, dated first century BCE.

The origins of the Yuezhi are a subject of intense debate, with many researchers believing they were Tocharians based on Greek sources that identify the Yuezhi with the *Tókharoi*, meaning Tocharians. An Indo-European language of the Agnean-Kuchean branch, Tocharian, was primarily spoken in the Tarim Basin until its extinction in the ninth century CE. However, other theories suggest that while the Tocharians were related to the Yuezhi, they were distinct groups, and we don't know for sure if the Yuezhi were Tocharians.

The earliest mention of the Yuezhi is from the same source as the Xiongnu, Sima Qian's *Shiji.* Further information comes from the *Book of Han* (*Han Shu*, the official history of the Han dynasty).

The *Book of Han* describes the Yuezhi's location and military capabilities as:

> "The Great Yuezhi was a nomadic horde. They moved about following their cattle and had the same customs as those of the Xiongnu. As their soldiers numbered more than a hundred thousand, they were strong and despised the Xiongnu. In the past, they lived in the region between Dunhuang and Qilian."

The Yuezhi were close allies of the Qin dynasty (221 BCE to 206 BCE), which unified China. They became influential by supplying jade and horses to the Qin and receiving silk in exchange. Chinese records describe the Yuezhi as nomadic pastoralists.

The Yuezhi's primary adversaries were the Xiongnu, as we learned in Chapter 15. To thwart the Xiongnu threat, the Yuezhi and the Chinese joined forces and pushed them beyond the Ordos region in Inner Mongolia. You may recall from the previous chapter that Modu[2] was a hostage of the Yuezhi; therefore, when he assassinated Touman and captured power, they were his primary target. During their initial clash, it isn't clear if the Xiongnu scored a decisive victory. They probably didn't, as a series of wars between the Xiongnu and the Yuezhi occurred throughout Modu's reign. In 203 BCE, Modu inflicted a severe defeat on the Yuezhi and captured a substantial portion of their territory. In 176 BCE, the Xiongnu again attacked the Yuezhi, scoring a significant victory. Modu boasted of his triumph in a

2 Refer to the Chapter 15 for more details on the Xiongnu.

letter to the Chinese emperor in 174 BCE. However, the Yuezhi were far from finished and continued to thrive in their homeland.

Later, Modu's son Laoshang (reign 174 BCE–166 BCE) dealt the Yuezhi a crushing defeat and evicted them from the Gansu region. According to Sima Qian, the Xiongnu killed the Yuezhi king and turned his skull into a drinking cup.

Defeated and out of options, the Yuezhi migrated west and arrived in Kazakhstan's Ili River Valley in 162 BCE. There, they met the Sakas, a nomadic eastern Iranian tribe, probably a branch of the Scythians.

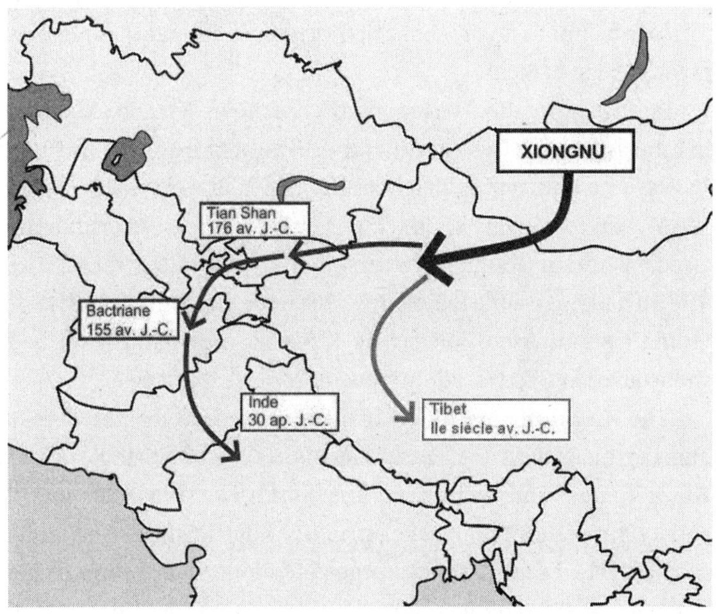

Yuezhi migrations after defeat at the hands of the Xiongnu.

The Yuezhi proved a formidable opponent for the Sakas, driving them south towards the Greco-Bactrian Kingdom, based in present-day Uzbekistan, Afghanistan, Tajikistan, and Turkmenistan. This victory over the Sakas had a domino effect as the Sakas raided the

Greeks of Bactria before turning to the lucrative but weakened Indo-Greek Kingdom in northwestern India and present-day Pakistan. The Sakas routed the Indo-Greeks, assimilated into India, and came to be known as Indo-Scythians.

The Yuezhi lived temporarily in the Ili River Valley. Their former neighbors and enemies, the Wusun,[3] cut short their stay. The Wusun were an Indo-European nomadic people who were rivals of the Xiongnu and the Yuezhi. But after Modu *Chanyu*'s rise, they submitted to the Xiongnu, hoping to maintain their regional autonomy. There's no consensus on their origin. Some scholars say they were Indo-Aryans, and Wusun is derived from "*Ashvin*." Others favor Tocharian origins, and some academics favor Iranian origins.

In 132 BCE, the Wusun, with the help of their Xiongnu overlords, routed the Yuezhi and drove them from the Ili River Valley. The devastating defeat at the hands of the Wusun forced the Yuezhi to migrate south. The Yuezhi entered the crumbling Greco-Bactrian Kingdom, weakened by the Saka raids. The Yuezhi had no trouble taking over this once-prosperous but now-fading Central Asian power. By 126 BCE, they had established themselves in Bactria, adopting a more settled lifestyle.

The Yuezhi also expanded on the fortifications that the Greeks and Parthians built in Central Asia. Forts in Uzbekistan, such as Kampir Tepe and Ayaz Kala, and Surkh Kotal in Afghanistan show signs of monumental constructions during the Kushan rule.

The Han Empire hadn't forgotten about its erstwhile trade partners. Seeking help to fight the Xiongnu, Emperor Han Wudi sent a delegation led by Zhang Qian to locate the Yuezhi and form an alliance. Unfortunately for him and the Chinese, the Yuezhi were more concerned with enjoying their opulent new territory than battling the Xiongnu. Qian describes the Yuezhi

---

3 Wusun means the grandson of the crow in ancient Chinese.

as having a vast force but unwilling to engage with the fearsome Xiongnu. But don't let the Yuezhi's refusal to lock horns with their arch-nemesis deceive you. They had an insatiable appetite for conquest. To the south and east were the wealthy cities of the Silk Road, and as a historic mercantile community, the Yuezhi recognized the potential of controlling this route.

THE RISE OF THE KUSHANS

Tetradrachm of Heraios, showing a Greek diadem and Greek inscriptions.

According to Chinese texts from the first century BCE, the Yuezhi were divided into five ruling clans, each led by a *yabgu*.[4] The yabgus produced coinage in their name and ruled over sub-domains. In the first century CE, Heraios, a yabgu of the Kushan[5] clan, seized control and defeated the other Yuezhi yabgus. We know little about Heraios besides his silver coins with Greek inscriptions. His coinage depicts a clean-shaven man wearing a Greek-style diadem with an elongated skull. During ancient times, Steppe tribes commonly practiced artificial cranial

4 *Yabgu* is a Turkic title equivalent to a viceroy.

5 Kushans are called Guishang in Chinese sources.

deformation, a custom observed among the Scythians, Huns, and Turks, Xiongnu, and the Yuezhi.

Heraios's successor, Kujula Kadphises (reign 30 CE–80 CE), consolidated authority and expanded the Kushan lands. Kadphises was the first of seven Kushan rulers identified by historians.

In 1993, a British humanitarian worker in Afghanistan saw Afghan rebels digging a trench on an artificial hill. The worker photographed the scene and sent the pictures to the British Museum. One photo caught the museum's attention. The image was of a stone with text in Bactrian and Greek. The rock was the Rabatak inscription, which contained the genealogy of four Kushan rulers. It was composed by Kanishka (reign 127 CE–153 CE), the most well-known Kushan emperor. N. Sims-Williams and J. Cribb, who deciphered the Rabatak inscription, describe Kanishka's lineage:

> "... for King Kujula Kadphises (his) great grandfather, and for King Vima Taktu (his) grandfather, and for King Vima Kadphises (his) father, and also for himself, King Kanishka."

Kujula Kadphises united all the Yuezhi tribes in Transoxiana.[6] They conquered the Kabul Valley, thus gaining control over the lucrative trading routes through the Khyber and Bolan Passes in the present-day Pakistan–Afghanistan border. His son, Vima Taktu, continued to expand east and attacked the Indo-Parthian Kingdom, which ruled present-day Pakistan and parts of northern India.

6 A historical region in Central Asia comprising eastern Uzbekistan, western Tajikistan, southern Kazakhstan and parts of Turkmenistan and Kyrgyzstan.

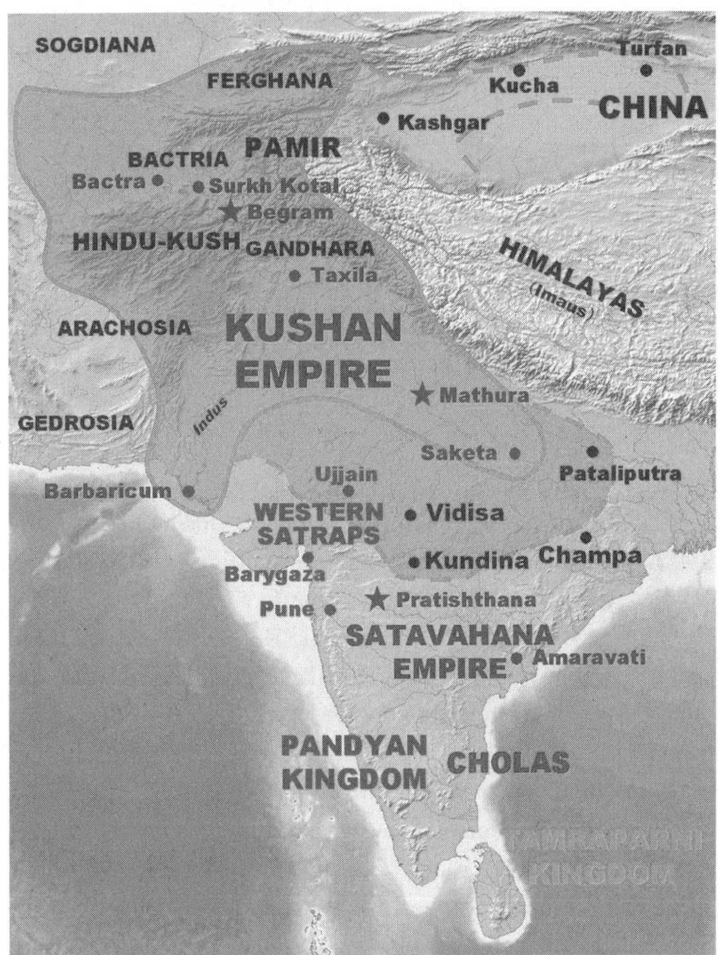

The Kushan Empire's greatest extent during the rule of Huvishka.

According to the *Book of Han*:

> "His (Kujula Kadphises) son, Yan Gaozhen (Vima Taktu), became king in his place. He returned and defeated Tianzhu (Northwestern India) and installed a General to supervise and lead it. The Yuezhi then became extremely

> rich. All the kingdoms call [their king] the Guishuang (Kushan) king, but the Han call them by their original name, Da Yuezhi (the Great Yuezhi)."

There is some ambiguity about whether Kujula Kadphises or Vima Taktu defeated the Indo-Parthians, as Vima was only 15 years old when he took the Kushan throne. Modern historians believe Kujula Kadphises was more likely to have invaded the Indo-Parthians.

Gondophares I, a Parthian[7] noble from the influential House of Suren,[8] established the Indo-Parthian Kingdom. Under his leadership, the Parthians invaded present-day Pakistan and northwest India. As he took charge of this new kingdom, he declared independence from the Parthians. During his rule, the Kushans expanded southward without getting into a full-scale conflict with the Indo-Parthians. But after the formidable ruler died, around 45 CE, the opportunistic Kushans wasted no time invading the prosperous Indo-Parthian Kingdom and making it their vassal. The conquest of northwestern India provided access to elephants, rhinoceroses, turtle shells, gold, silver, copper, iron, lead, and tin, making the Kushans wealthy.

The desire to control the wealthy trading routes of Central Asia meant that the Kushans were eager to work with their former allies, Han China. In 84 CE, Kushans helped the Chinese general Ban Chao crush a revolt supported by the Sogdians in the Tarim Basin town of Kashghar. Later, the Kushans also assisted the Han dynasty in conquering Turpan, another Tarim Basin Oasis

---

7 The Parthians were a nomadic people who migrated to Khorasan region of ancient Iran and ruled from 247 BCE to 224 CE.

8 One of the Surenas defeated the famous Roman general Crassus at the Battle of Carrhae in 53 BCE after luring the Roman army into the desert and picking them apart using horse archers and cataphract knights.

city. Emboldened, the Yuezhi demanded a Han princess, which the Chinese rejected. Enraged, they attacked Ban Chao with a force of 70,000 soldiers but were defeated. The Kushans realized their best bet was to work with the Hans rather than fight them; hence, they decided against expanding east, focusing instead on India and Central Asia.

The southward annexation policy continued under Vima Kadphises and Kanishka. According to the Rabatak inscription, Kanishka controlled a vast territory that stretched from present-day Uzbekistan to Pataliputra in eastern India, the former capital of the Mauryan Empire.

Kanishka's war with the Parthians was one of his most controversial campaigns. Vologases III, the Parthian ruler, attacked Kanishka because he was upset at the Kushan conquest of the Indo-Parthian Kingdom. The Kushans withstood the invasion, killing 900,000 Parthians in the counter-offensive. The loss of lives appalled Kanishka, and he resolved to give up war and embrace Buddhism.

Does the story sound familiar?

The account is akin to Mauryan Emperor Ashoka's remorse and conversion to Buddhism following the Kalinga War, which resulted in an immense loss of lives.[9]

Historians doubt the authenticity of Kanishka's conversion story. The only source for this war is a Chinese text from 470 CE, *A History of the Buddha's Successors,* written over three centuries after Kanishka's death. Although a clash with the Parthians probably occurred, the strong resemblance to Ashoka's penance suggests that the Buddhist writers may have grafted an earlier tale.

Why did the scribes do so?

---

9 Though Ashokan rock edicts mention regret for his conquest of Kalinga and his embrace of Buddhism, it is less clear if the two events were related as suggested by later texts. The process of conversion was gradual and probably based on political considerations.

Though later Buddhist scholars may have exaggerated the details of the campaign against the Parthians, Kanishka's patronage of Buddhism was genuine. His vast empire was home to several faiths and cultures. Like his predecessors, Kanishka welcomed them, but it is his special attention to Buddhism that we remember him for. However, this has often led to a widespread perception that the Kushans were Buddhists. Although we know very little about the original religion of the Kushans, in Bactria, they demonstrated patronage for various faiths, often following distinct practices or a blend of spiritual beliefs.

RELIGION UNDER KUSHAN RULE

A gold coin of Emperor Kanishka depicting Nana.

After migrating from China, the Kushans took over a kingdom governed by the Greeks, where the locals worshiped Hellenic and native Bactrian deities. The Rabatak inscription says Kanishka was a devotee of Nana, a Bactrian goddess. He exalts the goddess and says he "obtained his kingship from Nana and the other gods." In Kushan and earlier Bactrian art, artists depict Nana as a cosmic deity often shown with four arms, riding a lion. In Sogdian art, she's shown holding the sun and the moon in two of her hands. The Kushans saw Nana as a source of royal legitimacy, and the Rabatak inscriptions tell us that Kanishka claimed his kingship through her divine authority.

The flourishing trade with the Romans led to an influx of gold coins in the Kushan Empire. Vima Kadphises had them melted and minted in his name, starting a tradition continued by his successors. In these gold coins, we see evidence of diverse religious iconography. The coins feature over 30 deities from the Iranian, Indic (Hindu and Buddhist), and Greco-Roman pantheons. In the early years of Kushan rule, Iranian and Greco-Roman religious figures were popular, such as Oromozdo (Ahura Mazda), Ardoksho, Mithro (Mithra), Pharro, Elios (Helios), Rishti, and Zaoou (Zeus).

Oesho on a coin issued by Huvishka.

Following the conquest of India, Hinduism and Buddhism influenced the religious beliefs of the Kushans. Perhaps the most prominent depiction of one of the Kushan's chief deities, Oesho. He is believed to be an early depiction of the Hindu god Shiva, and was closely related to the Zoroastrian god Vayu, the god of wind. Like Shiva's *vahana* (vehicle), Nandi, he is depicted with a bull. Oesho's companion is Ommo (Uma/Parvati), and by the rule of Huvishka, he becomes one of the most prominent deities.

Kanishka began sponsoring Buddhism and convened the Fourth Buddhist Council around 100 CE. He was guided by Aśvaghoṣa, a monk known for composing Buddhist literature in Sanskrit. Before Aśvaghoṣa, Gandhari Prakrit was the common language used for Buddhist texts. A new tradition of writing texts in Sanskrit in the Brahmi script began. The shift in Buddhist literary tradition to Sanskrit in Brahmi script influenced the development of the writing systems of different people of Central Asia, such as the Sogdians, the Göktürks, and the Uyghurs, as we shall see in the next chapter. Before the Turkic script emerged, the Brahmi script spread widely, reaching as far as Mongolia, where archaeologists have uncovered inscriptions in Mongolian and Sogdian written with it. Kanishka encouraged the translation of Sanskrit works into Tocharian and helped Indian literature spread across Asia.

The Kushan emperor promoted the Mahayana (Sanskrit for "great vehicle") school of Buddhism. Mahayana philosophy believes anyone can attain nirvana and break the cycle of rebirths, even if they haven't taken ascetic vows. This interpretation appealed to the masses, as people didn't have to join a monastic order to be Buddhist.

Kanishka also built a large stupa in Purusapura, near present-day Peshawar, to house Buddhist relics. His successors extended the shrine to a height of 120 m. The original stupa didn't survive, though we have several later accounts from Chinese travelers, such as Faxian (337 CE–422 CE) and Xuanzang (602 CE–664 CE),[10] who mention it as a grand monument. The last person to describe it was the Muslim polymath Al-Biruni, who mentions

A copy of Kanishka's casket from the British Museum. Indra and Brahma surround the Buddha.

10 Faxian, formerly romanized as Fa-hien, and Xuanzang as Hiuen-tsung.

a great stupa built by King Kanak (a reference to Kanishka). The exact circumstances surrounding the stupa's destruction remain unclear, with various theories suggesting that it was struck by lightning or by invading forces. Historical accounts indicate that the stupa was rebuilt three times after being struck by lightning; however, it is unknown when it was permanently destroyed. Since Al-Biruni saw it, we can assume its destruction occurred after the tenth century CE.

In the early twentieth century, archaeologists led by David Brainerd Spooner discovered the ruins of Kanishka's stupa and a shrine containing three bone fragments of the Buddha. The stupa's base was 87 m in diameter. Near the base, he found a casket showing the Buddha surrounded by Indra and Brahma. The casket's inscription tells us it was Kanishka's incense box. The artwork uniquely blended Iranian, Indian, and Greek elements.

Promoting the aesthetics of Buddhism was vital for Kanishka. He wanted people to experience the faith, which led to a new fusion art style centered around the Buddha, known as Gandhara Art. Like his casket, Gandhara Art incorporated various artistic traditions that met on the Silk Road.

GANDHARA ART: THE BUDDHA MEETS HERCULES

Greek art in Central Asia predates the Kushans. In 327 BCE, Alexander conquered Bactria and Gandhara (present-day northern Pakistan and eastern Afghanistan). His successors established the Greco-Bactrian Kingdom (256 BCE–120 BCE) in Central Asia and the Indo-Greek Kingdom (200 BCE to 10 CE) in the Indian subcontinent. These kingdoms had trade connections to the Greco-Roman world. As they became wealthier, their citizens developed a craving for luxury. From the first century CE, Bactrian art began to show signs of Hellenistic influence.

Between the first centuries BCE and CE, Hercules became a subject of Bactrian art. The following dish depicts an intoxicated Hercules in Gandhara attire, embracing two women.

An intoxicated Hercules embracing two women, an example of Greco-Bactrian art, second century BCE to first century CE.

Buddhism reached Central Asia during the rule of Ashoka (reign 268 BCE to 232 BCE) and received patronage from the Indo-Greeks. Mauryan art was the first to portray scenes from the Buddha's life. However, the Mauryas chose not to show the Buddha. Instead, artists used symbols, such as the Bodhi tree under which the Buddha achieved enlightenment, to represent him.

The earliest anthropomorphic images of the Buddha appeared during the Kushan era. They show him as an Indian man dressed in a himation (a Greek toga-like garment), emphasizing the Hellenistic influence. Throughout the Mauryan era, the dhoti, a traditional Indian loincloth, was commonly worn by Buddhist figures. The Buddha's distinctly Greek appearance marked a dramatic shift in how the Kushans viewed Buddhist icons.

Hercules as Vajrapani protecting Buddha, second to third century CE.

A prominent theme in Gandhara art is the depiction of Hercules as Vajrapani, one of the earliest boddhisattvas, holding a club and protecting the Buddha. A bodhisattva is an individual on their path to "bodhi" or enlightenment.

Besides Hercules, there are other depictions of deities from the Greco-Roman pantheon as Buddhist figures, such as the representation of the Greek goddess Tyche as Hariti, a Buddhist fertility deity.

Gandhara art also featured famous scenes from Greek mythology, such as a panel depicting the Trojan War, dated between the second and third centuries CE, and discovered in present-day northwestern Pakistan.

Trojan War scene depicted in Gandhara art.

Gandhara art represents a microcosm of the Kushan legacy. Archaeologists have found several artifacts from the Kushan Empire in Central Asia. A gold hoard at Tillya Tepe, Afghanistan, known as Bactrian Gold, contained 22,000 golden objects, including belts, crowns, and coins.

Crown belonging to a female, Tillya Tepe Gold Hoard.

The Bactrian Gold is a spectacular archaeological discovery from northern Afghanistan. It dates back to the early first century BCE to the first century CE, as demonstrated by coins found in the site of the Roman Emperor Tiberius's (coins minted between 16 CE and 21 CE), Parthian ruler Mithridates II (123 BCE–88 BCE), and Yuezhi chieftain Sapadbizes (20 BCE–20 CE). The Yuezhi most likely built the site, but Scythian (Saka) or Parthian origins are also possible.

The treasure trove comprises valuable coins and artifacts that demonstrate a variety of cultural influences. Notable discoveries include gold coins of Tiberius, Parthian imitations, and a Buddhist coin with a figure turning a wheel, probably an early portrayal of the Buddha. Archaeologists observed ritual skull deformation among the buried individuals at Tillya Tepe, which connects them to Central Asian nomads. Hellenistic artistic themes, such as images of Athena, together with Scythian-influenced objects like elaborately designed daggers and crowns, reveal the site's wide cultural contacts.

The hoard's history encompasses both loss and dramatic rediscovery. In 1989, President Mohammad Najibullah instructed the Afghan authorities to place the treasure in an underground vault in Kabul, from where it disappeared only to reappear in 2003 following the fall of the Taliban. As of August 2021, after the return of the Taliban, the hoard has gone missing again. Its last known international exhibition was at the Hong Kong History Museum from November 2019 to February 2020.

The finds at Tillya Tepe reveal the refined tastes of the Kushans. They were keen on developing the artistic traditions of the previous rulers and blended their styles. They welcomed diverse influences, which added to the beauty of their art. While researching this enigmatic Silk Road empire, I wondered: "If we have so much proof of a sophisticated civilization, why don't we know more about it?"

A FORGOTTEN LEGACY

The Kushan Empire crumbled after Kanishka's grandson, Vasudeva (reign 190 CE–230 CE), died. The Sassanids rose to power in Iran and overthrew the Parthians.

The Persians attacked the Kushans in an attempt to revive the once-mighty Achaemenid Empire (550 BCE to 330 BCE). By the mid-fourth century CE, India saw a new imperial power rise from the Gangetic Plains: the Gupta dynasty. The Guptas and the Sassanids proved to be formidable for the declining Kushnas, and they carved up the once mighty Silk Road empire.

The Kushans shaped a new era in human history. Under their influence, the Silk Road experienced significant growth and prosperity. They brought together Eastern and Western artistic traditions, playing a pivotal role in the global spread of Buddhism. So, why are they rarely discussed?

The Kushans left a legacy that does not fit nationalist historical narratives. A syncretic civilization with multiple faiths and languages peacefully coexisting was unprecedented. Their tolerance of religious plurality clashes with modern nationalism. Later monarchs, including the Sassanid shahs and Arab caliphs, rejected the Kushan legacy because of theological differences. This ideological clash continued till recent times, as evidenced by the Taliban's 2001 demolition of the Bamiyan Buddha sculptures. Scholars believe that the Hephthalite Huns, a branch of the Huns who ruled over Central Asia, Persia, and India, possibly built the Bamiyan Buddhas. The Hephthalites carried on the Kushan legacy, as did their successors, the Göktürks. But this chapter of Afghanistan's history was uncomfortable for the Taliban, who sought to remove any remnants of a once-thriving, tolerant civilization in the heart of the Silk Road.

The Kushans faded from memory, yet their legacy endures. The Yuezhi migrations gave birth to the Silk Road, the world's oldest active trade route. Thanks to Kanishka and his successors, Buddhism has grown to become the fourth most widely followed religion globally, with approximately 530 million adherents. Successor states promoted their unique Gandhara art style. Today, museums and archaeologists around the globe are fighting to save Central Asia's Buddhist heritage.

17

Children of the Wolf: The Rise of the Göktürks

WHEN YOU THINK OF AN EMPIRE BUILT BY THE TURKS, WHAT comes to mind? The most common answer is the Ottoman Empire, Europe's arch-nemesis for controlling the Middle East, the Balkans, and the Mediterranean Sea. But long before the Ottomans, a group of blacksmiths in the Eurasian Steppes forged the world's first and largest Turkic empire. They were the Göktürks.[1]

In the sixth century CE, the First Turkic Khaganate stretched from Siberia in the East to the shores of the Black Sea in the West, making it the largest empire in the world. The Göktürks were the first to use the term "Turk" to refer to a specific cultural, linguistic, and political group. They set the stage for the rise of later Turkic powers such as the Uyghurs, Khazars, Ghaznavids, Seljuks, and Ottomans, who ruled different parts of Asia, Europe, and Africa, dominating world politics from the Middle Ages to modern times. The rise of the Göktürks was far from certain. Had it not been for an insult by their overlords, we may have had a different course in history. In our quest to discover lost

1 Romanized from *Kök Türük* meaning "celestial" or "blue" Turks.

Göktürk petroglyphs from Mongolia, sixth to eighth century CE.

empires, our final destination is the Orkhon Valley in Mongolia, where we'll learn about the legendary origins of a people who profoundly influenced world history during the Middle Ages.

BORN FROM THE WOLF

The histories of the people of the Eurasian Steppes have been poorly understood thanks to a lack of surviving written records. The Göktürks were the first Steppe people to document their history in the Orkhon inscriptions,[2] which Bilge Khagan and his brother Kul Tigin commissioned in 732 CE. However, the record was almost 200 years after the Turks first appeared as a political force. Chinese sources such as the *Book of Zhou* and the *History of the Northern Dynasties* claim that the Turks were a "detached

2 Refer to the section "language to unite an empire" later in this chapter for a detailed discussion on the Orkhon inscriptions.

branch of the Xiongnu." Historians have questioned the claim, but a loose connection isn't inconceivable. Modern research suggests the Xiongnu elite were primarily Turkic or Yeniseian speakers. Chinese texts also discuss the mythical origins of the Turks. The most famous story is the legend of the abandoned child raised by a wolf.

The tale is of a young boy who is the victim of a brutal attack by enemies and is left to die in a swamp. The child is rescued and nursed back to health by a she-wolf, and they seek refuge in a cavern. After a few years, the boy, now a young man, impregnates the wolf. They have ten half-human, half-wolf boys. Several generations later, the first Turks arrive on the scene, descended from the half-human, half-wolf men. These men became the blacksmiths of the Juan Juan or the Rouran Khaganate.[3] *Book of Zhou* has a differently worded version of this legend, but the theme of the Turks descending from a wolf is the same.

The last legend, popularly known as the "Spirit of the Lake," appears in Chinese sources around 860 CE. According to this myth, the ancestor of the Turks, Shê-mo-shê-li, lives in a cavern and has an affair with the daughter of the lake spirit. One day before a hunt, she tells She-mo: "Tomorrow during the hunt, a white deer with golden horns will come out from the cavern where your ancestors were born. If your arrow hits the deer, we will keep in touch as long as you live, but if you miss it, our relationship will end."

During the hunt, one of She-mo's followers kills the stag with the golden horns, and the man is immediately decapitated. An angry She-mo punishes the guilty man's tribe and orders them to

---

3 Rouran is a Chinese transliteration of possibly Mongolian *nökör*, which is similar to *nokar* in Persian, *nyögér* in Hungarian and *naukar* in Hindi. The term means companion or friend who abandons their family to serve their lord. In the Rouran context, it is believed the term emerged from the companions of the early "Rouran" leaders, who helped build the Rouran state.

send a victim for human sacrifice every year, a custom the Chinese sources mention remains "till this day" (ninth century CE).

These legends are essential for our understanding of the origins of the Turks. The story of the abandoned child raised by a wolf reads like a traditional creation myth, but, based on historical and archaeological evidence, we can confirm that the tale was metaphorical. The early Turks were blacksmiths living near Central Asia's Altai Mountains. They produced high-quality weapons and armor that were sought after by armies across Asia. The cavern where the young boy and the wolf sought refuge could symbolize an iron ore mine.

The legend also highlights the importance of the wolf in Turkic mythology. A wolf-themed myth is common in several cultures across the Eurasian Steppes besides the Turks, such as the Indo-Europeans and the Mongols. Descending from the wolf was an essential part of Turkic beliefs, as seen in the Bugut inscription[4] (c. 584 CE), a wolf-crowned stele depicting a she-wolf with a human under her belly, reminiscent of Remus and Romulus and the foundation of Rome.

The origin myths are also crucial in establishing a link between the early Turks and the Kyrgyz, whom the same sources claim do not belong to the "race of wolf." However, they mention that the Kyrgyz also lived in caverns. They were expert miners and played an essential role in the politics of the Steppes during the rise of the Göktürks.

THE RISE OF THE FIRST TURKIC KHAGANATE

In the fourth century CE, a new power in the Steppes emerged, known as the Rourans, a proto-Mongolic people related to the

4 Refer to the section "language to unite an empire" later in this chapter for a detailed discussion on the Bugut Inscription.

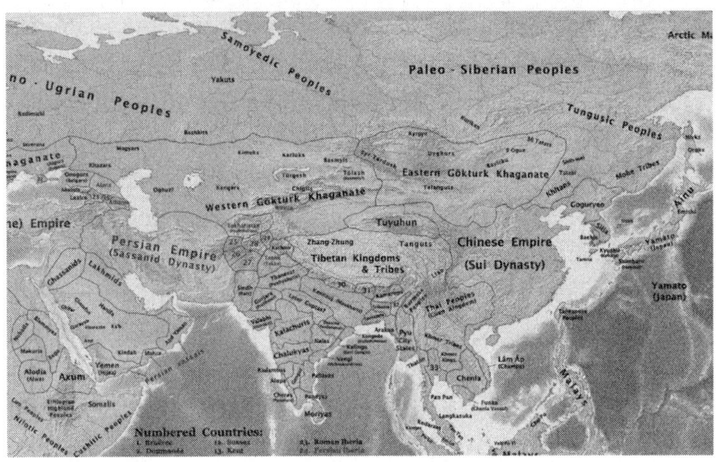

A map of Eurasia showing the First Turkic Khaganate (Eastern and Western) in 600 CE.

Donghu.[5] In 402 CE, Yujiulu Shelun united the Rouran tribes. No longer plagued by infighting, the Rourans locked horns with the Northern Wei dynasty, which ruled North China, in a legendary conflict. You may be familiar with this clash if you've seen the Disney movie *Mulan* (1998). The Huns shown in the film were Rourans. The Northern Wei dynasty, although depicted in the movie as ethnic Han Chinese, was founded by the Touba clan of the Xianbei, one of the descendants of the Donghu. As we discussed in Chapter 15, on Modu and the Xiongnu, the arch-nemesis of nomadic powers was primarily a rival tribe, rather than a settled people. The Rouran–Wei conflict was essentially a clash between two proto-Mongolic people rather than Hun vs. Han Chinese as *Mulan* depicts.

The Rourans were the first Steppe power to use the term *Khagan*[6] to refer to an emperor. Later, the title Khagan became popular among the Turks and Mongols, and its usage continued

5 For more details on Donghu refer to Chapter 15.

6 *Khagan* is pronounced "Kha'an"; the "g" is silent.

until the twentieth century. The Rourans controlled the lucrative Silk Road trade. Around 460 CE, they settled the Ashina clan of the Göktürks along the eastern foothills of the Altai Mountains and on the Steppes east of Lake Issyk, hiring them to make weapons and armor for their soldiers. However, since the Turks were also talented warriors with a deep understanding of military tactics, they found service in the Rouran army.

The earliest mention of the Ashina clan is from the *Book of Sui,* which describes the Northern Wei Emperor defeating Juqu Mujian, ruler of Northern Liang,[7] and 500 Ashina families fleeing west to seek refuge in Rouran lands. According to Chinese sources, the Ashina emerged from the Xiongnu Empire. Other scholars have suggested Indo-European origins of the Ashina clan, as the term "Ashina" probably has a Tocharian or East Iranian root. Limited DNA analysis supports the Xiongnu origins of Ashina. A 2023 genetic study by Xiaoming Yang et al. on an early Ashina elite (Empress Ashina)[8] found that she had 97.7 percent Northeast Asian ancestry with a minor 2.3 percent of West Eurasian component. The admixture between the two groups occurred around 1000 BCE, and like the Xiongnu, the Ashina and Göktürk elite were likely a heterogeneous group.

Legend has it that Bumin, head of the Ashina clan, put down a rebellion for the Rouran Khagan, Yujiulu Anagui, in 551 CE. Bumin then asked for the princess's hand in marriage. The Rouran chief laughed at the request and rejected it, claiming that a woman of noble birth would never marry a blacksmith slave.

Insulted and humiliated, Bumin allied with the Northern Wei, who were ever ready to strike at an opportunity to create

7 Northern Liang (397 CE to 439 CE) was one of the 16 kingdoms of ancient China.

8 Empress Ashina (c. 581 CE to 582 CE) was the queen of the Xianbei led Northern Zhou dynasty. She was the daughter of Muhan and the granddaughter of Bumin, founder of the Göktürk Khaganate.

chaos in the Rouran realm. He married a Chinese princess and united the Turks and, with the Wei's help, revolted against Anagui in 552 CE.

Bumin routed the Rourans, captured their capital, and declared himself Khagan. Anagui, pained by the humiliation, committed suicide.

The Göktürks spread west and east, raiding affluent Silk Road frontier towns in Central Asia and China. Bumin's brother, Ishtemi, ruled the empire's western half and took the title of *Yabgu*, equivalent to a viceroy. The primary seat of power remained in the eastern half of the empire. Ishtemi inflicted further defeats on the Rourans, who fled to Central Europe and were later known as the Avars.

Bumin died in 552 CE, a few months after establishing the Göktürk Khaganate. His son, Issik, succeeded him. Issik's reign didn't last long, as he died within three months of ascending the throne. Bumin's second son, Muhan, assumed power, ushering in a new era for the Turkic people.

EXPANSION, DIPLOMACY, AND TRADE

The two realms of the Turkic Khaganate, east and west, provided a unique opportunity for Muhan and Ishtemi. Uncle and nephew could go in different directions and target wealthy empires in the Middle East, Central Asia, and northern China without relying on each other for orders. The fluid command structure helped in the rapid expansion of the Göktürks.

Muhan conquered the nomadic kingdom of the Khitans in the east and the Kyrgyz in the south. His conquests are poorly documented beyond this point. We have a better understanding of Ishtemi's exploits because his forces came into contact with Persians and Romans (Byzantine), who recorded the historical events.

Initially, Ishtemi allied with the Sassanid Persians to conquer the Hephthalite Huns, also known as the White Huns.[9] The Göktürks held a grudge against the Hephthalites because they had shielded the Rouran nobles fleeing from the Turks. The Sassanids had come under the heavy cosh of the Hephthalites, who had inflicted a series of defeats on the Persians. In 484 CE, somewhere near present-day Balkh, Afghanistan, Persian Emperor Peroz and his entire army were killed by the Huns, who successfully lured the Sassanians into a trench.

The Persians were looking to avenge Peroz's death. Hence, his grandson, Khusrow I, welcomed an alliance with Ishtemi. A joint Persian and Göktürk army attacked the Hephthalites near Bukhara in 560 CE. In an epic eight-day battle, the Hephthalites, led by Gatfar, defended the city valiantly. But his heroics were not enough, as the Persian–Turk alliance proved formidable, and Bukhara was sacked.

Ishtemi's goal wasn't just to punish the Hephthalites for shielding the Rourans. He had an eye on taking over the lucrative Silk Road trade. Despite his initial alliance with the Persians, things soon turned sour. The Persians didn't allow the Göktürk envoys to sell silk in their empire, and on one occasion, they seized a Turkic cargo and burned all their textiles. The trade hostilities escalated into a full-fledged conflict, and the next 50 years saw repeated clashes between the Persians and the Turks, with victories on both sides but no significant shifts in territorial boundaries. The wars with the Persians didn't prevent the Turks from gaining wealth and finding new allies.

---

9 In Hunnic society, white represented the western direction, black indicated north, blue symbolized east, and red signified south. The black and blue Huns held a higher status than their red and white counterparts. Attila's Huns, for example, used black.

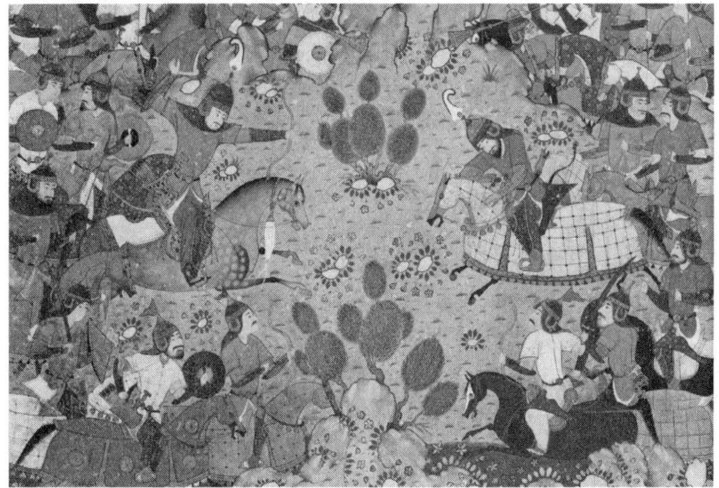

An illustration from *Shahnameh* depicts a conflict between Persians and Turks.

Maniah, a Sogdian diplomat, convinced Ishtemi to bypass the Persians and trade directly with the Romans, the world's largest buyers of silk. In 568 CE, the Eastern Roman Emperor Justin II received a Göktürk delegation at Constantinople. The following year, the Turks warmly welcomed a Roman envoy. With the Romans they formed a military, commercial, and diplomatic alliance. This new partnership benefited both during their conflicts with the Persians.

Sogdian merchants played a crucial role in helping the Göktürks establish themselves as a commercial power. The Sogdians were an Iranian people who lived in Sogdiana, a region that spans modern-day Tajikistan and Uzbekistan. Diplomatically adept, they also aided the Turks in creating the Old Turkic alphabet, the foundation of the Turkic writing system. Archaeologists have discovered inscriptions in Old Turkic as far west as the Balkans and Hungary.

In the east, after Muhan died in 572 CE, his brother Taghpar took over as Khagan. Once a devout follower of the ancient

Sogdian noble An Jia (*right*) brokering a deal with a Turkic aristocrat (*left*).

Turkic religion of Tengrism, Taghpar converted to Buddhism. He began an ambitious project to construct monasteries and study centers. Taghpar sponsored the Sogdian and Turkic translations of Buddhist canonical works. During his reign, Sogdian and Brahmi,[10] the ancient script of India, were widely used, and we have the best-preserved evidence in the Bugut inscription.

LANGUAGE TO UNITE AN EMPIRE

In 1889, Nikolai Mikhailovich Yadrintsev, a Russian archaeologist, discovered Karakorum, the capital of the Mongol Empire, in

10 Brahmi reached the Göktürk Khaganate from India through the Silk Road trade. Sogdian merchants are believed to have introduced it to the Turkic nobility.

The Orkhon inscription, the first recorded history of the Turkic people, Orkhon Museum, Mongolia.

Övörkhangai Province, Mongolia. But one of his other finds is vital for us. In Mongolia's Orkhon Valley, Yadrintsev unearthed two gigantic monoliths containing the earliest undisputed proof of a written language in the Steppes. In 1893, Vasily Vasilyevich Radlov, a schoolteacher from Siberia with an interest in Turkic languages, heard about Nikolai Yadrintsev's discovery of the Orkhon inscriptions. Radlov published the Orkhon inscriptions, and we remember him as one of the leading figures who started the discipline of Turkology, the scientific study of Turkic languages.

Radlov's publication caught the eye of Danish linguist Vilhelm Thomsen. In the same year, Thomsen deciphered the Orkhon inscriptions, thereby forever changing our understanding of writing in nomadic societies. Before Thomsen decoded the Old Turkic script, historians believed that the Turks and their preceding nomadic powers lacked a written script or depended on other literate people, such as the Chinese and Sogdians, for official communications.

The Orkhon Valley lies 320 km west of Mongolia's capital, Ulaanbaatar. The area was the seat of power of the Göktürks and the Xiongnu. In 732 CE, Göktürk rulers Bilge Khagan and his brother Kul Tigin constructed two colossal monoliths in the region. Bilge Khagan was the fourth ruler of the Second Turkic Khaganate, which arose after the collapse and subjugation of the First Turkic Khaganate by the Tang dynasty of China.

Though the Orkhon inscriptions are the earliest surviving form of Old Turkic, there is evidence that the script may be even older. According to the seventh century *Book of Zhou*, which documents the histories of China's western Wei and northern Zhou dynasties, the Turks employed a writing system similar to that of the Sogdians.

Besides Sogdian, the Brahmi-derived Tocharian script also influenced the Old Turkic writing system. Brahmi was the primary script of ancient India, popularized in Central Asia by Buddhist monks. Before the full-fledged use of Old Turkic, Brahmi may have been the Turks' default script. The Bugut inscription in Mongolia, written during the reign of Taghpar in 582 CE, was in Sogdian and Brahmi. The language of the Brahmi script was once assumed to be Sanskrit, but in 2014, linguists concluded it was an early version of Mongolian. Surprisingly, the Bugut inscription did not contain any Turkic language. Besides Bugut, there are other inscriptions in Mongolic Brahmi. The Hüis Tolgoi inscription, dated to the early seventh century CE and possibly commissioned by Niri Khagan, was also in Mongolic Brahmi, demonstrating that the Turks had a script before establishing their own.

Another theory suggests that Old Turkic had its roots in the Xiongnu's Hu script.[11] Archaeologists have discovered over 20 Hu script-carved characters at a burial site in Noin-Ula, near Lake Baikal, in Mongolia. These characters resemble the Old Turkic alphabet, but the links are tenuous at best.

The evidence for the widespread use of the Hu script across the Steppes is limited. We don't know if it significantly impacted the development of Old Turkic. In contrast, archaeologists have unearthed over 200 inscriptions written in Old Turkic across Eurasia. The writing system introduced by the Göktürks laid the foundation for the development of scripts among Steppe peoples, including the Uyghurs, Khitans, Mongols, and Manchus. The successor states put a greater emphasis on written records for communication, which became integral to empire-building.

COLLAPSE

After Taghpar died, his son, Apa, was supposed to be the Khagan. Nivar, Taghpar's brother, usurped the throne. Apa asked Tardu, the Yabgu from the west, for help to get rid of Nivar. He routed Apa and Tardu's combined army. However, Apa would not abandon his dream of ruling an empire. He betrayed Tardu and took over the Western Turkic Khaganate, dividing the first Turkic empire into two independently ruled parts, East and West, in 603 CE.

11 More on the Hu script in Chapter 15.

The schism in the Khaganate did not mark the end of Turkic rule over Central Asia, but the Turks were weaker than before.

Yet despite their waning power, the Göktürks were poised to take advantage of the political chaos in China. The transition from the Sui to the Tang dynasty (613 CE–628 CE) was bloody and resulted in a reduced influence of the Chinese in the politics of the region. The Turks took advantage of the chaos to launch raids deep inside China.

In 626 CE, Illig, the Khagan of the Eastern Turks, marched on the Chinese capital, Chang'an, forcing the Tang ruler Li Shimin, better known as Taizong, to accept a peace treaty. Taizong is one of the most well-known rulers in Chinese history, and he wouldn't forget the humiliation at the hands of the Turks.

In 629 CE, Taizong declared war against the Turks, and the Chinese crushed the Göktürks in the Battle of Yinshan in 630 CE. Illig was captured and taken as a prisoner. China absorbed the eastern half of the Turkic Khaganate. The western half of the Khaganate was conquered in 657 CE. The Turks recognized Emperor Taizong as "Khagan of Heaven," making him the first Chinese emperor to achieve such a title and rule over the nomadic tribes of the Eurasian Steppes.

After being absorbed by the Tang dynasty, the power of the Göktürks waned. The Tang forced them to provide troops for combat and take part in military campaigns. The Turks had a complex relationship with the Tangs, and the Turkic scribes lamented their loss of freedom. The Orkhon inscriptions ask the Turks to shun Chinese luxuries, living in walled cities, and encourage a nomadic lifestyle in felt tents[12] in the open Steppes. The stele sums up the dire situation of the Turks:

12 Felt tents are known as *gers* (Mongolian) or *yurts* (Russian).

Bust of Kul Tigin, National Museum of Mongolia, Ulaanbaatar.

"The sons of the nobles became the bondsmen of the Chinese people, their unsullied daughters became its slaves. The Turkic beys gave up their Turkic names, and bearing the Chinese names of Chinese beys, they obeyed the Chinese Emperor and served him for fifty years. For him, they waged war in the East towards the sun's rising,

> as far as Bokli kagan; in the West, they made expeditions as far as Taimirkapig; for the Chinese Emperor, they conquered kingdoms and power. The whole of the common Turkic people said thus: 'I have been a nation that had its own kingdom; where is now my kingdom? For whom do I win the kingdoms, they said. I have been a people who had their own khagan; where is my khagan? Which khagan is it I serve?"

In 679 CE, Ashina Nishufu, the leader of a Turkic faction, had had enough of Chinese overlordship and revolted against the Tang. But the revolt was unsuccessful, and in 680 CE, Nishufu's men, unhappy with his leadership, assassinated him.

Ashina Funian, another member of the royal Ashina clan, rebelled with limited success. However, Ilterish Khagan and his trusted aide, Tonyukuk, led the Turks to triumph over the Chinese, establishing the Second Turkic Khaganate in 682 CE, with its capital at Ötüken in the Orkhon valley.

This resurgent state lasted until 744 CE, when a civil war broke out between the Ashina clan and one of their vassals, the Uyghurs, led by Qutlugh Bilge Kol. Qutlugh joined forces with the Karluks and attacked Ötüken, defeating and beheading the last Göktürk Khagan, Ozmish. Following the conquest of Ötüken, the Uyghurs constructed Ordu-Baliq, their new city, atop the foundations of the former Göktürk metropolis. Ordu-Baliq, also known as Karabalasagun,[13] had a significant impact on the design of the Mongol capital Karakorum centuries later.

With the collapse of the Ashina clan's control, a new Turkic Khaganate, the Uyghur Khaganate, emerged.

13 Karabalasagun is a distinct city from Balasagun, which we discussed in Chapter 12.

Uyghur princes wearing Chinese-style robes, Bezeklik Caves.

The Uyghurs maintained a profitable alliance with the Tang dynasty. They assisted the Tang emperor in putting down the An Lushan rebellion (755 CE–763 CE), which ravaged China. According to some estimates, China lost 36 million people or nearly one-sixth of the global population. An Lushan was a Tang general of Sogdian and Turkic origin. Tensions, distrust of the Tang court officials, personal ambition, and an indulgent emperor were the perfect recipe for a brewing revolt. During the catastrophic conflict between the Tang and An Lushan's forces, the Uyghurs played a crucial role in supplying horse archers and horses to the Chinese cavalry, albeit at a steep cost. China provided silk, copper coins, and food to the Uyghurs and, subsequently, princesses to forge matrimonial alliances. Unlike the Xiongnu and the *heqin* policy we discussed in Chapter 15,[14] this arrangement was voluntary, as Chinese women continued their customs even after marriage. They wouldn't sacrifice themselves with their Turkic husbands following the latter's death. The last Tang princess to marry an Uyghur Khagan even returned to China after his death.

The Uyghurs built upon the legacy of the Göktürks, and Ordu-Baliq became a flourishing city of international commerce. Writing was vital for the Uyghurs, and they developed a script based on the Brahmi script used in the Tarim Basin with the help of the Sogdians. The Uyghur script became a prototype for the Mongol and Manchu scripts centuries later.

In 840 CE, Kulug Bagha, an ambitious Uyghur minister, fled to the Yenisei Kyrgyz and invited them to attack the Uyghur Khaganate. A century after they triumphed over the Göktürks, the Uyghurs had weakened because of internal conflict. The Kyrgyz were vassals of the Uyghurs who lived northeast of the Altai Mountains. The relationship between the two parties was frosty. Hence, the Kyrgyz didn't need much persuasion to muster a force of 80,000 horsemen and attack Ordu-Baliq. In a repeat of the events a century ago, the city was razed. The Kyrgyz executed the last Uyghur Khagan and sent his head to the Tang court. Uyghurs fled the Orkhon Valley and migrated to present-day Xinjiang. The unified rule of Turks over the eastern and western Eurasian Steppes ended. But the story of the Göktürks didn't end yet.

The Göktürks ruled a vast territory and controlled a profitable trade route for almost 200 years. Their legacy, however, lasted well into the modern era. Following the break-up of the Turkic

14 Xiongnu's *heqin* policy involved the Chinese paying mandatory tribute of silk and princesses in exchange for a few horses, refer to Chapter 15 for more details.

Khaganate, various Turkic tribes that emerged from this realm significantly influenced the politics of Europe, Asia, and North Africa until the twentieth century. The successors of the Turkic Khaganate, the Ghaznavids, Qara-Khanids, Uyghurs, Khazars, Seljuks, and Ottomans, played a vital role in world politics from the Middle Ages till the modern era.

Today, there are over 200 million speakers of Turkic languages worldwide, and they can trace their origins to a band of blacksmiths living in the foothills of the Altai Mountains.

EPILOGUE

In the summer of 2022, I returned to the Indian Museum in Kolkata, where I had seen Kanishka's statue in a special exhibition when I was ten years old. I hadn't been to the museum since then. This time, another exhibition was taking place, focusing on the Indus Valley Civilization. As I made my way through the artifacts, a pot caught my attention. The ceramic was from Mehrgarh, a bichrome piece painted in white and dark red with distinct depictions of three fish (refer to Chapter 4, page 77). Reflecting on my time at the Indian Museum, I see that the two artifacts described in my book's opening and closing sections appear in reverse order to the way I first came upon them.

The most challenging part for me was how to come up with a narrative that tells the story of human progress since the early days, while focusing only on the chapters of the past which popular discourse seldom highlights.

The earliest *Homo sapiens* fossil, dating back 300,000 years, was discovered in the Jebel Irhoud archaeological site in Morocco. We began chronicling our lives between 7,000 and 5,000 years ago, depending on whether I convinced you that a script existed in the Balkans or if you favor the traditional narrative of writing originating from Mesopotamia. Between

Jebel Irhoud and the Vinča culture, humans lost a substantial amount of their history. Widespread writing and recording across the globe came considerably later, as we saw throughout the book, leaving us with numerous advanced societies, such as those of the Eurasian Steppes, that did not leave written records until the sixth century CE. The absence of documentation has frequently discouraged the public from becoming interested in these exceptional cultures and their accomplishments.

Forgotten Footprints is a humble attempt to change this perception.

We began our journey in Czechia, where people established the first permanent settlements and produced the earliest known ceramics. They showed us that being human is about more than just surviving in the frigid conditions of the Ice Age. Art and creativity are a constant in our lives. They were equally relevant 27,000 years ago as they are today. We saw the emergence of megaliths at Göbekli Tepe before the arrival of full-fledged farming in the Near East. Çatalhöyük pioneered modern urban living. Its residents had a different perspective on death than we did. At Mehrgarh, we watched the world's first cotton farmers try an early form of dentistry, showing that caring for one's health has always been a human priority.

We then witnessed the rise of civilizations, where we challenged several popular ideas about what a civilization means. Writing may have originated in the Balkans before Mesopotamia; Peru could have the world's oldest dated pyramids rather than Egypt; the wheels of war and modern horses that revolutionized transportation were traced to an obscure settlement at the foothills of the Urals; and the so-called "Old World" had a fifth river valley civilization, discovered only in the 1970s.

We then investigated the urbanization stage of human progress. Tell Brak tells us about the gradual development of an agrarian society into a sophisticated city that was densely packed but not as crowded as a typical Fertile Crescent metropolis. In contrast, at Nekhen we saw a rapid transformation, as Egypt's first farmers built sophisticated cities and laid the groundwork for the pyramids within just 1,500 years of the earliest evidence of farming. The city gave us a rare story of the rise of Egyptian Civilization as it happened. We defied conventional notions about cities in the Americas by exploring the history of urbanization and agriculture in the Amazon. We saw a megapolis on the banks of the Mississippi, which rivalled the population of Paris and London in the twelfth century CE. The Steppes, which we often imagine as empty grasslands, were once the home to a city deemed the center of the universe.

In the final section, we saw how the Assyrians established the world's first transcontinental empire and paved the way for future empires.

Modu's rise and the impact the Xiongnu and their Hunnic descendants had on the histories of China, Persia, India, and Europe are underrated. Their adversaries, the Yuezhi, were also significant in the Silk Road trade and established a magnificent civilization that merged Greek and Indian art and served as a crossroads for faiths from east and west. Finally, we concluded with the Göktürks, the first Steppe Empire to invent a native writing system.

I want to attract attention to these lesser-known civilizations and cultures for more than just the stories they have to offer. I aim to emphasize the political, environmental, and socioeconomic risks that these neglected civilizations face. In the Kushans chapter, we covered how Bactrian Gold has vanished since 2021, and some of us will remember the horrific destruction of the Bamiyan Buddhas in 2001. At Cahokia we saw how a financial dispute between the government and the private property owner resulted in the unfortunate demolition of the Powell's Mound.

In 2013, property developers damaged many of the pyramids at the El Paraíso archaeological site, which are even older than Caral's. Police intervened to prevent further destruction. Grave robbers have looted

Nekhen's wine-rich tomb of King Scorpion and several burials from the Oxus Civilization. Expanding agriculture and mining operations pose a severe threat to the Amazon rainforests.

Let us ask ourselves, would it be possible to demolish the pyramids of Giza or the Colosseum as easily as Powell's Mound or the pyramids at El Paraíso? The answer is no. I am confident that the events leading to the demolition of Powell's Mound wouldn't occur in today's world, where there is a greater interest in the histories of the Indigenous peoples of the Americas.

What makes me hopeful is that technological advancement is making it possible for scholars to reconstruct the past in ways we may not have imagined before. Maybe Percy Fawcett would've admired LiDAR and imaging of Amazon's lost cities instead of fading into the wilderness, had he been alive today. LiDAR has also revealed that we have scratched only the surface of the extent of Mayan urbanization in Mesoamerica.

At the same time, technology has also made human altercations deadlier.

Recent conflicts across the globe have revealed the devastating effects of new technologies in warfare. Bombs level ancient cities, drones can precisely target archaeological sites and can erase our heritage in the blink of an eye. The cost of human conflicts is not just in terms of lives lost, but also in silencing civilizations and the voices of the past. Yet, in the face of these horrific clashes, some remain defiant. I am reminded of Syrian archaeologist Khaled al-Assad, who, when ISIS demanded the location of Palmyra's treasures, refused. His execution was a tragedy, but his defiance became a testament: that some would rather die than allowing the erasure of their heritage.

As a storyteller, I wield no chisel to carve monuments, no brush to restore faded murals, but I have words. And with them, I can resurrect buried cities, rekindle the ambitions of forgotten dreamers, and shield fragile truths from the erosion of time. History is not static; it is a fire, and every story we tell is an ember keeping it alive. If these pages have sparked your curiosity, then you, too, hold a link in this chain: a promise that no voice from the past will go unheard.

ACKNOWLEDGEMENTS

I WOULD LIKE TO THANK MY FAMILY FOR THEIR SUPPORT IN helping me write this book. In particular, I acknowledge my mother's vital role during the editing process by patiently reviewing the manuscript multiple times.

Being a student of history, she has a keen eye for identifying areas of improvement, helping me provide you with a better reading experience. Whenever I've doubted myself, my wife Satabdi has been my pillar of strength. She always pushed me to aim higher and pursue my love for the past. My father has been supportive of my endeavors and ensured I worked on the book in a peaceful environment. I owe them immense love and gratitude.

My sincere thanks to Dr. Jon Hunner, Dr. David Miano, and Sam Dalrymple for reviewing my manuscript and providing me with invaluable feedback. I truly appreciate them taking the time to endorse my work.

Dr. Hunner deserves a special mention for introducing me to the fascinating world of ancient Americas through his travelogues and graciously agreeing to write the foreword for the book. Dr. Miano is a popular figure among ancient history enthusiasts because of his engaging educational content at *The World of Antiquity* YouTube channel. I've looked up to his work as an inspiration. Hence, it means a lot to me that he chose to endorse my book. Sam Dalrymple is a brilliant historian and author, best known for his bestselling Substack *Travels of Samwise* and his recent debut bestseller *Shattered Lands: Five Partitions and the Making of Modern Asia*. I've been following his work for a long time, and am grateful that despite a hectic schedule, he read the book on short notice and showed his support.

A special thanks to Hachette India's editorial team, especially Anirban Sarkar and Shubhali Chopra, for helping me bring my vision for *Forgotten Footprints* to life.

I would like to express my sincere thanks and gratitude to the Belgrade City Museum for granting me access and permission to use exclusive images related to the Vinča culture. I would especially like to thank Miloš Spasić, Jelena Medaković, and Predrag Đidić for their cooperation and support.

My Substack and Medium readers have been my source of strength, as their regular feedback enabled me not only to improve my writing, but they've also drawn my attention to unexplored worlds and works that I otherwise may not have known about. Hence, I'm thankful to my readers, particularly those who regularly engage with me, for broadening my horizons. I would like to thank all those who supported me since I began my writing journey, especially Dr. Shamik Chakravarty, Dr. John M. Palka, Inge E. Knudsen, Yuri Minamide, Amy Harlib, Lalipa Hongladarom Nilubol, Promit Sengupta, Karen L. Randall, Jackson Houser, David Livingston, M. Thomas Robertson, Rituparna Goswami, Matthew K. Buening, M.E. Rothwell, Vivek Das, James Benson Sarsgard, Prester John Andrews, Devayani Khare, and Kelly Miller. Lastly, I thank you, the reader, for joining me on this fascinating journey as we peel back the layers of time and listen to the stories the past has been whispering to us all along.

I hope you enjoyed this work.

Prateek Dasgupta.

REFERENCES

SECTION 1: DAWN OF CIVILIZATION

Chapter 1

- Maria Dobrovolskaya, Michael Richards, and Erik Trinkaus, 'Direct radiocarbon dates for the Mid Upper Paleolithic (eastern Gravettian) burials from Sunghir, Russia', *Bulletins et mémoires de la Société d'anthropologie de Paris*, 24 (1–2): 96–102, 2011.
- Janusz K. Kozłowski, 'The origin of the Gravettian', *Quaternary International*, 2015.
- A. Revedin, L. Longo, M. Mariotti Lippi, E. Marconi, A. Ronchitelli, J. Svoboda, E. Anichini, M. Gennai, and B. Aranguren, 'New technologies for plant food processing in the Gravettian', *Quaternary International*, 2015.
- Robert Power and Domigo Salazar-García,'Dental calculus evidence of Gravettian diet and behaviour at Dolní Věstonice and Pavlov', Dolní Věstonice II: Chronostratigraphy, Paleoethnology, Paleoanthropology, Academy of Sciences of the Czech Republic, 2016.
- Q. Fu, C. Posth, M. Hajdinjak, M. Petr, S. Mallick, D. Fernandes, A. Furtwängler, W. Haak, M. Meyer, A. Mittnik, B. Nickel, A.

Peltzer, N. Rohland, V. Slon, S. Talamo, I. Lazaridis, M. Lipson, I. Mathieson, S. Schiffels... D. Reich, 'The genetic history of Ice Age Europe', *Nature...*, 2016.

- Mihael Budja, 'Ceramics among Eurasian hunter-gatherers: 32 000 years of ceramic technology use and the perception of containment', *Documenta Praehistoric*, 2016.
- A. Mittnik, C. Wang, J. Svoboda, and J. Krause, 'A Molecular Approach to the Sexing of the Triple Burial at the Upper Paleolithic Site of Dolní Věstonice', *PLoS ONE*, 2016.
- N. Reynolds, R. Dinnis, A.A. Bessudnov, T. Devièse, T. Higham, 'The Kostënki 18 child burial and the cultural and funerary landscape of Mid Upper Palaeolithic European Russia', *Antiquity*, 2017.
- D.G. Drucker, Y.I. Naito, S. Péan, S. Prat, L. Crépin, Y. Chikaraishi, N. Ohkouchi, S. Puaud, A. Yanevich, and H. Bocherens, 'Isotopic analyses suggest mammoth and plant in the diet of the oldest anatomically modern humans from far southeast Europe', *Scientific Reports,* 2017.
- C. Posth, H. Yu, A. Ghalichi, H. T Tougier, I. Crevecoeur, Y. Huang, H. Ringbauer, A.B. Rohrlach, K. Nägele, R. Radzeviciute, T. Ferraz, A. Stoessel, R. Tukhbatova, D.G. Drucker, M. Lari, A. Modi, S. Vai, T. Saupe, C.L. Scheib, J. Krause, 'Palaeogenomics of Upper Palaeolithic to Neolithic European hunter-gatherers', *Nature*, 2023.
- J-C Svenning, R.T. Lemoine, J. Bergman, et al, 'The late-Quaternary megafauna extinctions: Patterns, causes, ecological consequences and implications for ecosystem management in the Anthropocene', *Cambridge Prisms: Extinction*, 2024.
- J. Baker, S. Rigaud, D. Pereira and L.A. Courtenay, 'Evidence from personal ornaments suggest nine distinct cultural groups between 34,000 and 24,000 years ago in Europe', *Nature Human Behaviour*, 2024.
- Don Hitchcock, Don's Maps: https://donsmaps.com/ (Accessed Jan 2025).

Chapter 2

- Steven Mithen, 'After the ice: A Global Human History', 2003.
- Klaus Schmidt, 'Göbekli Tepe: A Neolithic Site in Southwestern Anatolia', *The Oxford Handbook of Ancient Anatolia: (10,000–323 BCE)*, eds. Sharon R. Steadman; Gregory McMahon, Oxford University, 2011.
- Richard A. Herrmann, Klaus Schmidt, 'Göbekli Tepe – Investigations into the extraction and use of water in the area of the Stone Age mountain sanctuary', 2012.
- Jens Notroff, Oliver Dietrich, Klaus Schmidt, 'Building Monuments – Creating Communities', *Early monumental architecture at Pre-Pottery Neolithic Göbekli Tepe*, In: James Osborne (Hrsg.), Approaching Monumentality in the Archaeological Record. Albany: SUNY Press, 83-105, 2014.
- M. Benz, J. Bauer, 'On Scorpions, Birds and Snakes — Evidence for Shamanism in Northern Mesopotamia during the Early Holocene', *Journal of Ritual Studies*, 2015.
- J. Notroff, O. Dietrich, K. Schmidt, 'Gathering of the Dead? The Early Neolithic Sanctuaries of Göbekli Tepe, Southeastern Turkey', *Death Rituals, Social Order and the Archaeology of Immortality in the Ancient World: 'Death Shall Have No Dominion.'*, In: eds. C. Renfrew, M.J. Boyd, I. Morley, Cambridge University Press, 2015.
- L. Dietrich, J. Meister, O. Dietrich, J. Nostroff, J. Kiep, J. Heeb, A. Beuger, & B. Schütt, 'Cereal processing at Early Neolithic Göbekli Tepe, southeastern Turkey', *PLoS ONE, 14(5)*, 2019.
- E. Özdoğan, 'The Sayburç reliefs: a narrative scene from the Neolithic', *Antiquity*, 2022.
- S. Mithen, 'Shamanism at the transition from foraging to farming in Southwest Asia: sacra, ritual, and performance at Neolithic WF16 (southern Jordan)', *Levant*, *54*(2), 158–189, 2022.
- Edward B. Banning, 'Paradise Found or Common Sense Lost? Göbekli Tepe's Last Decade as a Pre-Farming Cult Centre', *Open Archaeology*, vol, 2023.

- Peter Frankopan, *The Earth Transformed: An Untold History,* Bloomsbury, pp. 58–59, 2023.
- L. Clare, 'Inspired individuals and charismatic leaders: Hunter-gatherer crisis and the rise and fall of invisible decision-makers at Göbeklitepe', *Documenta Praehistorica, 51, 2–39,* 2024.
- Prateek Dasgupta and Devyani Khare, *'Did Hunter-Gatherers Build Göbekli Tepe?'*, Published in Forgotten Footprints and Geosophy, via Substack, 2024.
- Website consulted: Tepe Telegrams: Official Blog of the Göbekli Tepe Research Project.

Chapter 3

- J. Mellaart, 'Çatal Hüyük a Neolithic City in Anatolia', *Proceedings of the British Academy*, 51, pp. 201–13, 1965.
- S.J. Mithen, *After the Ice: a global human history, 20,000–5000 BC.* Cambridge, Massachusetts: Harvard University Press, 2004. Weidenfeld & Nicolson, London, 2003.
- Ian Hodder, *The Leopard's Tale: Revealing the Mysteries of Çatalhöyük*. London; New York: Thames & Hudson, 2006.
- P. Andrews and S. Bello, 'Pattern in human burial practice' eds. R. Gowland and C. Knüsel. *Social archaeology and funerary remains,* Oxford: Oxbow Books, pp. 14–29, 2006.
- M.A. Pilloud and C.S. Larsen, 'Official' and 'practical' kin: Inferring social and community structure from dental phenotype at Neolithic Çatalhöyük, Turkey. *American Journal of Physical Anthropology, 145*(4), 519–530. https://doi.org/10.1002/ajpa.21520, 2011.
- Başak Boz and Lori Hager, 'Living above the Dead: Intramural Burial practices at Çatalhöyük.' 2013.
- W. Palaver, Death in Çatalhöyük, ed. I. Hodder, *Violence and the Sacred in the Ancient Near East: Girardian Conversations at Çatalhöyük*, Cambridge University Press; *41–59,* 2019.
- E.M. Schotsmans, G. Busacca, S.C. Lin, M. Vasić, A.M. Lingle, R. Veropoulidou, C. Mazzucato, B. Tibbetts, S.D. Haddow, M. Somel, C.J. Knüsel, & M. Milella. 'New insights

on commemoration of the dead through mortuary and architectural use of pigments at Neolithic Çatalhöyük, Turkey'. *Scientific Reports*, *12*(1), 1–19. https://doi.org/10.1038/s41598-022-07284-3, 2022.

- Web sources: https://archaeologymag.com/2023/12/ancient-skull-trepanation-in-catalhoyuk/
- https://news.stanford.edu/stories/2016/09/archaeologists-find-8000-year-old-goddess-figurine-central-turkey

Chapter 4

- L. Costantini and A. Lentini, 'Studies in the Vegetation History of Central Baluchistan, Pakistan: Palynological Investigations of a Neolithic Sequence at Mehrgarh', in M. Taddei & G. De Marco (eds.) South Asian Archaeology 1997, pp. 133–159, 2000.
- J. F. Jarrige, 'Mehrgarh Neolithic: New Excavations', in M. Taddei & G. De Marco (eds.) South Asian Archaeology 1997, pp. 259–283, 2000.
- C. Moulherat, M. Tengberg, J. Haquet and B. Mille, *First Evidence of Cotton at Neolithic Mehrgarh, Pakistan: Analysis of Mineralized Fibres from a Copper Bead*, Journal of Archaeological Science, 29(12), 2002.
- V.N. Misra, 'The Mesolithic Age in India', in S. Settar & R. Korisettar (eds.) Indian Archaeology in Retrospect, Prehistory: Archaeology of South Asia, I, pp. 111-125, New Delhi: ICHR Manohar, 2002.
- S.J. Mithen, *After the Ice: A Global Human History, 20,000–5000 BC,* Weidenfeld & Nicholson, 2003.
- J.F. Jarrige, Mehrgarh Neolithic, Pragdhara 18: 136–154, 2008.
- L. Constantini, The first farmers in Western Pakistan: the evidence of the Neolithic agropastoral settlement of Mehrgarh. Pragdhara 18: 167–178, 2008.
- K. Gangal, G.R. Sarson, and A. Shukurov, *The Near-Eastern Roots of the Neolithic in South Asia*. PLOS ONE, 9(5), 2014.

- Robin Coningham; Ruth Young, *The Archaeology of South Asia: From the Indus to Asoka, c.6500 BCE–200 CE*, Cambridge University Press, 2015.
- M. Thoury, B. Mille, T. Séverin-Fabiani, L. Robbiola, M. Réfrégiers, F. Jarrige and L. Bertrand, High spatial dynamics-photoluminescence imaging reveals the metallurgy of the earliest lost wax cast object, *Nature Communications, 7,* 13356, 2016.
- Vasant et al, *An Ancient Harappan Genome Lacks Ancestry from Steppe Pastoralists or Iranian Farmers.* Cell, Volume 179, Issue 3, 2018.
- V.M. Narasimhan, N. Patterson, P. Moorjani, N. Rohland, R. Bernardos, S. Mallick, I. Lazaridis, N. Nakatsuka, I. Olalde, M. Lipson, A.M. Kim, L.M. Olivieri, A. Coppa, M. Vidale, J. Mallory, V. Moiseyev, E. Kitov, J. Monge, N. Adamski, ...D. Reich, *The Formation of Human Populations in South and Central Asia*, Science (New York, N.Y.), *365*(6457), 2019.

SECTION 2: RISE OF CIVILIZATIONS

Chapter 5

- Colin Renfrew, Before civilization: The radiocarbon revolution and prehistoric Europe, 1973.
- Marija Gimbutas, *The Goddesses and Gods of Old Europe, 6500–3500 BC: Myths and Cult Images* (New and updated ed.), Berkeley: University of California Press, 1974.
- A. Marija Gimbutas (ed.)., *Neolithic Macedonia as reflected by excavation at Anza, southeast Yugoslavia,* Los Angeles: Institute of Archaeology, University of California, 1976.
- Sham M.M. Winn, *The Signs of the Vinca Culture*, 1973.
- Sham M.M. Winn, Pre-writing in Southeast Europe: The Sign System of the Vinca culture, 1981.
- John Chapman, *The Vinča culture of south-east Europe: Studies in chronology, economy and society (2 vols)*, BAR International Series, Vol. 117, Oxford, 1981.

- J. Makkay, *Early Stamp Seals in South-East Europe*, Budapest, 1984.
- Denise Schmandt-Besserat, Before Writing, University of Texas Press, Austin, Volume I: From Counting to Cuneiform, 1992.
- Gareth A. Owens, 'Balkan Neolithic Scripts', *Kadmos,* 1999.
- Marco Merlini, Gheorghe, Lazarovici, 'Settling discovery circumstances, dating and utilization of the Tărtăria tablets'. *Acta Terrae Septemcastrensis,* 2008.
- Adam N. Crnobrnja, Marko Jankovic, Simić Zoran, Late Vinča culture settlement at Crkvine in Stubline: Household organization and urbanization in the Late Vinča culture period, 2009.
- Adam N. Crnobrnja, Arrangement of Vinča culture figurines: a study of social structure and organisation, 2011.
- Miloš Spasić: A Group Find of Neolithic Figurines of the Vinča Culture from Stubline, Serbia, 2014.
- Gheorghe Lazarovici; Marco Merlini, 'Tărtăria Tablets: The Latest Evidence in an Archaeological Thriller'. In Nikolova, Lolita; Merlini, Marco; Comsa, Alexandra (eds.). *Western-Pontic Culture Ambience and Pattern: In memory of Eugen Comsa*. Warsaw, Poland: De Gruyter Open Poland. pp. 53–142, 2016.
- Miljana Radivojević, Paint It Black: The Rise of Metallurgy in the Balkans, Journal of Archaeological Method and Theory, 23 (1): 200, 2016.
- Mark Lipson, 'Parallel palaeogenomic transects reveal complex genetic history of early European farmers', *Nature*. 551 (7680), 2017.
- D. Borić, B. Hanks, D. Šljivar, M. Kočić, J. Bulatović, S. Griffiths, R. Doonan, & D. Jacanović, Enclosing the Neolithic World: A Vinča Culture Enclosed and Fortified Settlement in the Balkans, *Current Anthropology*, 2018.
- Harald Haarmann, The Mystery of the Danube Civilisation, 2020.
- M. Porčić, Observations on the origin and demography of the Vinča culture, *Quaternary International, 560-561*, 57-64, 2020.

- R. Hofmann, & N. Müller-Scheeßel, Orientation of Neolithic dwellings in Central and Southeast Europe: Common denominator between the Vinča and Linearbandkeramik worlds, *Quaternary International, 560-561*, 142-153, 2020.
- Benjamin W. Roberts; Miljana Radivojević; Miroslav Marić, 'The Vinča culture: an overview', In Radivojević, Miljana; Roberts, Benjamin (eds.), The Rise of Metallurgy in Eurasia: Evolution, Organisation and Consumption of Early Metal in the Balkans, Summertown, Oxford, 2021.
- K. Rassmann; M. Furholt, 'The social organisation of the Vinča culture settlements. New evidence from magnetic and archaeological excavation data', In Radivojević, Miljana; Roberts, Benjamin (eds.), *The Rise of Metallurgy in Eurasia: Evolution, Organisation and Consumption of Early Metal in the Balkans,* Summertown, Oxford: Archaeopress, 2021.
- P. Raczky, Review of Wolfram Schier & Florin Drašovean (Eds.), *Uivar 'Gomilă': A prehistoric settlement in the Romanian Banat. Vol. I: Site, architecture, stratigraphy and dating* (Prähistorische Archäologie in Südosteuropa, Vol. 32), 2024.

Chapter 6

- M.E. Moseley and G.R. Willey, Aspero, Peru: A Reexamination of the Site and Its Implications. *American Antiquity*, *38*(4), 452–468. 1973.
- T.F. Lynch, R. Gillespie, J. A. J. Gowlett, & R.E.M. Hedges, Chronology of Guitarrero Cave, Peru. *Science*. 1985
- Ruth Shady Solis, Jonathan Haas; Winifred Creamer, 'Dating Caral, a Preceramic Site in the Supe Valley on the Central Coast of Peru' *Science*. 292 (5517): 723–726. 2001.
- Heather Pringle, 'The First Urban Center in the Americas'. *Science*. 292 (5517): 621. 2001.
- Hanna Hoag, 'Oldest evidence of Andean religion found.' *Nature News,* 2003.

- Jonathan Haas, Winifred Creamer; Alvaro Ruiz, 'Dating the Late Archaic occupation of the Norte Chico region in Peru.' *Nature*, 23 December 2004.
- Charles C. Mann, 'Oldest Civilization in the Americas Revealed', *Science*, 2005.
- Ruth Shady Solís, *Caral Supe, Perú: the Caral–Supe civilization: 5,000 years of cultural identity in Peru*, Lima: Instituto Nacional de Cultura, 2005.
- Ruth Shady Solis, America's First City? The Case of Late Archaic Caral, 2006.
- Charles C. Mann, *1491: New Revelations of the Americas Before Columbus*. Vintage Books, 2006.
- D.H. Sandweiss, R.S. Solís, M.E. Moseley, D.K. Keefer, & C.R. Ortloff, Environmental change and economic development in coastal Peru between 5,800 and 3,600 years ago, *Proceedings of the National Academy of Sciences of the United States of America, 106*(5), 1359. 2009.
- J. Haas, W. Creamer, L. Huamán Mesía, D. Goldstein, K. Reinhard, & C.V. Rodríguez, Evidence for maize (*Zea mays*) in the Late Archaic (3000–1800 B.C.) in the Norte Chico region of Peru, *Proceedings of the National Academy of Sciences, 110*(13), 4945-4949, 2013.
- L. Pezo-Lanfranco, M. Machacuay, P. Novoa, R. Peralta, E. Mayer, S. Eggers, & R. Shady, The diet at the onset of the Andean Civilization: New stable isotope data from Caral and Áspero, North-Central Coast of Peru, *American Journal of Biological Anthropology, 177*(3), 402-424, 2022.
- Peter Frankopan, The Earth Transformed: An Untold History, Bloomsbury, pp 92-93, 2023.
- Jessica Rawnsley, 'Archaeologists unveil 3,500-year-old city in Peru', BBC News, Accessed July 2025, 6 July 2025.

Chapter 7

- David W. Anthony, *The Horse, the Wheel And Language. How Bronze-Age Riders From the Eurasian Steppes Shaped The Modern World,* Princeton University Press, 2007.

- Elena E. Kuzmina, ed. J.P. Mallory, *The Origin of the Indo-Iranians*, BRILL, 2007.
- David W. Anthony and R. Brown Dorcas, 'The Secondary Products Revolution, Horse-Riding, and Mounted Warfare,' *Journal of World Prehistory*, 2011.
- Morten E. Allentoft, et al, 'Population genomics of Bronze Age Eurasia', *Nature*, 2015.
- I.V. Chechushkov and A.V. Epimakhov, '*Eurasian Steppe Chariots and Social Complexity During the Bronze Age*', *Journal of World Prehistory*, 2018.
- Peter de Barros Damgaard, et al, 'The first horse herders and the impact of early Bronze Age steppe expansions into Asia', *Science*, 2018.
- Orlando Ludovic, et al. 'The origins and spread of domestic horses from the Western Eurasian Steppes', *Nature*. 2021.
- Ivan Semyan and Spyros Bakas, 'Archaeological Experiment on Reconstruction of the "Compound" Bow of the Sintashta Bronze Age Culture from the Stepnoe Cemetery', EXARC Journal Issue 2021/2, 2021.
- I.V. Chechushkov, et al, 'From adaptation to niche construction: Weather as a winter site selection factor in northern Mongolia, the Quebec Lower North Shore, and the southern Urals', *Journal of Anthropological Archaeology*, 2021.
- W. T. T. Taylor and C.I. Barrón-Ortiz, '*Rethinking the evidence for early horse domestication at Botai*', *Sci. Rep*, 11, 2021.
- E. Casanova, et al, Direct 14 C dating of equine products preserved in archaeological pottery vessels from Botai and Bestamak, Kazakhstan. *Archaeol. Anthropol. Sci.* 14, 175, 2022.
- Alexander Lubotsky, 'Indo-European and Indo-Iranian Wagon Terminology and the Date of the Indo-Iranian Split', In Willerslev, Eske; Kroonen, Guus; Kristiansen, Kristian (eds.). *The Indo-European Puzzle Revisited: Integrating Archaeology, Genetics, and Linguistics*, Cambridge: Cambridge University Press, pp. 257–262, 2023.

- W. Powell, G. Barjamovic, and C. Pulak, 'Copper for the early oxhide ingots traced to the South Urals', *Journal of Archaeological Science: Reports*, *56*, 104583, 2024.
- P. Librado, G. Tressières, L. Chauvey, A. Fages, N. Khan, S. Schiavinato, M.A. Kusliy, C. Gaunitz, X. Liu, S. Wagner, C. Der Sarkissian, A. Perdereau, J. Aury, J. Southon, B. Shapiro, O. Bouchez, C. Donnadieu, Y. R. Collin, K. M. Gregersen, ... L. Orlando, Widespread horse-based mobility arose around 2200 bce in Eurasia. *Nature*, *631*(8022), 819-825. 2024.

Chapter 8

- V.M. Masson and V.I. Sarianidi, Central Asia: "Turkmenia before the Achaemenids, London", *Thames and Hudson*. 1972.
- H.P. Francfort,"Note on some Bronze Age Petroglyphs of Upper Indus and Central Asia," *Pakistan Archaeology*, 26: 125–135, 1991.
- H.P. Francfort, "The central Asian Dimension of the Symbolic System in Bactria and Margia", *Antiquity*, vol. 28, no. 259, pp. 406–418, 1994.
- V.I. Sarianidi, "Preface", In F.T. Hiebert (ed.), *Origins of the Bronze Age Oasis Civilization of Central Asia*, Cambridge: Harvard University Press, 1994.
- V.I. Sarianidi, "Soviet Excavations in Bactria: The Bronze Age". In G. Ligabue; S. Salvatori (eds.), *Bactria: An ancient oasis civilization from the sands of Afghanistan*. Venice: Erizzo, 1995.
- History of Civilizations of Central Asia, Vol I, UNESCO Publishing, 1997
- J.P. Mallory, D.Q. Adams, "BMAC". *Encyclopedia of Indo-European culture*. London: Fitzroy Dearborn, 1997.
- A. Lubotsky, "Indo-Iranian substratum" (PDF), In Christian Carpelan (ed.). *Early Contacts between Uralic and Indo-European*. Helsinki: Suomalais-Ugrilainen Seura, 2001.
- Joan Aruz (ed), *Art of the First Cities: The Third Millennium B.C. from the Mediterranean to the Indus*, pp. 347–375,Metropolitan Museum of Art (New York, N.Y.), 2003.

- Philip L. Kohl, *The Making of Bronze Age Eurasia*, Cambridge University Press, 2007.
- Kai Kaniuth, "The Metallurgy of the Late Bronze Age Sapalli Culture (Southern Uzbekistan) and its implications for the 'tin question'", in Iranica Antiqua 42, p. 26, 2007.
- Asko Parpola, *The Roots of Hinduism: The Early Aryans and the Indus Civilization*, Oxford University Press Incorporated, 2015.
- Massimo Vidale, *Treasures from the Oxus: The Art and Civilization of Central Asia*, Bloomsbury Publishing, 2017.
- Vagheesh M. Narasimhan; Nick Patterson; Priya Moorjani; Nadin Rohland; Rebecca Bernardos; Swapan Mallick; Iosif Lazaridis; Nathan Nakatsuka; Iñigo Olalde; Mark Lipson; Alexander M. Kim; Luca M. Olivieri; Alfredo Coppa; Massimo Vidale; James Mallory, "The formation of human populations in South and Central Asia". *Science*. 365. 6 September 2019.
- Nadezhda A. Dubova, "Gonur Depe – City of Kings and Gods, and the Capital of Margush Country (Modern Turkmenistan)", in: *Urban Cultures of Central Asia from the Bronze Age to the Karakhanids*, Harrassowitz Verlag, Wiesbaden, 2019.
- Bertille Lyonnet and Nadezhda A. Dubova, "Introduction", in Bertille Lyonnet and Nadezhda A. Dubova, (eds.), *The World of the Oxus Civilization*, Routledge, London and New York, 2020a.
- Bertille Lyonnet and Nadezhda A. Dubova, "Questioning the Oxus Civilization or Bactria- Margiana Archaeological Culture (BMAC): an overview", in Bertille Lyonnet and Nadezhda A. Dubova (eds.), 2020b.
- Julio Bendezu-Sarmiento, "Horse domestication history in Turkmenistan and other regions of Asia.", 2021.
- Daniel Berger, "The rise of bronze in Central Asia: new evidence for the origin of Bronze Age tin and copper from multi-analytical research", *Frontiers in Earth Science*, 2023.

SECTION 3: LOST CITIES

Chapter 9

- Max Edgar Lucien Mallowan, *Twenty-Five Years of Mesopotamian Discovery (1932–1956)*, British School of Archaeology in Iraq, 1959.
- David Oates, "The Excavations at Tell Brak, 1976.", Iraq 39.2, 1977.
- David Oates, "Excavations at Tell Brak, 1978–81.", Iraq 44.2, 1982.
- David Oates, "Excavations at Tell Brak, 1983–84.", Iraq 47, 1985.
- David Oates, "Excavations at Tell Brak 1985–86.", Iraq 49, 1987.
- David Oates and Joan Oates, "Excavations at Tell Brak 1990-91.", Iraq 53, 1991.
- David Oates and Joan Oates, "Excavations at Tell Brak. v. 1: The Mitanni and Old Babylonian periods", McDonald Institute for Archaeological Research, British School of Archaeology in Iraq, 1997.
- Giorgio Buccellati, "Urkesh and the Question of Early Hurrian Urbanism", In Michael Hudson; Baruch Levine (eds.), *Urbanization and Land Ownership in the Ancient Near East*, Peabody Museum Bulletin. Vol. 7. Harvard University Pres, 1999.
- Geoff Emberling, "Political Control in an Early State: The Eye Temple and the Uruk Expansion in Northern Mesopotamia", In Lamia Al-Gailani Werr; John Curtis; Harriet Martin; Augusta McMahon; Joan Oates; Julian Reade (eds.), *Of Pots and Plans: Papers on the Archaeology and History of Mesopotamia and Syria presented to David Oates in Honour of his 75th Birthday*, NABU Booksellers, 2002.
- Jean M. Evans, "Tell Brak in the Akkadian Period". In Joan Aruz; Ronald Wallenfels, (eds.), *Art of the First Cities: The Third Millennium B.C. from the Mediterranean to the Indus*, Metropolitan Museum of Art, 2003.

- Peter M.M.G. Akkermans; Glenn M. Schwartz, *The Archaeology of Syria: From Complex Hunter-Gatherers to Early Urban Societies (c.16,000-300 BC)*, Cambridge University Press, 2003.
- Augusta McMahon, Joan Oates; Salam al-Quntar, Salam; Colantoni, Carlo; Hald, Mette Marie; Karsgaard, Philip; Khalidi, Lamya; Sołtysiak, Arkadiusz; Stone, Adam; Weber, Jill (2007). "Excavations at Tell Brak 2006–2007". *Iraq*. 69.
- Trevor Bryce, *The Routledge Handbook of the Peoples and Places of Ancient Western Asia*. Routledge, 2009.
- Maria Eugenia Aubet, *Commerce and Colonization in the Ancient Near East*, Translated by Mary Turton, Cambridge University Press, 2013.
- Augusta McMahon, "North Mesopotamia in the Third Millennium BC", In Harriet Crawford (ed.), *The Sumerian World*, Routledge, 2013.
- Rita Dolce, "Equids as Luxury Gifts at the Centre of Interregional Economic Dynamics in the Archaic Urban Cultures of the Ancient Near East", *Syria: Archéologie, Arte et Histoire,* 2014.
- Minna Silver, "Equid burials in archaeological contexts in the Amorite, Hurrian and Hyksos cultural intercourse.", 2014.
- Geoff Emberling, "Mesopotamian Cities and Urban Process, 3500–1600 BCE", In Norman Yoffee (ed.), *The Cambridge World History, Volume 3: Early Cities in Comparative Perspective 4000BCE-1200CE,* Cambridge University Press, 2015.
- E. Andrew Bennett; Jill Weber; Wejden Bendhafer; Sophie Chaplot; Joris Peters; Glenn M. Schwartz; Thierry Grange; Eva-Maria Geigl, "The genetic identity of the earliest human-made hybrid animals, the kungas of Syro-Mesopotamia", *Science Advances*, 2022.

Chapter 10

- James H. Breasted, "The predynastic union of Egypt", *Bulletin de l'Institut Français d'Archéologie Orientale*, 1931.

- Michael Allan Hoffman, *"Before the Pharaohs: How Egypt Became the World's First Nation-State"*, The Sciences, New York Academy of Sciences, 1988.
- Donald B. Redford, *Egypt, Canaan, and Israel in Ancient Times,* Princeton: University Press, 1992.
- Peter A. Clayton, *Chronicle of the Pharaohs,* London: Thames and Hudson, 1994.
- Ian Shaw and Paul Nicholson, *The Dictionary of Ancient Egypt,* London: British Museum Press, 1995.
- Günter Dreyer, *Umm El-Quaab I: Das prädynastische Königsgrab U-j und seine frühen Schriftzeugnisse* (Umm El-Quaab I: The predynastic royal tomb U-j and its early written records). Mainz: Zabern, 1998.
- Nancy C. Lovell, "Egyptians, physical anthropology of", In Kathryn A. Bard; Steven Blake Shubert (eds.), *Encyclopedia of the Archaeology of Ancient Egypt,* London: Routledge, 1999.
- J.C. Darnell, D. Darnell, R. Friedman, and S. Hendrickx, *Theban Desert Road Survey in the Egyptian Western Desert, Volume 1: Gebel Tjauti Rock Inscriptions 1-45 and Wadi el-Hôl Rock Inscriptions 1-45*, Oriental Institute, Chicago, 2002.
- Ian Shaw, *The Oxford History of Ancient Egypt,* Oxford: Oxford University Press, 2003.
- S.J. Mithen, *After the Ice: a global human history, 20,000–5000 BC,* Cambridge, Massachusetts: Harvard University Press, 2004, Weidenfeld & Nicolson, London, 2003.
- Jason Thompson, *A History of Egypt: From Earliest Times to the Present,* American University in Cairo Press, 2008.
- Emily Teeter, *Before the Pyramids,* Oriental Institute, Chicago, 2011.
- John Romer, *A History of Ancient Egypt Volume 1: From the First Farmers to the Great Pyramid,* Allen Lane, 2012.
- Lorraine Boissoneault, *"UNCHARTED Leopards, Hippos, and Cats, Oh My! The World's First Zoo",* JSTOR, 2015.
- Ian Shaw, *Ancient Egyptian Warfare: Tactics, Weaponry and Ideology of the Pharaohs,* Open Road Media, 2019.

- Christopher Ehret, *Ancient Africa: A Global History, to 300 CE*, Princeton: Princeton University Press, 2023.

Chapter 11

- M.J. Heckenberger, A. Kuikuro, T. Kuikuro, J.C. Russell, M. Schmidt, C. Fausto, and B. Franchetto, Amazonia 1492: Pristine Forest or Cultural Parkland? *Science*, 2003.
- Charles C. Mann, *1491: New Revelations of the Americas Before Columbus,* 2nd edition, Vintage, 2005.
- John H. Walker, "The Llanos de Moxos" in *Handbook of South American Archaeology*, ed. by Helaine Silverman and William H. Isbell, New York, Springer, p. 927; Block, David (1994), *Mission Culture on the Upper Amazon,* Lincoln: University of Nebraska Press, 2008.
- Clark L. Erickson, "Amazonia: The Historical Ecology of a Domesticated Landscape" in *Handbook of South American Archaeology* edited by Helaine Silverman and William H. Isbell, New York: Springer, 2008.
- David Grann, *The Lost City of Z: A Tale of Deadly Obsession in the Amazon*, Doubleday, 2009.
- D. Renard, J. Iriarte, J.J. Birk, S. Rostain, B. Glaser, and D. McKey, "Ecological engineers ahead of their time: The functioning of pre-Columbian raised-field agriculture and its potential contributions to sustainability today", *Ecological Engineering*, Vol 45, 2012.
- H. Prümers, C.J. Betancourt, J. Iriarte, M. Robinson, and M. Schaich, Lidar reveals pre-Hispanic low-density urbanism in the Bolivian Amazon. *Nature, 606*(7913), 325, 2022.
- Brian Handwerk, "Lost Cities of the Amazon Discovered From the Air", *Smithsonian Magazine,* 25 May 2022.
- S. Rostain, A. Dorison, H. Prümers, L.L. Pennec, F.M. Mejía, A.M. Freire, J.R. Pagán-Jiménez, and P. Descola, Two thousand years of garden urbanism in the Upper Amazon, *Science*, 2024.
- Elliot Stein, *"The discovery of the Americas' long-lost 'Rome'"*, BBC, January 2024.

Chapter 12

- Charles E. Nowell, "The Historical Prester John", *Speculum*, 28, No. 3, 1953.
- Ata-Malik Juvayni, *The History of The World Conqueror*, Harvard University Press, 1958.
- René Grousset, *The Empire of the Steppes: A History of Central Asia*, Rutgers University Press, p. 160, 1970.
- Robert Devereux, "Yūsuf Khāss Hājib, Wisdom of Royal Glory (Kutadgu Bilig): A Turko-Islamic Mirror for Princes, Robert Dankoff, trans., Publications of the Center for Middle Eastern Studies, No. 16 (Chicago: University of Chicago Press, 1983), Pp. 291", *International Journal of Middle East Studies*, 17 (4): 577–579, 1985.
- Michal Biran, "Like a Mighty Wall: The armies of the Qara Khitai". *Jerusalem Studies in Arabic and Islam*, 25: 44–91, 2001.
- Michal Biran, *The Empire of the Qara Khitai in Eurasian History: Between China and the Islamic World*, Cambridge Studies in Islamic Civilization, Cambridge, 2005.
- C. Edmund Bosworth, *Historic Cities of the Islamic World*, 2007.
- Peter Roudik, The History of the Central Asian Republics, Greenwood Press, 2007.
- W. Barthold, "Balāsāghūn or Balāsaḳūn", In P. Bearman; Th. Bianquis; C.E. Bosworth; E. van Donzel; W.P. Heinrichs (eds.), *Encyclopaedia of Islam*, Brill, 2008.
- James A. Millward, *Eurasian Crossroads: A History of Xinjiang*, Hurst, p. 54, 2010.
- Peter Frankopan, *The Silk Roads: A New History of the World*, Bloomsbury, 2015.
- "*Silk Roads: the Routes Network of Chang'an-Tianshan Corridor.*" *UNESCO World Heritage Centre*, United Nations Educational, Scientific, and Cultural Organization.

Chapter 13

- Warren L. Wittry, "An American Woodhenge", *Cranbrook Institute of Science Newsletter*, 33 (9): 102–107 – via *Explorations into Cahokia Archaeology*, Bulletin 7, Illinois Archaeological Survey, 1964.
- Timothy Pauketat, *The Ascent of Chiefs: Cahokia and Mississippian Politics in Native North America*, Tuscaloosa, AL: University of Alabama, 1994.
- Thomas E. Emerson, *Cahokia and the Archaeology of Power*, Tuscaloosa, AL: University of Alabama, 1997.
- Mark Rose, "Sampling Monks Mound", *Archaeology*, 52 (1), January–February 1999.
- Melvin L. Fowler; Jerome Rose; Barbara Vander Leest; Steven R. Ahler, *The Mound 72 Area: Dedicated and Sacred Space in Early Cahokia*, Illinois State Museum Society, 1999.
- W.I. Woods, "Population nucleation, intensive agriculture, and environmental degradation: The Cahokia example." *Agriculture and Human Values* 21, 255–261, 2004.
- Timothy R. Pauketat, *Ancient Cahokia and the Mississippians*, Cambridge University Press, 2007.
- John E. Kelly; Lucretia S. Kelly; James Brown, *Summary of 2008 Field Excavations to Locate the Copper Workshop in the Mound 34 Area*, Central Mississippi Valley Archaeological Research Institute, 2009.
- Timothy R. Pauketat, *Cahokia: Ancient America's Great City on the Mississippi*, Penguin Books, 2010.
- William R. Iseminger, *Cahokia Mounds: America's First City*, History Press, 2011.
- Charles C. Mann, *1491: New Revelations of the Americas before Columbus*, 2nd ed., Vintage, 2011.
- S.E. Munoz, K.E. Gruley, A. Massie, D.A. Fike, S. Schroeder, and J.W. Williams, Cahokia's emergence and decline coincided with shifts of flood frequency on the Mississippi River, *Proceedings of the National Academy of Sciences, 112*(20), 6319-6324, 2015.

- Melissa Mattioli, "The Ramey Incised Pottery of Cahokia (IL) USA: Diffusion and Reinterpretation of its Iconographic Message", *Zea Books,* 2020.
- C.G. Rankin, C.R. Barrier, and T.J. Horsley, Evaluating narratives of ecocide with the stratigraphic record at Cahokia Mounds State Historic Site, Illinois, USA, *Geoarchaeology, 36*(3), 369-387, 2021.
- Peter Frankopan, The Earth Transformed: An Untold History, Bloomsbury, pp. 282-283, 2023.
- Timothy R. Pauketat, *Gods of Thunder: How Climate Change, Travel, and Spirituality Reshaped Precolonial America,* Oxford University Press, 2023.
- A.J. White, "Cahokia", *The Office of Resources for International and Area Studies,* UC Berkeley, 2024.
- Prateek Dasgupta and Jon Hunner, "*The Mystery of Cahokia's Mounds: America's Lost Ancient City.",* Published in "Forgotten Footprints" and "Driven by the Past" via Substack, 2025.
- Henry M. Brackenridge to Thomas Jefferson, National Archives, 25 July 1813.

SECTION 4: FORGOTTEN EMPIRES

Chapter 14

- E. Belibtreu and Biblical Archaeology Society, *Grisly Assyrian Record of Torture and Death,* https://faculty.uml.edu/ethan_spanier/teaching/documents/cp6.0assyriantorture.pdf, 1991.
- Stephanie Dalley, "Nineveh, Babylon and the Hanging Gardens: Cuneiform and Classical Sources Reconciled, 1994.
- C. Jeanette, Fincke "The British Museum's Ashurbanipal Library Project." Iraq, 2004.
- Francis Joannès, *The Age of Empires: Mesopotamia in the First Millennium BC,* Edinburgh: Edinburgh University Press, 2004.
- Lucien Polastron, "Books On Fire: The Tumultuous Story Of The World's Great Libraries", 2007.

- Irving Finkel; Michael Seymour, *Babylon: City of Wonders.* London: British Museum Press, 2008.
- John Julius Norwich, *The Great Cities In History*, London: Thames & Hudson, 2009.
- Stuart A.P. Murray, The Library: An Illustrated History, Chicago, IL: Skyhorse Publishing, 2009.
- Peter R. Bedford, "The Neo-Assyrian Empire", In Ian Morris; Walter Scheidel (eds.), *The Dynamics of Ancient Empires: State Power from Assyria to Byzantium*, Oxford: Oxford University Press, 2009.
- Stephanie Dalley, *The Mystery of the Hanging Garden of Babylon: An Elusive World Wonder Traced*, Oxford University Press, 2013.
- Mario Liverani, *The Ancient Near East: History, Society and Economy*, London: Routledge, 2014.
- Karen Radner, Ancient Assyria: A Very Short Introduction, 2015.
- Karen Radner, "Economy, Society, and Daily Life in the Neo-Assyrian Period", In E. Frahm (ed.), *A Companion to Assyria.* Hoboken: John Wiley & Sons, 2017.
- Ariel Bagg, "Assyrian Technology", In E. Frahm (ed.), *A Companion to Assyria*, Hoboken: John Wiley & Sons, 2017.
- Paul-Alain Beaulieu, "Assyria in Late Babylonian Sources", In E. Frahm (ed.), *A Companion to Assyria*, Hoboken: John Wiley & Sons, 2017.
- Stephanie Dalley, "Assyrian Warfare", In E. Frahm (ed.), *A Companion to Assyria*, Hoboken: John Wiley & Sons, 2017.
- Jeanette C. Fincke, "Assyrian Scholarship and Scribal Culture in Kalḫu and Nineveh", In E. Frahm (ed.), *A Companion to Assyria*, Hoboken: John Wiley & Sons, 2017.
- Sebastian Fink, "Invisible Mesopotamian royal women?", In Carney, Elizabeth D. Carney and Sabine Müller (eds.), *The Routledge Companion to Women and Monarchy in the Ancient Mediterranean World*, London: Routledge, pp. 137–148, 2020.
- Peter Frankopan, The Earth Transformed: An Untold History, Bloomsbury, 2023.

- K. Ulanowski, University of Gdańsk, and Faculty of Social Sciences, The Practical Dimension of Neo-Assyrian Militarism, Terror of War as Ideology of Power, In *Alcumena: Vol. Nr 3(15)/2023*, 2023.
- Eckart Frahm, Assyria: The Rise and Fall of the World's First Empire, Basic Books, 2023.

Chapter 15

- Otto, Maenchen-Helfen, The World of the Huns: Studies in Their History and Culture (1st ed.), Berkeley, CA: University of California Press, 1973.
- Thomas J. Barfield, The Perilous Frontier: Nomadic Empires and China, 221 BC to AD 1757, Basil Blackwell, 1989.
- Burton Watson, Records of the Grand Historian by Sima Qian, Columbia University Press, 1993.
- N. Ishjamts, "Nomads In Eastern Central Asia", In Janos Harmatta; et al. (eds.), History of civilizations of Central Asia, Volume 2: The Development of Sedentary and Nomadic Civilizations, 700 bc to ad 250, UNESCO, 1996.
- Nicola di Cosmo, "The Northern Frontier in Pre-Imperial China." In The Cambridge History of Ancient China from the Origins of Civilization to 221 B.C. Edited by Michael Loewe and Edward L. Shaughnessy, Cambridge, MA: Cambridge University Press, 1999.
- Sophia-Karin Psarras, "Han and Xiongnu: A Reexamination of Cultural and Political Relations", Monumenta Serica, 2003.
- Paola Demattè, "Writing the Landscape: Petroglyphs of Inner Mongolia and Ningxia Province (China)", In David L. Peterson; et al, (eds.), Beyond the steppe and the sown: proceedings of the 2002 University of Chicago Conference on Eurasian Archaeology, 2006.
- Christopher Beckwith, Empires of the Silk Road, Princeton University Press, 2009.

- Nicola di Cosmo, Ancient China and Its Enemies: The Rise of Nomadic Power in East Asian History, Cambridge University Press, 2010.
- Peter Golden, Central Asia in World History, Oxford: Oxford University Press, 2011.
- Valerie Hansen, The Silk Road: A New History, Oxford University Press, 2012.
- Hyun-Jin Kim The Huns, Rome, and the Birth of Europe, Cambridge, MA: Cambridge University Press, 2013.
- Hyun-Jin Kim, The Huns, Routledge, 2015.
- Christopher P. Atwood, "The Kai, the Khongai, and the Names of the Xiōngnú", International Journal of Eurasian Studies, 2015.
- John Man, Empire of Horses: The First Nomadic Civilization and the Making of China, W.W. Norton, 2019.
- Shevan Wilkin, Alicia Ventresca Miller, Bryan K. Miller, Robert N. Spengler, William T. T. Taylor, Ricardo Fernandes, Richard W. Hagan, Madeleine Bleasdale, Jana Zech, S. Ulziibayar, Erdene Myagmar, Nicole Boivin, Patrick Roberts, "Economic Diversification Supported the Growth of Mongolia's Nomadic Empires, Scientific Reports, 2020.
- Harl Kenneth W., Empires of the Steppes: A History of the Nomadic Tribes Who Shaped Civilization, Bloomsbury, 2023.

Chapter 16

- Victor Sarianidi, "The Treasure of Golden Hill." *American Journal of Archaeology*, Vol. 84, No. 2 (Apr., 1980), pp. 125–131, "The Treasure of Golden Hill", JSTOR.
- Craven Roy, *Indian Art: A Concise History*, Thames & Hudson (Praeger in USA), 1987.
- Victor Sarianidi, "Tilya Tepe: The Burial of a Noble Warrior." *PERSICA XIV*, 1990–1992, pp. 103–130, 1990–1992.
- Peter B. Golden, *An Introduction to the History of the Turkic Peoples,* 1992.

- Burton Watson, Records of the Grand Historian of China: Han Dynasty II. Columbia University Press, 1993.
- J.C. Harle, *The Art and Architecture of the Indian Subcontinent*, 2nd edn. 1994, Yale University Press Pelican History of Art.
- History of Civilizations of Central Asia, Vol II, UNESCO Publishing, 1994.
- Sims-Williams, Nicholas and Joe Cibb, "A New Bactrian Inscription of Kanishka the Great," Silk Road Art and Archaeology, volume 4, 1995–6.
- John E. Hill, The Peoples of the West from the Weilüe by Yu Huan: A Third Century Chinese Account Composed between 239 and 265 CE. English translation, 2003.
- Harry Falk, "The *Kaniṣka* era in Gupta records". *Silk Road Art and Archaeology X*. pp. 167–176, 2004.
- *The art of Gandhara in the Metropolitan Museum of Art*, 2007.
- Christopher I. Beckwith, *Empires of the Silk Road: A History of Central Eurasia from the Bronze Age to the Present*, Princeton University Press, 2009.
- John E. Hill, *Through the Jade Gate to Rome: A Study of the Silk Routes during the Later Han Dynasty, First to Second Centuries CE*, BookSurge, 2009.
- Valerie Hansen, The Silk Road: A New History, Oxford University Press, 2012.
- Cristoph Braumer, *The History of Central Asia* (Volume Two): *The Age of the Silk Roads*, I.B. Tauris, London, 2014.
- Peter Frankopan, *The Silk Roads: A New History of the World*, Bloomsbury, 2015.
- Kenneth W. Harl, Empires of the Steppes: A History of the Nomadic Tribes Who Shaped Civilization, 2023.

Chapter 17

- E. Denison Ross; Vilhelm Thomsen, "The Orkhon Inscriptions: Being a Translation of Professor Vilhelm Thomsen's Final Danish Rendering." Bulletin of the School of Oriental Studies, University of London, 1930.

- Peter B. Golden, An Introduction to the History of the Turkic Peoples, 1992.
- M.S. Asimov, *History of civilizations of Central Asia Volume IV The age of achievement: A.D. 750 to the end of the fifteenth century Part One The historical, social and economic setting,* UNESCO Publishing, 1998.
- Kemal Silay, An Anthology of Turkish Literature, 1996.
- History of Civilizations of Central Asia, Vol II, UNESCO Publishing, 1999.
- History of Civilizations of Central Asia, Vol III, UNESCO Publishing, 1999.
- Alexander Vovin, *"Did the Xiong Nu Speak a Yeniseian Language?",* Central Asiatic Journal, 44 (1), 2000.
- Francis Wood, *The Silk Road: Two Thousand Years in the Heart of Asia*. Berkeley, CA: University of California Press, 2002.
- James A. Millward, *Eurasian Crossroads: A History of Xinjiang,* Columbia University Press, 2007.
- Christopher I. Beckwith, Empires of the Silk Road: A History of Central Eurasia from the Bronze Age to the Present, Princeton, NJ: Princeton University Press, 2009.
- Peter B. Golden, *Central Asia in World History*, Oxford University Press, 2011.
- Marc S. Abramson, *Ethnic Identity in Tang China*. Encounters with Asia, University of Pennsylvania Press, 2011.
- Christoph Baumer, *The History of Central Asia: The Age of the Steppe Warriors,* 2012.
- Peter Frankopan, *The Silk Roads: A New History of the World,* Bloomsbury, 2015.
- Kenneth W. Harl, Empires of the Steppes: A History of the Nomadic Tribes Who Shaped Civilization, 2023.
- M. Yang, L. Meng, L. Zhang, Y. Yu, E. Allen, Y. Xia, Y. Zhu, X. Du, Y. Ren, X. Xiong, Y. Lu, Y. Ding, S. Han, P. Liu, L. Jin, C. Wang and Q. Wen, Ancient genome of Empress Ashina reveals the Northeast Asian origin of Göktürk Khanate, *Journal of Systematics and Evolution, 61*(6), 1056-1064, 2023.

IMAGE COPYRIGHT INFORMATION

Note: CCA-SA refers to the Creative Commons Attribution–Share Alike Wikimedia Commons/International Wikimedia Commons licences; Public Domain/PD: All public domain photographs have been sourced from: Wikimedia Commons/Public Domain.

Licences: Creative Commons - Wikipedia; Deed - Attribution 3.0 Unported - Creative Commons; Deed - Attribution-ShareAlike 4.0 International - Creative Commons; Deed - Attribution-ShareAlike 3.0 Unported - Creative Commons;Deed - Attribution-ShareAlike 2.5 Generic - Creative Commons; Deed - Attribution-ShareAlike 2.0 Generic - Creative Commons; Deed - Attribution-ShareAlike 1.0 Generic - Creative Commons; https://creativecommons.org/publicdomain/zero/1.0/deed.en; Deed - Attribution 2.5 Generic - Creative Commons; https://commons.wikimedia.org/wiki/Template:Copyrighted_free_use; https://creativecommons.org/licenses/by-sa/2.0/deed.en; Deed - Attribution-ShareAlike 3.0 Germany - Creative Commons; Flickr: The Commons; Deed - Attribution 3.0 Brazil - Creative Commons

PART 1

CHAPTER 1

6: CCA-SA 4.0 International/Wuselig/https://commons.wikimedia.org/wiki/File:MUT-9846.jpg; 7: CCA-SA 4.0 International/ पाटलिपुत्र/ Amcelxx/ https://commons.wikimedia.org/wiki/File:Sculptural_reconstruction_of_Homo_Sapiens_from_the_Kostenki_14_site_

by_M.M._Gerasimov.jpg; **8**: CCA-SA 4.0 International/Posth, C., Yu, H., Ghalichi, A. et al. Palaeogenomics of Upper Palaeolithic to Neolithic European hunter-gatherers. Nature 615, 117–126 (2023). https://doi.org/10.1038/s41586-023-05726-0/ https://creativecommons.org/licenses/by/4.0/; **9**: CCA-SA 4.0 International/Zde/ https://commons.wikimedia.org/wiki/File:Stone_tools,_Gravettian,_Anthropos,_Brno,_187963.jpg; **10**: Don Hitchcock, donsmaps.com; **11**: Shutterstock.com; **12**: CCA-SA 4.0 International/ Drucker, D.G., Naito, Y.I., Péan, S. et al. Isotopic analyses suggest mammoth and plant in the diet of the oldest anatomically modern humans from far southeast Europe. Sci Rep 7, 6833 (2017). https://doi.org/10.1038/s41598-017-07065-3/ https://creativecommons.org/licenses/by/4.0/; **14**: Illustration by Surojit Bhattacharjee/© Hachette India; **15**: CCA-SA 4.0 International/पाटलिपुत्र/User:Zde/https://commons.wikimedia.org/wiki/File:Female_face,_ivory_carving,_Doln%C3%AD_V%C4%9Bstonice,_Gravettian,_28_000_-_22_000_BP.jpg; **16**: CCA-SA 4.0 International/ पाटलिपुत्र/User:Zde/ https://commons.wikimedia.org/wiki/File:Reconstruction,_Doln%C3%AD_V%C4%9Bstonice.jpg; **18**: CCA-SA 2.5 Generic/Che/Petr Novák, Wikipedia/ File:Vestonicka venuse edit.jpg - Wikimedia Commons; **19**: CCA-SA 4.0 International/ Mustafagunes2/Jc Domenech/File:Venus of Impudique - 1.jpg - Wikimedia Commons; **20**: CCA-SA 4.0 International/Uspn/

Bjørn Christian Tørrissen/File:Venus of Willendorf - All sides.jpg - Wikimedia Commons; **21**: CCA-SA 4.0 International/Sarrasin75013/ Kleber Rossillon & Région Provence-Alpes-Côte d'Azur/Sources 3D MC/https://commons.wikimedia.org/wiki/File:Panneau_des_chevaux_-_Cosquer_M%C3%A9diterran%C3%A9e.jpg; **22**: CCA-SA 3.0 Unported/Thilo Parg/https://commons.wikimedia.org/wiki/File:Brillenhoehle_Blaubeuren_Schmuckanhaenger_Tafel17.jpg/ Thilo Parg/Wikimedia Commons; **23**: CCA-SA 4.0 International/ Thilo Parg/ Dagmar Hollmann / Wikimedia Commons/ https://commons.wikimedia.org/wiki/File:Loewenmensch1.jpg; **24**: CCA-SA 4.0 International/Zde/File:Dolni Vestonice II burial, Anthropos, Brno, 187988.jpg - Wikimedia Commons; **26**: CC0 1.0 Universal Public Domain Dedication/Lorenzo Donzelli/ https://commons.wikimedia.org/wiki/File:Resti_del_principe_delle_arene_candide.jpg; **27**: PD/Locutus Borg/José-Manuel Benito Álvarez/ https://commons.wikimedia.org/wiki/File:Sunghir-tumba_paleol%C3%ADtica.jpg;

CHAPTER 2

31: CCA-SA 3.0 Unported/Teomancimit/ https://commons.wikimedia.org/wiki/File:G%C3%B6bekli_Tepe,_Urfa.jpg; **33**: CCA 2.5 Genric/CCA-SA 4.0 International/Zunkir/German Archaeological Institute, photo E. Kücük./ Dietrich L, Meister J, Dietrich O, Notroff J, Kiep J, Heeb J, et al. (2019) Cereal processing at Early Neolithic Göbekli Tepe, southeastern Turkey. PLoS ONE 14(5): e0215214. https://doi.org/10.1371/journal.pone.0215214

Image: https://journals.plos.org/plosone/article/figure?id=10.1371/journal.pone.0215214.g001/Copyright: © 2019 Dietrich et al./ https://commons.wikimedia.org/wiki/File:The_archaeological_site_of_G%C3%B6bekli_Tepe_-_main_excavation_area.png; **34**: CCA-SA 4.0 International/𐱅𐰇𐰼𐰜/Cobija/File:Şanlıurfa Müzesi Göbeklitepe D Tapınağı.jpg - Wikipedia; **36**: CCA-SA 4.0 International/ पाटलिपुत्र/ Cobija/ File:Urfa man.jpg - Wikimedia Commons; **37**: CCA-SA 4.0 International/Beytullah eles/ https://commons.wikimedia.org/wiki/File:G%C3%B6beklitepe_%C5%9Eanl%C4%B1urfa.jpg; **39**: CCA 2.5 Genric/CCA-SA 4.0 International/पाटलिपुत्र/Iris Groman-Yaroslavski , Ehud Weiss, Dani Nadel/Composite Sickles and Cereal Harvesting Methods at 23,000-Years-Old Ohalo II, Israel/© 2016 Groman-Yaroslavski et al./File:Composite Sickles for Cereal Harvesting at 23,000-Years-Old Ohalo II, Israel.jpg - Wikimedia Commons; **44**: CCA-SA 3.0 Unported/ पाटलिपुत्र/Klaus-Peter Simon/File:Totem pole from Göbekli Tepe, Layer II, 8800-8000 BCE Sanliurfa Museum.jpg - Wikimedia Commons; **46**: CCA-SA 4.0 International/Dosseman/ https://commons.wikimedia.org/wiki/File:G%C3%B6beklitepe_Building_C_sept_2019_5373crop.jpg; **47**: CCA-SA 2.0 Generic/ Hypnôs/Sue Fleckney/File:Vulture Stone, Gobekli Tepe, Sanliurfa, South-east Anatolia, Turkey (cropped).jpg - Wikimedia Commons; **48**: CCA-SA 4.0 International/Dosseman/File:Urfa museum Animal statuette sept 2019 4754.jpg - Wikipedia; **49**: CCA-SA 4.0 International/ Pamputt/B. Köşker/File:Urn cambridge.org id binary 20221201181421541-0856 S0003598X22001259 S0003598X22001259 fig4.png - Wikimedia Commons;

CHAPTER 3

52: CCA-SA 4.0 International/Murat Özsoy 1958/File:Çatalhöyük, 7400 BC, Konya, Turkey - UNESCO World Heritage Site, 08.jpg - Wikimedia Commons; **54**: steve estvanik/Shutterstock.com; **56**:

CCA-SA 3.0 Unported, 2.5 Generic, 2.0 Generic and 1.0 Generic/ 120/ Nevit Dilmen/File:Seated Woman of Çatalhöyük on black background.jpg - Wikimedia Commons; **57**: Selcuk Oner/Shutterstock.com; **58**: Shutterstock.com; **59**: CCA-SA 3.0 Unported/Alonso de Mendoza/ Elelicht/File:Catal Hüyük EL.JPG - Wikimedia Commons; **62**: steve estvanik/Shutterstock.com; **63**: Illustration by Surojit Bhattacharjee/© Hachette India; **64**: CCA-SA 4.0 International/Dan Palraz/File:Jericho Statue.png - Wikimedia Commons; **67**: CCA-SA 4.0 International/ Murat Özsoy 1958/File:Çatalhöyük, 7400 BC, Konya, Turkey - UNESCO World Heritage Site, 11.jpg - Wikimedia Commons;

CHAPTER 4

71: CCA-SA 3.0 Unported/Capmo/Ashish_Premier/File:Mehrgarh ruins.jpg - Wikimedia Commons; **76**: CCA-SA 4.0 International/ Archaeodontosaurus/Didier Descouens/ File:Lazurite.jpg - Wikimedia Commons; **77**: CC0 1.0 Universal Public Domain Dedication/ Pharos/Gift of Alexander Götz, in honor of Martin Lerner's curatorship 1972–2004, 2003/ https://www.metmuseum.org/art/collection/search/72342/Metropolitan Museum of Art/ File:MET 2003 592 2 O.jpg - Wikimedia Commons; **79**: CC0 1.0 Universal Public Domain Dedication/ पाटलिपुत्र/Metropolitan Museum of Art/File:Seated Mother Goddess ,3000–2500 B.C. Pakistan (Baluchistan) Mehrgarh style.jpg - Wikimedia Commons; **81**: CC0 1.0 Global Dedication/Hamadshahazada/ https://he.wikipedia.org/wiki/%D7%A7%D7%95%D7%91%D7%A5:MEHRGARH_2.jpg; **82**: CCA 4.0 International/http://creativecommons.org/licenses/by/4.0/Thoury, M. et al. High spatial dynamics-photoluminescence imaging reveals the metallurgy of the earliest lost-wax cast object. Nat. Commun. 7, 13356 doi: 10.1038/ncomms13356 (2016); **83**: CC0 1.0 Universal Public Domain Dedication/पाटलिपुत्र/Gary Todd/ https://commons.wikimedia.org/wiki/File:Dancing_girl_of_Mohenjo-daro.jpg; **84**: CC0 1.0 Universal Public Domain Dedication/Madreiling/ Purchase from the J. H. Wade Fund/Cleaveland Museum of Art/ https://clevelandart.org/art/1973.160/File:Clevelandart 1973.160.jpg - Wikimedia Commons; **85**: CCA-SA 2.5 Generic, 2.0 Generic and 1.0 Generic/I, KENPEI/KENPEI/ File:Gossypium arboreum2.jpg - Wikimedia Commons;

PART 2

CHAPTER 5

93: CC0 1.0 Universal Public Domain Dedication/WikiEditor2004/ https://commons.wikimedia.org/wiki/File:Neolithic_vinca_culture_en.png; **94**: CCA-SA 3.0 Unported/Ario1234/Andrej Danković/ File:Prosomorphic lid 2.jpg - Wikimedia Commons; **95**: CCA-SA 3.0 Serbia/ShadowBrood84/Unknown author/Museum of Vojvodina/ File:Crvenokosa boginja, neolit, Donja Branjevina.tif - Wikimedia Commons; **96**: CCA-SA 3.0 Unported/Tekiii/Unknown author/ Institute for the Protection of Cultural Monuments of Serbia/ File:White Hill in Vinča, profile and approach.jpg - Wikimedia Commons; **98**: Belgrade City Museum; **99**: Belgrade City Museum; **100**: CCA-SA 4.0 International/CryolophosaurusEllioti/ File:Copper axes with modern replicas, National Museum of Serbia 04 2413-2423 (09).jpg - Wikimedia Commons; **102**: CC0 1.0 Universal Public Domain Dedication/ Ario1234/Museum of Vojvodina; **103**: CCA-SA 3.0 Unported, 2.5 Generic, 2.0 Generic and 1.0 Generic/User-duck/Michel wal/ British Museum/File:Vinca clay figure 02.jpg - Wikimedia Commons; **104**: CCA-SA 3.0 Serbia/Nikola Smolenski/https://commons.wikimedia.org/wiki/File:Vidovdanka.jpg; **105**: CCA-SA 4.0 International/ Albinfo/File:Prishtina Goddess on the Throne (cropped).jpg - Wikimedia Commons; **106**: CCA 3.0 Unported/Ario1234/FlorinCB/ File:Tartaria2.jpg - Wikimedia Commons; **107**: CCA 3.0 Unported/ Randona.bg/Unknown author/ https://www.europeana.eu/bg/item/2021502/jspui_handle_pub_83/File:Gradeshnitsa Tablet.jpg - Wikimedia Commons;

CHAPTER 6

114: CCA-SA 2.0 Generic/Edubucher/World Wide Gifts/Peru - Paracas National Reserve/ File:Desert of Paracas, Peru - Paracas National Reserve.jpg - Wikimedia Commons; **115**: PD–US/Smith609/ File:Humboldt current.jpg - Wikimedia Commons; **116**: CCA 2.5 Generic/I, Xauxa/Xauxa/Håkan Svensson Xauxa/File:PeruCaral01.jpg - Wikimedia Commons; **119**: CCA-SA 3.0 Unported/Ontrvet/ https://commons.wikimedia.org/wiki/File:Peru_site_locations.png; **121**: Shutterstock.com; **123**: CCA 2.5 Generic/I, Xauxa/Xauxa/ Håkan Svensson Xauxa/ https://commons.wikimedia.org/wiki/ File:PeruCaral22.jpg; **124**: CCA-SA 2.5 Generic, 2.0 Generic and 1.0

Generic/I, KyleThayer/KyleThayer/File:Caral 9.jpg - Wikimedia Commons; **125**: CCA 2.0 Generic/Infrogmation/Marc Davis/ https://www.flickr.com/photos/marcalandavis/45649160// File:Bolivia - Gate of the Sun detail - Tiwanaku or Tiahuanaco 04.jpg - Wikimedia Commons; **127: top**: CCA-SA 3.0 Unported/Eniol/ File:Caral - Caza - Ballena.jpg - Wikimedia Commons; **bottom**: CCA-SA 4.0 International/ Ineuw/ Dravinia/File:Aspero.jpg - Wikimedia Commons; **128**: PD; **129**: CCA 2.5 Generic/I, Xauxa/Xauxa/Håkan Svensson Xauxa/ https://commons.wikimedia.org/wiki/File:PeruCaral14.jpg; **130**: CCA 2.5 Generic/I, Xauxa/Xauxa/Håkan Svensson Xauxa/File:PeruCaral21.jpg - Wikimedia Commons; **131**: CCA-SA 4.0 International/Yhhue91/ File:Pirámide principal del sitio arqueológico El Paraiso-Perú 2.jpg - Wikimedia Commons;

CHAPTER 7

136: top: CCA-SA 4.0 International/Joshua Jonathan/File:From Corded Ware to Sintashta.jpg - Wikimedia Commons; **middle**: CCA-SA 4.0 International/Ario1234/Iwona Dembicz, Ivan I. Moysiyenko, Anastasia Shaposhnikova, Denys Vynokurov, Łukasz Kozub, Barbara Sudnik-Wœjcikowska/ Isolation and patch size drive specialist plant species density within steppe islands: a case study of kurgans in southern Ukraine (2016) Biodiversity and Conservation 25(12) DOI:10.1007/ s10531-016-1077-y

https://www.researchgate.net/publication/298898621_Isolation_and_patch_size_drive_specialist_plant_species_density_within_steppe_islands_a_case_study_of_kurgans_in_southern_Ukraine/ File:Kurgans in southern Ukraine.png - Wikimedia Commons; **137**: PD/Кабак В.О. User:Narada Lefvf; **139**: **top**: CCA-SA 3.0 Unported/Einsamer Schütze/File:Danneil-Museum 037.JPG - Wikimedia Commons; **bottom**: CCA-SA 3.0 Unported, 2.5 Generic, 2.0 Generic and 1.0 Generic/ Einsamer Schütze/File:Museum für Vor- und Frühgeschichte Berlin 031.jpg - Wikimedia Commons; **142**: CCA-SA 4.0 International/ Ario1234/Stanislav Grigoriev/ https://www.researchgate.net/publication/350632762_Andronovo_Problem_Studies_of_Cultural_Genesis_in_the_Eurasian_Bronze_Age/File:Sintashta culture, Arkaim and Sintashta settlement ground plans.png - Wikimedia Commons; **143**: CCA-SA 4.0 International/Ario1234/Stanislav Grigoriev/ https://www.researchgate.net/publication/350632762_Andronovo_Problem_Studies_of_Cultural_Genesis_in_the_Eurasian_Bronze_Age/ https://commons.wikimedia.org/wiki/File:Sintashta_culture_artefacts_1.

png; **146**: Illustration by Surojit Bhattacharjee/© Hachette India; **148**: CCA-SA 4.0 International/Ario1234/Lindner, S. (2020). Chariots in the Eurasian Steppe: A Bayesian approach to the emergence of horse-drawn transport in the early second millennium BC. Antiquity, 94(374), 361-380. doi:10.15184/aqy.2020.37/https://commons.wikimedia.org/wiki/File:Sintashta1_copy.jpg; **150**: CCA 2.0 Generic/Flickr upload bot/Lawrence/File:Wintercoat.jpg - Wikimedia Commons;

CHAPTER 8

156: CCA 2.0 Generic/पाटलिपुत्र/Ninara/File:Tepe Fullol bowl fragment (cropped), 3rd millennium BCE, National Museum of Afghanistan.jpg - Wikimedia Commons; **158**: CCA-SA 3.0 Unported/Dbachmann/File:BMAC.png - Wikimedia Commons; **159**: CCA 2.0 Generic/Russavia/David Stanley/https://www.flickr.com/photos/davidstanleytravel/5731107988/File:Gonur ruins.jpg - Wikimedia Commons; **163**: CC0 1.0 Universal Public Domain Dedication/Pharos/https://www.metmuseum.org/art/collection/search/324256/Rogers Fund, 1953/Metropolitan Museum of Art/File:Bactrian camel MET DP-14200-001.jpg - Wikimedia Commons; **165**: CC0 1.0 Universal Public Domain Dedication/Pharos/https://www.metmuseum.org/art/collection/search/329076/Purchase, Harris Brisbane Dick Fund, and James N. Spear and Schimmel Foundation Inc. Gifts, 1982/Metropolitan Museum of Art/File:Shaft-hole axe head with bird-headed demon, boar, and dragon MET 1982.5.jpg - Wikimedia Commons; **166**: CCA-SA 2.0/3.0 France/Rama/Louvre Museum/File:Bactrian princess-AO 22918-IMG 0239-black.jpg - Wikimedia Commons; **167**: CC0 1.0 Universal Public Domain Dedication/Pharos/https://www.metmuseum.org/art/collection/search/328593/Purchase, 2009 Benefit Fund and Friends of Inanna Gifts; Gift of Mr. and Mrs. Horiuchi, 2010/Metropolitan Museum of Art/File:Monstrous male figure MET dp22227.jpg - Wikimedia Commons; **168**: CC0 1.0 Universal Public Domain Dedication/Pharos/https://www.metmuseum.org/art/collection/search/327427/Gift of Norbert Schimmel Trust, 1989/Metropolitan Museum of Art/File:Beaker with birds on the rim MET DT866.jpg - Wikimedia Commons; **172**: CCA-SA 4.0 International/Ario1234/Molodin V.I., Mylnikova L.N., Ivanova D.P. A/ https://journal.archaeology.nsc.ru/jour/article/view/79/80

Molodin V.I., Mylnikova L.N., Ivanova D.P. A MORPHOLOGICAL ANALYSIS OF VESSELS FROM MIDDLE BRONZE AGE (EARLY 2ND MILLENNIUM BC) BURIALS AT VENGEROVO, IN THE

IRTYSH FOREST-STEPPE. Archaeology, Ethnology & Anthropology of Eurasia. 2014;58(2):44-66/File:Andronovo ceramics 4.png - Wikimedia Commons;

PART 3

CHAPTER 9

178: PD/Peter Philim/National Portrait Gallery, London/File:Agatha Christie and Max Mallowan in 1950.png - Wikimedia Commons/**179**: PD–Australia/PD–US/ITBF/Swan Watson, Andrew/The National Library of Australia/http://nla.gov.au/nla.pic-an23815428/ File:Gordon Childe.jpg - Wikimedia Commons; **182**: CC0 1.0 Universal Public Domain Dedication/Daderot/ https://commons.wikimedia.org/wiki/File:Copper_knife,_spearpoints,_awls,_and_spud,_Late_Archaic_period,_Wisconsin,_3000_BC-1000_BC_-_Wisconsin_Historical_Museum_-_DSC03436.JPG; **184**: CCA 3.0 Unported/ Bertramz/File:TellBrak-NE.jpg - Wikimedia Commons; **185**: CCA 3.0 Unported/पाटलिपुत्र/Jolle/File:Mesopotamian Prehistorical cultures.jpg - Wikimedia Commons/ Changes were made to the file, stripes, checkered pattern, polka dots and stars were added to distinguish the markings in black and white; **187**: PD/Helvetiker; **188**: CCA-SA 4.0 International/Attar-Aram syria/Sémhur/File:Near_East_topographic_map-blank.svg/File:First Eblaite Empire.png - Wikimedia Commons; **189**: CCA-SA 4.0 International/Codas/Davide Mauro/File:Calco di tavoletta in terracotta da Ebla - Museo d'Arte Orientale Roma.jpg - Wikimedia Commons; **190**: PD–UK/पाटलिपुत्र/Mallowan (1936) "The Bronze Head of the Akkadian Period From Nineveh", Iraq Vol. 3(1) pp. 104–110/File:Sargon of Akkad (1936).jpg - Wikimedia Commons; **191**: CCA 3.0 Unported/Bertramz/File:TellBrakNaramsinN.jpg - Wikimedia Commons;**192**: CCA-SA 2.0 Generic/ पाटलिपुत्र/ALFGRN/ https://www.flickr.com/photos/156915032@N07/47027390354/ File:Foundation tablet, dedication to God Nergal by Hurrian king Atalshen, king of Urkish and Nawar, Habur Bassin, circa 2000 BC Louvre Museum AO 5678.jpg - Wikimedia Commons; **193**: CCA-SA 3.0 Unported/ Morningstar1814/Sémhur, Zunkir, rowanwindwhistler/ File:Carte du Mitanni-en.svg - Wikimedia Commons; **194**: CCA 3.0 Unported/Bertramz/File:TellBrakMitanni.jpg - Wikimedia Commons; **195**: CCA 3.0 Unported/Bertramz/https://commons.wikimedia.org/wiki/File:TellBrakTW-W.jpg; **197**: CCA-SA 4.0 International/Zunkir/ File:Etendard d'Ur - char.jpg - Wikimedia Commons;

CHAPTER 10

199: CCA-SA 4.0 International/Neuroforever/Osama Shukir Muhammed Amin FRCP(Glasg)/BayernLB/State Museum of Egyptian Art/File:God Horus as a falcon wearing the Double Crown of Egypt. 27th dynasty. State Museum of Egyptian Art, Munich.jpg - Wikimedia Commons; **201**: CCA-SA 3.0 Unported, 2.5 Generic, 2.0 Generic and 1.0 Generic/Bibi Saint-Pol/ Jeff Dahl/File:Ancient Egypt main map.png - Wikimedia Commons; **203**: CC0 1.0 Universal Public Domain Dedication/ पाटलिपुत्र/Gary Todd/File:Al Fayum arrowheads.png - Wikimedia Commons; **204**: CC0 1.0 Universal Public Domain Dedication/ पाटलिपुत्र/akhenatenator/File:Badarian Burial.jpg - Wikimedia Commons; **205**: CC0 1.0 Universal Public Domain Dedication/User-duck/akhenatenator/File:Vase in the shape of a hippopotamus. Early Predynastic, Badarian. Fifth millennium BC. From Mostagedda.jpg - Wikimedia Commons; **206**: CCA-SA 1.0 Generic/Borislav/Aoineko/Louvre Museum/File:Egypte louvre 314.jpg - Wikimedia Commons; **208**: CCA 2.5 Generic/File Upload Bot (Kaldari)/Charles Edwin Wilbour Fund/Brooklyn Museum/ File:WLA brooklynmuseum Terracotta female figure.jpg - Wikimedia Commons; **209**: Open Access Public Domain/Rogers Fund, 1912/ Metropolitan Museum of Art; **211**: PD/PD–US/पाटलिपुत्र/Frederick William Green (March 21, 1869–1949); James Edward Quibell (1867-1935)/Hierakonpolis (Band 2) — London, 1902/File:Tomb 100 Hierakompolis, Naqada II culture (c. 3500-3200 BCE).jpg - Wikimedia Commons; **212**: **top**: PD/PD–US/पाटलिपुत्र/Frederick William Green (March 21, 1869–1949); James Edward Quibell (1867-1935)/ https://commons.wikimedia.org/wiki/File:Hierakonpolis_Tomb_100_Master_of_animals.jpg; **bottom**: CCA-SA 2.0 Generic/ पाटलिपुत्र/ALFGRN/ https://www.flickr.com/photos/156915032@N07/47463496632/ File:Gebel el-Arak Knife ivory handle (front top part detail).jpg - Wikimedia Commons; **214**: **top**: Copyrighted free use/Jeff Dahl/Jon Bodsworth/ https://commons.wikimedia.org/wiki/File:Hierakonpolis_Palette_fragment.jpg; **bottom**: Copyrighted free use/Jeff Dahl/Jon Bodsworth/British Museum/File:Battlefield palette.jpg - Wikimedia Commons; **216**: CC0 1.0 Universal Public Domain Dedication/ पाटलिपुत्र/ akhenatenator/File:Ceremonial mace-head of King Scorpion.jpg - Wikimedia Commons; **217**: CCA-SA 3.0 Unported/ Udimu/File:Kingscorpion.jpg - Wikimedia Commons; **218**: **top**: CCA-SA 2.0 Generic/ पाटलिपुत्र/Heidi Kontkanen/File:Detail from the mace-head of King Scorpion.jpg - Wikimedia Commons; **bottom**: CCA-SA 2.0 Generic/ पाटलिपुत्र/Heidi Kontkanen/File:Detail from the mace-head of King Scorpion.jpg - Wikimedia Commons; **219**:

Illustration by Surojit Bhattacharjee/© Hachette India; **220**: CCA-SA 3.0 Germany/Unported/Wdwdbot/Nephiliskos/ Eigene Anfertigung/ https://commons.wikimedia.org/wiki/File:Rockcutting.png; **222**: PD/PD–Art/Velatrix/http://www.studyblue.com/notes/note/n/art-midterm/deck/1189362/Egyptian Museum/File:Narmer Palette.jpg - Wikimedia Commons; **223**: CCA-SA 4.0 International/Maher166/ Quibell,1898, pl. 13/ https://upload.wikimedia.org/wikipedia/ commons/c/ca/Narmer_Palette%2C_recto.jpg/ File:Narmer Palette recto.svg - Wikimedia Commons; **224**: PD/Vorziblix; **225**: CCA-SA 4.0 International/Maher166/Quibell,1898, pl. 13/ https://upload.wikimedia.org/wikipedia/commons/6/6a/Narmer_Palette%2C_verso.jpg/ File:Narmer Palette verso.svg - Wikimedia Commons; **227**: **top**: Copyrighted free use/ Captmondo/Jon Bodsworth/https://commons.wikimedia.org/wiki/File:Narmer_Macehead.png; **bottom**: Flickr's The Commons/ पाटलिपुत्र/Budge, E. A. Wallis (Ernest Alfred Wallis), Sir, 1857-1934/File:Narmer Macehead drawing.jpg - Wikipedia;

CHAPTER 11

231: CCA-SA 4.0 International/Calderonbarco/Dominio publico/ https://www.thx-trailer.com/replica/indy4/Orellana/Orellana.htm/ File:Francisco-orellana.png - Wikimedia Commons; **232**: CCA-SA 3.0 Unported/Jkan997/File:Francisco de Orellana Amazon River voyage (1541-1542).svg - Wikimedia Commons; **233**: PD/Chris Winger; **235**: CCA 3.0 Brazil/Jurema Oliveira/Foto: Valter Campanato/ABr/Agência Brasil/File:Índios da etnia Kuikuro.jpg - Wikimedia Commons; **236**: PD/PD–Art/PD–US/Arjandb/ scanned from the book Albert Eckhout: een Hollandse kunstenaar in Brazilië ISBN 9040089299/Albert Eckhout/National Museum of Denmanrk; **238**: CCA-SA 3.0 Unported/ Smallchief/Klaus Ehlers/File:Llanos de Moxos.png/File:Llanos de moxos1.png - Wikimedia Commons; **239**: CCA-SA 2.0 Generic/Lupo/ Sam Beebe/File:Beni Department aérea 25.jpg - Wikimedia Commons; **240**: CCA-SA 4.0 International/Smallchief/Bruno Roux/https://commons.wikimedia.org/wiki/File:Pre-Columbian_man-made_causeway_in_Llanos_de_Moxos.jpg; **242**: CCA-SA 3.0 Unported/ Jlh249/ File:Rio Upano, Logroño.jpg - Wikimedia Commons; **243**: CC0 1.0 Universal Public Domain Dedication/Daderot; **246**: CCA-SA 3.0 Unported/FatAlbert/Albert Backer/File:Sangay2.jpg - Wikimedia Commons;

CHAPTER 12

250: CC0 1.0 Universal Public Domain Dedication/Bgag; **252**: PD/PD–Art/Bahatur; **253**: CCA-SA 4.0 International/Seasonsinthesun/SY/File:Kara-Khanid Khanate.png - Wikimedia Commons; **256**: PD/Dbachmann/Mahmud al-Kashgari; **259**: CCA-SA 3.0 Unported/**I, Sailko**/Sailko/ https://commons.wikimedia.org/wiki/File:Piatto_con_decorazione_di_castello_assediato,_arg,_samirechye,_da_bolshoe-anikovskaya,_IX-X_sec_su_orig_del_l%27VIII_sec.JPG; **260**: CCA-SA 4.0 International/Zossolino/File:2015-09-06-112644 - Balasagun - Burana-Turm.JPG - Wikimedia Commons; **262**: CC0 1.0 Universal Public Domain Dedication/Bgag/File:Burana Tower site 04.jpg - Wikimedia Commons; **263**: PD/Hux;

CHAPTER 13

265: PD–US/Achim55/Percy Frazer Smith; **267**: CCA-SA 4.0 International/Heironymous Rowe/ Herb Roe/ https://commons.wikimedia.org/wiki/File:Watson_Brake_Aerial_Illustration_HRoe_2014.jpg; **268**: CCA-SA 2.5 Generic/Chumwa/Maximilian Dörrbecker (Chumwa)/File:Louisiana - Poverty Point - Karte (English version).png - Wikimedia Commons; **269**: PD/SimpsonDG/David G. Simpson; **270**: CCA-SA 3.0 Unported, 2.5 Generic, 2.0 Generic and 1.0 Generic/Heironymous Rowe at English Wikipedia/Heironymous Rowe/Herb Roe/File:Mound City Chillicothe Ohio HRoe 2008.jpg - Wikimedia Commons; **272**: CCA-SA 3.0 Unported/Herb Roe/Ras67/Heironymous Rowe/https://commons.wikimedia.org/wiki/File:Mississippian_cultures_HRoe_2010.jpg; **275**: CCA-SA 3.0 Unported/Herb Roe/Heironymous Rowe/ https://commons.wikimedia.org/wiki/File:Woodhenge_motif_black_drink_beaker_HRoe_2013.jpg; **276:** CCA-SA 3.0 Unported/Herb Roe/Quibik/Herb Roe, www.chromesun.com/ File:Chunkeyplayer painting HRoe 2006.jpg - Wikimedia Commons; **277**: PD/TimVickers; **279**: CCA-SA 3.0 Unported/Grolltech/Skubasteve834/File:Monks Mound in July.JPG - Wikipedia; **280**: CCA-SA 3.0 Unported/Herb Roe/Heironymous Rowe/File:Mississippian culture mound components HRoe 2011.jpg - Wikimedia Commons; **281**: CCA-SA 3.0 Unported/Herb Roe/Heironymous Rowe/Herb Roe, www.chromesun.com/File:Spiro Wulfing and Etowah repousse plates HRoe 2012.jpg - Wikimedia Commons; **282**: CCA-SA 3.0 Unported/Herb Roe/Heironymous Rowe/File:Mound 72 Woodhenge diagram HRoe 2013.jpg - Wikimedia Commons; **283**: CCA-SA 3.0 Unported/Herb Roe/

Herb Roe, www.chromesun.com/ File:Cahokia Birdman tablet HRoe 2012.jpg - Wikimedia Commons; **285**: CCA-SA 4.0 International/ Herb Roe/Heironymous Rowe/File:Cahokia Aerial HRoe 2015.jpg - Wikimedia Commons; **286**: CCA-SA 3.0 Unported/Herb Roe/Herb Roe, www.chromesun.com/ https://commons.wikimedia.org/wiki/ File:Cahokia_reconstructed_palisade_HRoe_01.jpg;

PART 4

CHAPTER 14

291: CCA-SA 4.0 International/TYalaA/File:LammasuChicago.jpg - Wikimedia Commons; **293**: CCA-SA 4.0 International/Neuroforever/ Osama Shukir Muhammed Amin FRCP(Glasg)/File:Wall relief depicting the God Ashur (Assur) from Nimrud..JPG - Wikimedia Commons; **294**: CC0 1.0 Universal Public Domain Dedication/ पाटलिपुत्र/Gary Todd; **296**: PD/Capmo/Ningyou; Changes were made to the file, stripes and stars were added to distinguish the markings in black and white; **297**: PD/Soerfm/Capillon/British Museum; **299**: CC0 1.0 Universal Public Domain Dedication/User-duck/Gary Todd; **303**: CCA 4.0 International/Mharrsch/Allan Gluck/File:Assyrian Relief of the Banquet of Ashurbanipal From Nineveh Gypsum N Palace British Museum 01.jpg - Wikimedia Commons; **308**: PD–US/Ichthyovenator/ SSgt Noreen L. Feeney, 318th Public Affairs Operation Center (PAOC), US Army/File:Seal of Queen Hama of Assyria, Nimrud (transparent). png - Wikimedia Commons;

CHAPTER 15

313: CCA-SA 2.5 Generic, 2.0 Generic and 1.0 Generic/**I, PHGCOM**/ World Imaging/ File:QinEmpireWithOrdos.jpg - Wikimedia Commons; **316**: CCA-SA 4.0 International/KoizumiBS/File:Modu Chanyu.jpg - Wikimedia Commons; **318**: CC0 1.0 Universal Public Domain Dedication/Gary Lee Todd; **320**: PD/Adece033090/ http:// earlyworldhistory.blogspot.com/2012/03/liu-bang.html; **321**: CCA-SA 3.0 Unported/**I, Sailko**/Hzh/File:Periodo edo, kosumi morihage, wang zhaojun, XVII sec. 02.JPG - Wikimedia Commons; **324**: PD/ Barefact; **325**: CCA-SA 3.0 Unported/Nm900110/https://commons. wikimedia. org/wiki/File:%E7%BB%9F%E4%B8%87%E5%9F%8E% E9%81%97%E5%9D%80.jpg; **327**: PD/PD–Art/Shyoon1;

CHAPTER 16

332: CC0 1.0 Universal Public Domain Dedication/Daderot; **333**: CCA-SA 2.0 Generic/पाटलिपुत्र/ALFGRN/File:Khalchayan Prince, side view.jpg - Wikimedia Commons; **335**: CC0 1.0 Universal Public Domain Dedication/Vintotal; **337**: CCA-SA 3.0 Unported/Classical Numismatic Group, Inc. http://www.cngcoins.com/पाटलिपुत्र/CNG Coins/File:Heraios coin.jpg - Wikimedia Commons; **339**: CCA-SA 2.5 Generic, 2.0 Generic and 1.0 Generic/World Imaging/PHGCOM/File:Kushanmap.jpg - Wikimedia Commons; **342**: CCA-SA 3.0 Unported/Classical Numismatic Group, Inc. http://www.cngcoins.com/पाटलिपुत्र/CNG Coins/File:Kanishka I with Nana.jpg - Wikimedia Commons; **343**: CCA-SA 3.0 Unported/**I, PHGCOM**/World Imaging/ PHGCOM/File:CoinOfHuvishkaWithOisho.JPG - Wikimedia Commons; **345**: CCA-SA 2.0 Generic/ पाटलिपुत्र/Anthony Huan/https://www.flickr.com/photos/anthonyhuan/28173285998/File:Kanishka casket, Asia, G33 South Asia.jpg - Wikimedia Commons; **347**: Open Access Public Domain/Samuel Eilenberg Collection, Gift of Samuel Eilenberg, 1987/Metropolitan Museum of Art; **348**: CCA-SA 3.0 Unported/World Imaging/File:Buddha-Vajrapani-Herakles.JPG - Wikimedia Commons; **349**: PD/World Imaging; **350**: CCA-SA 2.0 Generic/पाटलिपुत्र/H Sinica/https://commons.wikimedia.org/wiki/File:Tillya_Tepe_crown.jpg;

CHAPTER 17

354: PD/File Upload Bot (Magnus Manske)/English: The Göktürks; **357**: CCA-SA 3.0 Unported/ 배우는사람/East-Hem_600ad.jpg: Thomas Lessman (Contact!), derivative work: 배우는사람 (talk)/File:Part of East-Hem 600ad.jpg - Wikipedia; **361**: PD/Fæ/Los Angeles County Museum of Art; **362**: PD/PD–Art/पाटलिपुत्र/Photography: Shaanxi Provincial Institute of Archaeology, Xi'an Bei Zhou An Jia mu; **363**: CCA-SA 4.0 International/Vezirtonyukuk/File:Kultigin Monument of Orkhon Inscriptions.jpeg - Wikimedia Commons; **367**: CC0 1.0 Universal Public Domain Dedication/पाटलिपुत्र/Gary Todd from Xinzheng, China; **369**: PD/PD–Art/पाटलिपुत्र.

INDEX